THE MANAGEMENT OF SERVICE OPERATIONS

Also available from Cassell:

Evans: *Supervisory Management*
Johns and Lee-Ross: *Research Methods in Service Industry Management*
Wild: *Essentials of Production and Operations Management*, 4th Edition
Wild: *Production and Operations Management*

The Management of Service Operations

J. Nevan Wright

CASSELL

Cassell

Wellington House
125 Strand
London WC2R 0BB

370 Lexington Avenue
New York
NY 10017-6550

www.cassell.co.uk

First published 1999

British Library Cataloguing-in-Publication Data
A catalogue record for this book is available from the British Library.

ISBN   0-304-70528-4

Designed and typeset by Kenneth Burnley, Wirral, Cheshire.
Printed and bound in Great Britain by Redwood Books, Trowbridge, Wiltshire.

Contents

Preface

This book will be of practical use for:

- managers;
- students of management at undergraduate and postgraduate level (especially MBA students);
- anyone engaged in a service industry (private or public sector).

It is based on the theory of operations management but links theory to practical everyday management of performance; its purpose is to provide an understanding of the management of service industries and to show how to turn policy and objectives into reality.

The book's central philosophy is that people make the difference in providing an efficient and 'quality' service. It might seem trite to say that people are any organization's *greatest* resource, but nonetheless it is true – and especially true – for service industries. It is also true to say that people in service industries will generally be the most *expensive* resource. However, this book is not designed as a human resource manager's handbook: it is designed for the general manager, and in particular the operations manager, so that they can make the most effective use of resources – primarily by the involvement and motivation of the people with whom they work, including suppliers of goods and services through to the end user of the service.

The text contains tools and techniques for developing and implementing strategies, and draws on everyday examples to provide basic day-to-day 'tips' in making the most efficient use of resources to gain a competitive edge through a focus on customer satisfaction. The book concludes with chapters on how to develop measures that will make a difference, and how to change the culture of an organization in order to self-motivate the people of the organization.

CD ROM CASE STUDIES

In addition to the everyday examples given in the book, additional case study material (including questions and answers) is given in the CD ROM included with the book. This CD ROM is edited by Professor Ray Wild, Principal of Henley Management College. The cases, which were selected by Ray and myself, illustrate and reinforce the book and provide an additional basis for study. Questions are included with the cases that are designed for you to check your understanding and to relate theory to practical management situations.

J. NEVAN WRIGHT

Acknowledgements

I am indebted to Professor Ray Wild for encouraging me to write this book and for the many hours he freely gave to read the draft of each chapter and for his helpful suggestions and comments. The final version is, however, my effort, and therefore any errors or omissions are my responsibility alone.

My original intention was to write a companion book for Ray Wild's definitive work *Production and Operations Management* (5th edition, 1995) but specifically based on service industries. While it is true that much of the material in *The Management of Service Operations* is derived from *Production and Operations Management*, much has been re-ordered to fit the service environment, and much new material is introduced which will not be found in that book. This has led to a new book which, although it does not differ in basic philosophy, cannot be considered as just the 'service' version of *Production and Operations Management*. I do however wish to acknowledge Ray's generosity in allowing me to quote so freely from his book.

Readers of *Total Manufacturing Solutions* (1998), written by Ron Basu and myself, will recognize the same theme of a holistic approach to the management of organizations. *The Management of Service Operations* freely draws on sections of *Total Manufacturing Solutions* where appropriate to service industries (direct quotations are acknowledged where possible). Again I wish to acknowledge Ron's friendship and the fun we had in writing *Total Manufacturing Solutions*.

Above all this book is drawn from my own experiences, the experiences of others and from a wide reading of contemporary management issues. It would not be possible to acknowledge the source of all the concepts that have been used: in some cases the source has been lost in the mists of time, on other occasions I have read ideas and suggestions which I am almost sure I first propounded in past lectures or articles! Suffice to say I have made every endeavour to credit materials and ideas of others (see References at the end of the book). I offer apologies to the authors of any works that I have failed to mention.

My thanks go also to David Barker, Helena Power and the team at Cassell. It is obvious that they know the meaning of good service.

I dedicate this book to Joy,
my wife and my best friend,
who put in many hours proof-reading.
(Naturally any mistakes will be mine.)

Introduction

Growth of service industries

It is generally agreed that 75 per cent of the workforce in the United Kingdom are engaged in service industries. This high percentage is not unique to the United Kingdom: it is representative of employment statistics for developed nations throughout the world. Indeed the US Bureau of the Census (1990: 395) shows that 80 per cent of the workforce in the United States is employed in service industries. Although a shift back to manufacturing industries has been identified (Basu and Wright, 1998), it is obvious that the greater percentage of the workforce of developed nations will continue to be employed in service-type activities. There are two reasons for this:

1. Continual advances in technology mean that manufacturing is considerably less labour intensive than in previous times. Automation, robotics, advanced information technology, new materials and improved work methods all have led to the decimation of manual labour.
2. For larger organizations, manufacturing has become internationalized. For example a company such as Xerox, once an American-based manufacturer of photocopiers, now regards itself primarily as a marketing and service company, with its manufacturing being supplied by contractors or allied companies situated all round the world.

Additionally, organizations can no longer regard themselves as being purely in manufacturing and hope to survive. The market first and foremost now demands quality of product *and* service. Market expectations of the level of quality are driven by perceptions of what technology is promising and by perceptions of what the competition is offering.

Organizations now operate in a global market where national barriers, tariffs and customs duties no longer provide protection for a home market. Any manufacturer, even if it has concentrated its efforts on supplying a local market, is in reality competing on the world stage. Competition is no longer limited to other local organizations, and the fiercest competition in the home market will be from goods produced overseas. This fact alone has meant that manufacturers can no longer make products to suit their engineering strengths, but must now be aware of what the market wants and what global competition is offering. And what the competition is offering is service, in the form of delivery on time, marketing advice, training, installation, project management, or whatever else is required to provide a total service as well as a reliable product.

Finally, it has to be recognized that never before in history has the customer been better travelled, more informed and had higher expectations. Many of these expectations for continuously improved product and service have arisen from global competition, and the well-publicized total quality management (TQM) drive of the 1980s, and the success of quality crusaders such as the charismatic Tom Peters.

Customers expect, and take for granted a reliable, high-quality product for their money, and most organizations realize that their products actually differ very little from those of their competitors, and any technological improvement is soon copied; thus the difference – the 'competitive edge' – comes from service.

Service separated from production operations

If no serious operation can ignore market demands for service and world-class quality, why bother to try and separate manufacturing from service in the study of operations management? Indeed for a manufacturing organization aspiring to world-class status I would agree, most emphatically, that the operations managers of such organizations must concern themselves with service and quality if they are to compete on the world stage.

But operations managers in service industries such as health, retail, distribution, education, travel, real estate, consultation, brokering, law, accounting, administration of central and local government, transportation of goods or people – where no direct manufacturing is involved, or where the manufacturing is light and simple (such as in a restaurant) – do not have to know much about manufacturing. Although all the above industries are reliant on manufacturers to varying degrees for the equipment they use, or in the case of a retailer for the goods they sell, the actual physical heavy work of making the goods is not their concern. The analogy is that of a driver of a car: one can be a very good driver without knowing very much about what happens under the bonnet. Some knowledge of when to change gear, and the danger of overheating due to lack of oil or water will be of advantage, but not much more is really necessary. Likewise with the operations manager in the service industry, a detailed knowledge of line balancing for a high-tech mass production line of washing machines is not necessary for a retailer of white wear. Some knowledge of lead times for deliveries, operating instructions and the capacity of the washing machine will be sufficient for the salesperson as a basis for good service to the customer.

Thus there can be a separation of operations management into two distinct streams: the management of operations management in production including service, and the management of operations in service industries (for whom this book is written) where only some rudimentary knowledge of manufacturing is required.

The operations manager that is involved directly in production and manufacturing needs to be well versed in strategies, tactics and methodologies of production operations management and also has to be very aware of what constitutes service and quality from the customer's point of view. Books such as *Production and*

Operations Management (Wild, 1995) or *Total Manufacturing Solutions* (Basu and Wright, 1998) are recommended for operations managers who need to take a total operations approach to providing a quality product coupled with the service required to better the competition.

On the other hand, operations managers who are primarily engaged in service industries do not need a detailed knowledge of production systems and methodologies. What they want is a book that specifically covers managing service operations as efficiently as possible and providing better service than the competition. Indeed over recent years more and more members and associates at Henley Management College have asked me to recommend an operations management book that is specifically designed for the service industry practitioner. I was not able to recommend one book alone that met this requirement, and as a result, at my students' request, I undertook to write this book.

At Henley Management College it is believed that it is important that members of programmes are able to apply course material to their own working environment. Therefore *The Management of Service Operations* is designed so that those employed in service industries will find this book practical, and user friendly. The 'theory' is brought to life by the use of carefully researched case studies from a wide spectrum of service industries which are presented on the attached CD ROM edited by Professor Ray Wild.

Theme of the book

The underlying theme of this book is the elimination of non-value-adding activities and the provision of customer satisfaction in service industries. The book takes a whole systems approach, from supplier through service provider to customer, and back again. Above all, it is stressed that particularly in a service industry, people are an organization's greatest resource. People include management and staff at all levels. It is concluded that if the organizational culture is 'right' there is little that an organization cannot achieve. The final chapter therefore deals with how to attain the 'right' culture: this has been reached when any member of the staff, when faced with an unusual or difficult problem, reacts instinctively in the manner in which management would have hoped they would act.

Part One

Part One is the foundation for the rest of the book. This part consists of two chapters.

- **Chapter 1** begins with some basic definitions, establishes the framework in which operations managers work, looks at the constraints of policy, and shows how what can be achieved is limited by resources and systems structure.

  The intangible nature of service is introduced.

- **Chapter 2** considers the dimensions of customer satisfaction, competition and resource utilization.

  The inherent conflict between achievement of customer satisfaction and efficient resource utilization is identified.

Chapter 1

Making it happen

Objectives for this chapter

Issues covered in this chapter are:

- The mission of a service organization.
- The theme of a whole systems approach.
- Definitions for service organizations.
- The importance of systems structure.

Introduction

In this chapter we consider the role of the operations function and the operations manager in service organizations. We look at the important role the customer plays as an input into the service operation. A framework for analysing the structure of the operating system is introduced.

The mission

Customer service is the mission – the reason for existence – of service organizations. Operations management is the function within a service organization which interacts with and delivers services to customers, and therefore efficient operations management is crucial to the success of the organization. The role of a manager of operations is to provide customer satisfaction within the framework of the organization's policy, and to use resources as efficiently as possible. Simply put: the operations manager 'makes it (the mission) happen'.

Techniques and strategies

This book tells you how operations managers make the service mission happen, and introduces techniques to make the service operations manager's life easier. Some of these techniques are new, but most of them are tried and proven. All of the techniques covered have a particular relevance to service organizations. Operations managers do not work in a vacuum; their options are influenced by factors over which they may have little control. These influencing factors and how to recognize their operational significance are considered, and strategies that can be adopted to make the most of operational situations are given.

Theme

The overall theme of this book is the elimination of non-value-adding activities within a service organization and the provision of excellent customer service. A whole systems approach, from supplier through to the successful delivery of service to the customer, is taken.

Definitions

The terms *operating system* and *operations management* will be referred to throughout the book. Service organizations – the focus of the book – is also referred to. We need to begin by defining these terms.

Definition 1: Service organization

> A service organization is when two or more people are engaged in a systematic effort to provide services to a customer, the objective being to *serve* a customer.

A service organization exists to *interact* with customers and to satisfy customers' service requirements. For any service to be provided, there has to be a customer. Without a customer, and interaction between customer and the service organization, the objective of providing service cannot exist.

The degree of intensity of interaction between the customer and personnel within a service organization varies and depends on the type of service offered. For example, a specialist medical consultant will have a high degree of 'face-to-face' interaction with the customer, and so will a hairdresser. Further down the scale of face-to-face interaction is a restaurant where the customer will judge the quality of service by the level of interaction (wine waiter's knowledge, waiting staff's attentiveness) as well as by the standard of the goods provided (wine and food). The restaurant in turn will, however, have a higher degree of personal interaction than will a fast-food takeaway. A scale of personal interaction is shown in Figure 1.1. The bottom of the scale on Figure 1.1 is automatic 'cashpoint' banking where customer interaction is purely with a machine.

Irrespective of the level of 'face-to-face' interaction, without some customer interaction, service cannot be provided. However, this does not mean that the customer always has to be present when the service is being provided. For example, when a car is being serviced by a mechanic, the owner of the car need not be present; but without the owner providing the car and giving instructions ('Grease and oil-change, ready at five?') no service can be provided.

 YOUR TURN!

Using a scale of 1 (low) to 10 (high) where would you rate the following service industries for personal interaction?

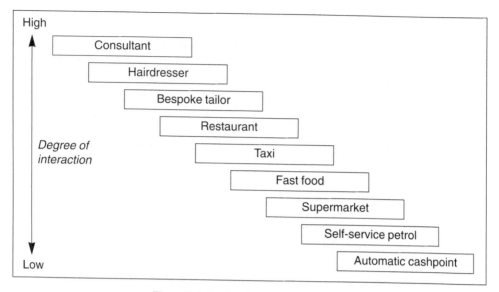

Figure 1.1: Scale of personal interaction

Retail shop
Tax Office
Ambulance
Dentist
Furniture removal
Fire Service
Emergency ward
Laundrette
Hotel
Commuter bus
Architect
Insurance broker

Where does your own organization lie on the scale?

Definition 2: Service operating system

A service operating system is the manner in which *inputs* are organized and used to provide service *outputs*.

Inputs

As shown above, without a customer the objective of service cannot be delivered, and therefore the customer must be regarded as an input to the system which provides the service. The role of the customer as an input to the system is discussed in detail later in this chapter under the heading 'System structures'.

Other inputs into the system are resources. Resources include:

- *Materials.* Materials used by the operating system include utilities such as energy, water and gas. Materials also include goods that are consumed by the system, goods that are transformed by the system, and goods held for sale. Transformation refers to changing the shape or form of inputs to produce an output. For example, by placing lettuce leaves, a beefburger and a slice of tomato between two halves of a bun, we have combined and transformed several goods to produce a new good, commonly known as a hamburger.
- *Machines/equipment.* These include computers, communication equipment, plant, fittings, vehicles, display racks, etc., and real-estate property available to the operating system.
- *People.* People not only means the number of people employed in the operating system, but includes knowledge and skill levels, and also includes the intangibles of dependability and attitude.

All of the above represent either a capital investment or an ongoing expense to the organization. Tangible inputs are physical and can be seen and touched, and the amount or rate of use can be measured in quantifiable terms.

Intangible inputs, which cannot be seen or touched, include:

- time;
- information.

Measurement of effective use of time and information is less obvious than for the tangible resources. Nevertheless, the amount of time and information available will be important issues for the operations manager.

With today's technology, information would seem to be readily available. The concern of the operations manager, however, will be *knowing* what information is required, and then being able to *interpret* and *use* information so as to achieve the organization's operational objectives.

The flow of resources through the operating system is shown in Figure 1.2. Customer and resources are brought together to provide a service output.

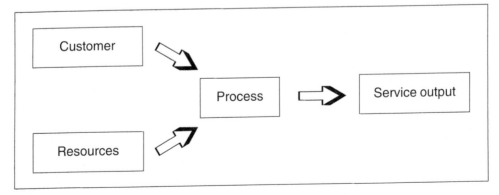

Figure 1.2: Service industry: customer-driven

EXAMPLES

- *Bus service.* A bus can travel on its advertised route, but until a passenger is carried, the function of the bus service is not achieved. Without a passenger the mission of the bus service – to carry passengers – cannot be fulfilled. An empty bus travelling on the bus route is nothing more than an unutilized, or 'stored', resource. Apart from the bus itself, other resources such as fuel, and the time (wages) of the driver are being used.

- *Hotel room.* Until a guest checks in, the service function of the hotel cannot be performed. The room can be 'serviced' and prepared in advance, but until a guest arrives there is no service output.

- *Restaurant.* With a restaurant it is possible for the chef to make up salads, and even to prepare and cook meals in advance, before any customer is seated. This may not be the policy (strategy) of a topline restaurant but nonetheless the decision (strategy) can be changed, i.e. it is not essential to have a customer before a meal is prepared. However, the mission of the restaurant is not to *prepare* meals, it is to *serve* meals, and the delivery of service cannot take place without the customer – it is not possible for the meal to be served unless there is a customer who has placed an order.

All three examples – the bus travelling on its route, the prepared hotel room, and the partly prepared meal in the restaurant – involve stored resources waiting for the input of a customer. Without customer input no service output will be delivered.

Definition 3: Service operations management

Operations management is the ongoing activities of designing, reviewing and using the operating system, or systems, to achieve service outputs as determined by the organization for customers.

The operations manager is a decision-maker. Decisions range from long-term strategy to short-term day-to-day operational concerns. As the operations manager is at the hub of, and responsible for 'making it happen', it follows that the most pressing decisions are of a day-to-day nature.

The operations manager will be limited in the decisions that can be made. The limitations are set, on the one hand, by the objectives of the organization, and on the other by what is feasible with the resources available and by the *structure* of the system.

In short, decision-making is limited by what is:

- *Desired* by the organization (mission and policy of the organization).
- *Feasible* with the amount and quality of resources (tangible and intangible) available, and given the nature – in particular the structure – of the operating system being used.

Figure 1.3: Making it happen

Figure 1.3 shows the constraints of an operations manager. The mission and policy of the organization set the scope of the operations manager. How business policy is determined is covered in Part Two (Chapter 3). Once the policy has been decided, then what is desirable is expressed as the objectives of the organization, and what is feasible is limited by the resources and structure of the organization.

The more demanding the objectives, the fewer the resources and the more limiting the structure, the less choice the operations manager will have in making decisions, and *vice versa*. The aim of the operations manger will be to use resources as *efficiently* as possible to achieve the highest level of *customer satisfaction* within the constraints of policy objectives, available resources and the system structure.

System structures

In considering system structures we find it convenient to use the following symbols:

O = the process of combining resources to add value.
V = 'store' of resources, or queue of customers waiting to enter the system.
⇨ = the flow of resources through the system.
C = the customer. Note, the customer does not have to be external to the organization, but may be an internal customer.

The 'internal customer' can be defined as the next person, or department, in the process.

Overall there are three basic service structures (Figures 1.4, 1.5, 1.6), but often organizations will consist of a combination of systems. The structures and the form of notation have been adapted from Wild (1995).

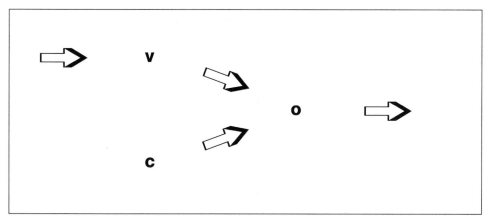

Figure 1.4: Service direct from resource to customer

Figure 1.4 shows service being provided direct to the customer from a stock of resource. The stock of resource could be the bus moving from stop to stop, an accident ward waiting for patients, a fire brigade waiting for a call-out, a restaurant waiting for diners, an accountant waiting for customers, or a betting shop waiting for punters. In this structure the customer does not normally wait: the resources do.

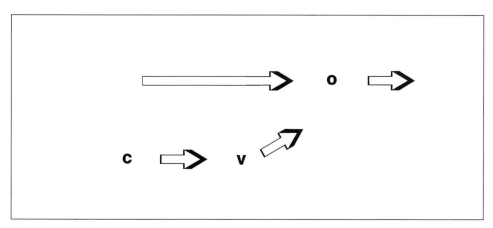

Figure 1.5: Customers form a queue for services

Figure 1.5 shows how most service providers would like to operate. Customers form a queue for services. An example is the dentist. Customers phone in for service, and are given an appointment. The dentist then draws patients from a stock of customers, with no waiting (by the dentist) between jobs. Evidence of this type of system can be seen at banks, post offices and supermarkets. Refuse collection is another example; the customer puts the wheelie bin out and the bin 'waits' to be emptied.

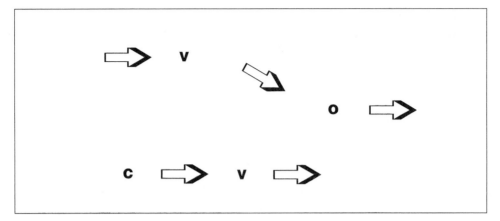

Figure 1.6: Spare resource waiting for customers; queues also form

Figure 1.6 shows a structure where there is spare resource waiting for customers, and customer queues also form.

In reality, the dentist, the accountant, the lawyer, the real-estate agent, the taxi driver, the travel agent, and the social service worker operate in this manner. In effect all inputs are stocked and customers accumulate in queues. Although the dentist would prefer not to wait for customers but to draw customers from the accumulated stock in the appointment book, in practice the dentist will be obliged to set aside some time each day for emergency treatment. If no patient arrives during the time set aside for emergency patients then the dentist will become an unused resource.

Some readers will ask why a service system could not be 'just in time', i.e. no spare resource and no customer queues. The answer is that if customers are never kept waiting there has to be spare resource, or alternatively if resources are going to be fully utilized with no idle time, there has to be a stock of customers to be drawn from. From time to time a perfectly balanced system might appear to exist but this will only be a temporary phenomenon.

Combined structures

Although three basic service system structures are shown above, in reality most organizations will employ a combination of structures.

The structures we have looked at so far are customer 'push' systems. Another type of structure is a customer 'pull' system, which occurs where activities take place in anticipation that eventually a customer will arrive. Sometimes the projected demand is known with a fair amount of certainty in advance, and activities can therefore be safely scheduled in advance. In this scenario the expected demand 'pulls' the system, rather than waiting for direct customer input to 'push' the system.

EXAMPLE

Motel

A small motel consists of twenty rooms. Occupancy varies but is on average 80 per cent. Some guests book in advance but mainly the motel relies on passing traffic. Each day, previously occupied rooms are cleaned and linen changed in anticipation of guests arriving. The system structure can be depicted as in Figure 1.7.

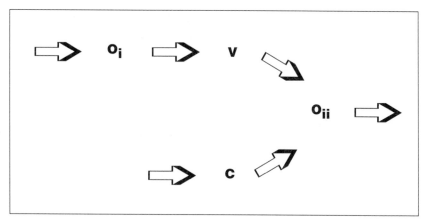

Figure 1.7: A customer 'pull' structure

In Figure 1.7, 'Oi' is the preparation of a room, 'V' represents that cost has been incurred and resources transformed and held – 'stored' – in anticipation of a customer. The service operation doesn't actually occur until 'Oii', i.e. a guest, arrives ('C') and a room is allotted.

Importance of structures

It is important to realize which structure(s) applies to your organization. The structure employed will determine what is feasible, and an understanding of the structures which are in force will enable consideration to be given to changing structures so as to best meet the aims and objectives of the organization.

For example it will be a policy decision that decides that:

1. resources will be stored in advance of customer requirements: such a structure implies some surplus capacity in the system;
2. no surplus resource will be held and that it is accepted that customers will queue for service.

YOUR TURN!

Consider your organization and identify the structures that apply.

CHAPTER SUMMARY

In this chapter we have defined operations management as the function within a service organization which interacts with customers and delivers service to customers. The role of the operations manager was shown to be to use resources as efficiently as possible to achive the highest level of customer satisfaction within the constraints of policy objectives, available resources and systems structures. The chapter concluded with an explanation of the three basic systems structures that can exist in a service organization, and it was shown how system structure would determine what is feasible.

Chapter 2

Operations objectives

Objectives for this chapter

Issues covered in this chapter are:

- Basic service requirements.
- The importance of stakeholders and their needs.
- Dimensions of resource utilization and efficiency.

Introduction

Managers of operations have two key objectives. The first is to satisfy customers' wants. Without customers the organization will cease to exist. The second key objective is the efficient use of resources. If an organization cannot afford the level of service it is providing, it will soon go out of business. The twin objectives of an operations manager must therefore be the provision of customer satisfaction combined with efficient use of resources. This chapter considers the dimensions of customer satisfaction and resource utilization.

Customers are sophisticated

Never before has the customer been more travelled, better informed and had higher expectations. Customers now take it as a matter of right that they will get a reliable, high-quality product and courteous, well-informed service. World-class organizations know that new products, services and technological improvements are quickly copied and improved upon and thus offer only a short-term advantage in the marketplace. They also know that the 'competitive edge' comes from providing a higher level of customer satisfaction than does the competition.

The role of competition

The quality of product and the level of service provided in a competitive market must at least equate to what the competition is providing or is perceived to be providing. Customers' expectations are influenced by what they have previously experienced, by what the competition is claiming to provide in advertisements, by what the media is saying, and by the promises of technological improvements.

Basic service requirements

When introducing the concept of customer satisfaction, it has to be understood that the basic requirements of any service, for the customer, are that the service must meet their specification and secondly that it will meet time and cost requirements.

Specification – providing the customer with what they expect to receive or are prepared to accept – is the essential requirement.

Time and cost are the next requirements. The service has to be provided at a time that is acceptable to the customer, and the price must be reasonable.

What is acceptable or reasonable will always be open to question, and will depend on the circumstances of how important the service is to the customer and the alternatives available.

EXAMPLE

Consider a commuter bus service – if a bus is not going from near where we live ('A') to near where we work ('B') then we will not catch it; and if the service does not get us to work on time and quickly, we will not use it. Also, if the cost is too high we will seek alternatives. Thus the essential dimension of customer satisfaction is specification (the bus must be going from 'A' to 'B'). In this example, if the specification is not right, time and cost are irrelevant.

Usually customers will accept, or tolerate, a service that does not perfectly meet their requirements. The amount of tolerance will be dependent on what the competition is offering or, if there is no immediate competition, what the alternatives are. Customers might be prepared to trade some specification for cost or timing, for instance the passenger may be prepared to walk an extra block to catch a train, rather than take the bus, if the train fare is considerably cheaper.

Provider's perspective

From the perspective of a services provider, what is provided has to be what can be afforded, and must be at least up to the same standard as the competition. The determination of what to provide is based on economic considerations rather than altruism. Customers are needed for income, but in the long term the organization cannot afford to run at a loss. Many an organization has failed to survive although customers have received excellent service. (Efficient use of resources is covered later in this chapter.)

Competitive advantage

As described in the opening sentences of this chapter, in today's environment of world-class standards and sophisticated customers, and where new services are quickly copied and improved upon by the competition, often the only competitive advantage will be from the level of service provided. Thus customer satisfaction goes past the basics of specification, time and cost to include the *quality* of service. Quality has two dimensions: customer satisfaction and efficient use of resources. What constitutes quality, how it is judged and controlled, and the culture of quality is detailed in Chapter 10. However, because of the importance of the quality of service in gaining a competitive edge, our discussion on customer service would be incomplete if we were to ignore the rudiments of what can be done to enhance the basic attributes of specification, cost and time.

In our example of the bus service, having offered a service that attracts customers – specification, cost and time are acceptable – it will be possible to look at ways of adding a perception of increased service without adding to the cost.

Adding value

Generally some perception of added service can be provided at very little cost. Using our bus service as an example; assuming that specification, cost and timing meet the customer's basic needs (the bus is going to the right place, at the right time and the price is right) additional quality service attributes which probably would be appreciated by the passengers might include punctuality, clean bus, friendly and well-presented driver, and consistency of service. A punctual service will be achieved by good planning and should not cost the company any extra to achieve; keeping the bus clean might add marginally to the cost (cleaning materials and wages). Issuing the driver with a smart uniform will obviously be a cost, and training a driver to be courteous and well-groomed might also incur some cost. Although all such costs are minimal when compared to the total operating cost of a bus company, the overall perception will be an improved service, *although the basics of specification, timing and costs have not changed.*

It is important to recognize that, above all, customers expect a reliable and consistent service. A service that is sometimes excellent and sometimes indifferent will only confuse the customer. Once a service level has been established, then the standard must be maintained.

For any organization, increased service at little or no cost will require a special culture. The workforce has to be enthusiastic and has to have some authority to make limited operational decisions. Creating a quality culture resulting in staff motivated to reduce inefficiencies and to give friendly and consistent service is covered in Chapter 10.

Reverting to our bus service, if having achieved the basics – right route, right time, right price, clean bus, friendly well-presented driver – the customers were now surveyed, it might be found that they would also like a more frequent service, sheltered waiting areas and more comfortable buses. Additional service at this level, such as a bus every ten minutes rather than one bus every half-hour, the provision of bus shelters, and an upgrade of the fleet will add an appreciable amount of cost, and the economics of doing so, rather than what the customer wants, will determine if such additional services are provided.

In Chapter 9 we examine scheduling strategies and techniques, but suffice to say that for this example it might be possible (if we have sufficient buses and drivers) to provide a ten-minute service at peak periods and to reduce the service to once an hour at other times without adding to the overall operating cost *and* at the same time providing a better service for peak-hour passengers.

To recap, customer satisfaction has three levels:

- The basics of specification, cost and timing have to be acceptable to the customer.
- The perception of an improved quality service can be achieved at very little cost, i.e. cleanliness, consistency, reliability, friendly and helpful front-line staff, etc.
- Added tangible value will cost money.

What is offered has to be affordable and sustainable.

We will now concentrate on determining who the customer really is, who are stakeholders, and how to rank the relative importance of the various requirements of customers and influential stakeholders.

Who is the customer?

In Chapter 1 we established that the customer is an input into the process. Quite simply, without a customer no service can be performed (see Figure 2.1).

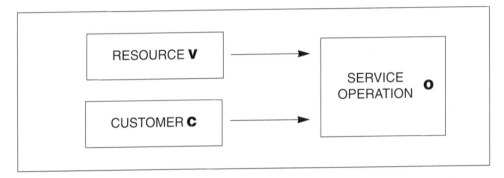

Figure 2.1: The role of the customer

Internal customers

In Chapter 10 we discuss the philosophy of total quality management (TQM). Some of the proponents of TQM consider the customer to be the next step in the operating process. For example with TQM a writer when passing a manuscript to a word-processing person would consider the *word processor* to be the customer. The TQM approach would appear to conflict with our stance which is that in a service industry the customer is an *input* into the process, rather than the *next step* in the process; thus we would show the *writer* as the customer.

The TQM concept of the internal customer was always a contrivance, initially aimed to get factory workers on an assembly line to reduce waste and to pass on a good job to the next operator in the process. It was easy to say that without customers we will not sell our goods, and without sales the factory will close, but for the operator wielding the screwdriver, faced with a seemingly never-ending assembly line, the customer was remote and faceless. Making the next person on the line the customer gave the customer a face. We do not criticise this approach: anything that serves to make work more meaningful, gives people more esteem and reduces costs, has to be applauded. However, in reality it has to be accepted that the factory worker has very little control over the quality of the product – the worker does not decide on the quality of the material used or decide on how many coats of paint will be applied, and even if a worker tried to take a craft worker's approach to the job, the time available to add the finishing touches to his or her small step in the overall process will be restricted by the speed of the line. Suffice to say that the suggestion that the next step in the process is an internal customer will not help to determine what the end user (the true customer) of the product or service really wants, *nor will it help when trying to analyse the structure of an operating service system.*

There can, of course, be customers drawn from within an organization.

EXAMPLE

A large organization with its own research department has moved to establish cost/profit centres. Previously the research department relied on other departments of the organization for research projects. The research department was not proactive in seeking work. The operating structure is shown in Figure 2.2.

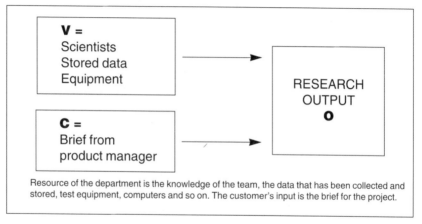

Resource of the department is the knowledge of the team, the data that has been collected and stored, test equipment, computers and so on. The customer's input is the brief for the project.

Figure 2.2: Research department operating structure

Using our systems structure approach it is apparent that without input from the customer no research would begin, and it is also likely that the product manager and his or her staff will be consulted at various stages as the research proceeds; therefore the customer, although internal to the organization, is more (in TQM terms) than just the next step in the process. To limit the department to being the next step in the process does not encourage proactivity, but encourages the department to think of themselves as the 'customer'. As a 'customer', the culture would not be to go out looking for work but to wait for work to come to them.

Once it is realized that the customer is an input, rather than the next stage in the process, it will be appreciated that the department cannot afford to passively wait for briefs from other departments. To survive, the research department will have to be proactive. They will need to promote themselves within the organization, and if sufficient customers are not available from within there should be no reason why they should not promote themselves outside the organization, i.e. look for work external to the organization.

EXAMPLE

A pension fund department of a water board is now seeking to manage funds for outside companies. Even two years ago this would not have been contemplated by the department, and even if such a suggestion had been put forward – 'to go outside the organization for pension customers' – it is likely that the board would not have sanctioned such a move. This is just another example of how the move towards deregulation and privatization around the world has set the environment for government-type organizations to become commercially orientated.

Satisfying the stakeholders or who pays the ferryman?

A stakeholder is anyone who has an interest in what an organization does. This might seem a very broad definition, and indeed it is. Knowing who stakeholders are and how their concerns might affect the operation of an organization is, however, becoming more and more critical.

With some organizations, usually public sector-type operations such as education, health and social welfare, the person with the direct input into the system – the student, the patient, the welfare beneficiary – has to be satisfied. Without these people (the direct customers) the need for the service will disappear. However, in many cases the direct customers do not personally pay for the service they receive. Funds for the operation come from the government, or in some cases charitable trusts. The body that provides the funds (government or charitable organization) obviously has a *stake* in the efficiency of the operation. These stakeholders, the fund providers, should, and increasingly do, seek value for money. In their eyes value for money will not only include providing a level of service to the customer but will also include efficient use of resources. There are also other stakeholders who do not directly provide money, such as the general public in the guise of taxpayers; they also are concerned that their money is being spent wisely.

EXAMPLE

For a government-funded university the customer is the student (the direct input into the teaching process). A major stakeholder is the government (major source of funds) and their concern will be that they are getting value for money. Other providers of funds include fee-paying students and their sponsors (parents or work organizations) and business houses who make grants or sponsor a chair. All these stakeholders have a stake in the *quality* of the outputs. There are still other stakeholders who do not directly provide funds for the university, but who will have a very real interest in the quality and relevance of the teaching provided. If the university offers law and/or accountancy degrees then relevant professional bodies and societies will have a special interest, and perhaps even some direct say, in what is taught. Likewise others who may not directly contribute funds, such as some parents, employers and prospective employers of graduates, and the staff of the university are all stakeholders. Each group of stakeholders is likely to have different priorities in judging the service provided. Some fund providers and taxpayers will be anxious that resources are being efficiently utilized (money is not being wasted); others will be more concerned with what is being taught, and the value of qualifications (perceived standard or status of the university).

Determining stakeholders

For commercial businesses a stakeholder is anyone with a pecuniary interest in the organization (such as shareholders, banks, financiers, investors, suppliers of goods and services, and the people who work in the organization and their families). Other more general stakeholders include investors in the share market, local bodies in the district of the operation, people who live and work in the operation's general neighbourhood, and the green movement. For government and quasi-government organizations, charitable trusts and other like bodies, stakeholders are fund providers, bankers, suppliers, people who work in the organization and their families, and the community at large.

YOUR TURN!

Identify the stakeholders for your organization and their concerns. (Identifying stakeholders and determining their concerns should prove to be an interesting exercise.)
Now rank their importance.

Customer/stakeholder priorities

Customer satisfaction therefore has two elements:

1. We have to *know* exactly what the customers want in terms of specification, price and timing.
2. We have to ensure that what is being offered and the manner in which we operate, to satisfy the customer, is not conflicting with the interests of stakeholders.

The matrix in Figure 2.3 is designed to allow a service industry to analyse customers' and stakeholders' needs. An example will best show the use of such a matrix.

EXAMPLE

The direct customers for the Refuse Collection Department of the Highvale Borough Council are considered to be householders. The service provided is a weekly collection of refuse. The Borough Council

	Specification	Timing	Price
Direct customers			
Stakeholders a			
b			
c			
d			
Total			

Figure 2.3: A service industry matrix

has recently decided to add a surcharge to the rates to partly offset the cost of refuse collection; until now there has not been a separate charge. The commercial (or business) district of the town also has refuse collected by the department, but commercial organizations are charged separately for this, and some organizations use alternative means of rubbish disposal. No competition yet exists for household refuse collection, but two private refuse collectors operate in a neighbouring town. The fee that will be charged by the Highvale Borough Council does not cover the full cost of the service and is much cheaper than neighbouring independent operators. Local body elections are due in eighteen months' time.

The operations manager (the manager of the Refuse Department) is worried that the charging of a fee by the Council suggests they are concerned with the cost of running the department. His other worry is that if householders are to pay for the service, they might become more critical and demand a higher service. In other words the Council have indicated that they are concerned with the cost of running the department, and customers are now likely to expect a higher level of service. The other worry for the operations manager is that the Council might consider out-sourcing (buying in) the service.

To determine what is wanted by the direct customers and by the Council, and to see if there are any other stakeholders, the operations manager commissioned a survey. The survey was designed to determine, first, what the customers and stakeholders (if any) wanted; and second, their perceptions of what they are currently getting. Results of the survey are tabulated in Figure 2.4.

Requirements
The results of the survey by the customer/stakeholder group showed that:

1. Householders' requirements are as follows:

    Specification

    Householders require a good service (ideally bins always fully emptied and left in a tidy manner with no rubbish scattered on the road).

    Timing

    Timing is important – householders want a regular service (same day each week).

    Price

    Price is most important to the customers. They rate price above service, and they do not see a need for the Council to make a profit on refuse collection (being close to budget is sufficient).

2. Council requirements are:

    Specification

    To maintain a reasonable service (they are not concerned if the occasional bin is missed).

Desired service (rating: 1 = very important; 2 = important; 1 = not important):

	Bins emptied	Timing	Price	Keep to budget
Direct customers	2	2	3	1
Stakeholders:				
Council	2	1	1	2
Commercial				
ratepayers	1	1	1	3

Perceptions of present service (rating: 3 = excellent; 2 = acceptable; 1 = not good):

	Bins emptied	Timing	Price	Keep to budget
Direct customers	3	3	2	2
Stakeholders:				
Council	3	3	2	1
Commercial				
ratepayers	3	3	1	1

Figure 2.4: Desired service

Timing
Timing is not vital.

Price
Keeping to budget is regarded as essential.

3. Requirements of important stakeholders:

    Commercial ratepayers see that keeping to budget is essential. Some
    even suggested that the Refuse Department should actually run at a
    profit, and others suggested that the service should be outsourced.
    Commercial ratepayers provide 70 per cent of the Council's income,
    and have a strong lobby group. They believe that they are subsidising
    the householders.

4. Other stakeholders' requirements
    The concern of the people who work in the department, and their
    immediate families, is with job security. They are confident that they
    can improve the efficiency of the service, and already some useful
    suggestions have been made.

Perceptions of existing service
Customers and all the stakeholders see the service as excellent. If the
operations manager was only concerned with what the customers want
then he would have been very pleased with the outcome of the survey. But
as the other stakeholders do not rate service as being the critical area of
measurement, this suggests a rethink of the priorities of the department.

From this analysis, the operations manager can see that the Council
cannot afford to run the service at a loss. Prior to this analysis, as the
Council was not suggesting an increase in fees for the commercial sector,
the operations manager had not realized that the commercial ratepayers
had an interest in the service for householders, and he had certainly not
considered that the commercial sector could actually threaten the future
of the department.

The results of the survey indicate that if the department cannot keep
to budget, the Council will put the price up or perhaps consider sub-
contracting to private providers. Likewise householders are very price
conscious and if the Council does contemplate a price increase the
householders could themselves well lobby for private subcontractors.
Now that the operations manager realizes the importance for the
department of not only keeping to budget but actually reducing costs, he
is looking to see if some efficiencies are possible. Until now regular and
high-level service rather than cost had been his main objective; keeping to
budget had been of secondary importance.

Adaptation of matrix

This type of matrix analysis can be adapted to any service industry. Even if there are no stakeholders, and there are only customers to be satisfied, then the analysis can be extended to include different groups or segments of customers. Pareto analysis will be a useful tool (see Chapter 3) where it may be found that a vital few will account for up to 80 per cent of the business.

Stakeholders such as banks and creditors (suppliers of goods and services) will generally only be interested in the financial security of the business. Other stakeholders such as people living in the neighbourhood of the operation will have other concerns such as pollution, noise and perhaps even heavy traffic flows. If local concerns are known in advance then action can be taken to prevent offence. Actions that have to be taken as a result of protests or legal initiatives not only taint an organization's reputation but will prove more costly than if the operation had been set up correctly and stakeholders' concerns addressed in the first place.

Composite customer service rating

Christopher (1992) gives another method of rating customer service, as illustrated in Table 2.1.

Service index	Weighting %	Performance %	Weighted score
	(a)	(b)	(a × b)
Order fill	45	70	0.315
On time	35	80	0.28
Invoice accuracy	10	90	0.09
Returns	10	95	0.095
	100		0.78
Composite customer service rating			*78%*

Table 2.1: Rating customer service

In this example the key criterion has been established as filling orders (specification): this is the most important criterion and has been given a rating of 45/100. On-time delivery is the next most important, and other important criteria (but of lesser rating) are invoice accuracy and the number of returns (return represents faulty goods).

Column 'b' shows that 70 per cent of orders are filled, 80 per cent of orders are sent on time, the accounts department are 90 per cent accurate, and 5 per cent of goods are faulty. Christopher's composite customer service rating is calculated against internally set standards of service, and is also calculated on internally gathered data, rather than on feedback from customers.

However, no matter how good or how relevant we think our own internal measures are, such as Christopher's composite service rating, there is no better method than to ask the customer. Ideally, internal measures should be set against targets established by the customer.

What might seem trivial to the business could, in the customer's eyes, be seen as a major problem. For example we might find that an important customer claims that they can never get through on the phone. Once we appreciated this we could then set the target that the phone must be answered within three rings. We might also do away with automatic recorded telephone answering: leaving a message on voice-mail is a very poor option. To stress the point that we are easy to communicate with, we could also set a target that all faxes and e-mails are replied to on the day received. No internal measures of such targets are needed if the culture of the organization is such that the staff are all driven by a desire to satisfy the customer (see Chapter 10).

Gap analysis

The level of service offered stems from the business policy which, in turn, to a large extent is driven by what the competition is doing or is threatening to do. When deciding upon and specifying a level of service, management tends to rely on the advice of the marketing function. If the marketing function does not correctly interpret the requirements of the customer then there will be a *gap* between the level of satisfaction the organization believes it is providing and what the customer believes he or she is getting. The concept of service gaps arose from the research of Berry (1988) and his colleagues (Parasuraman *et al.*, 1985, 1991; Zeithaml *et al.*, 1990). As Lewis (1994: 237) says 'They defined service quality to be a function of the gap between consumers' expectations of a service and their perceptions of the actual service delivery by an organization, and suggested that this gap is influenced by a number of other gaps which may occur in an organization.'

The magnitude of the gap will be compounded by the number of steps in the service process and by the distance of the operational function from the customer.

EXAMPLE

Suppose that the marketing department's interpretation of what the customer wants is only 90 per cent correct, then the actual performance can never be better than 90 per cent of what the customer really wants. If, however, business policy is such that it is deemed suffficient to provide resources to meet 90 per cent of customers' requirements (this 90 per cent will be set on the understanding that marketing is 100 per cent correct) then at best the customer will now only get 81 per cent of what they want. Let us assume that the operation consists of a back office and a front office. Supposing the back office slightly misinterpret what management want and also set themselves an internal target of 90 per cent, and then further suppose that the front office is so resourced that to the best of their ability they can only achieve 95 per cent of the standard set, this means the final result will be that the customer satisfaction is at best only 70 per cent. The calculation is shown in Table 2.2.

Unless gap analysis is attempted, management will firmly believe that the overall result is somewhere near 90 per cent of what the customer wants. And each department when queried will fervently believe that they are reaching between 90 and 95 per cent of required performance levels.

CUSTOMER REQUIREMENT	100
Marketing misinterpret (they get it 90% right)	90
Business policy sets target at 90% of 100 (but this actually equates to 90% of 90)	81
Under-resourced back office set internal standard of better than 90% of target. Due to slight ambiguity and misunderstanding of management target, even when 92% of internal target is reached, it is only 90% of what was set by management (90% of 81 = 73)	73
Front office, also under-resourced, are 95% on target (95% of 73 = 69)	69

Table 2.2: Gap analysis

If an organization is close to its customers and aware of what the competition is doing, then a gap of this magnitude should not happen. The larger the organization and the greater the delineation of responsibilities between departmental functions, and the further the operations function is removed from the customer and from consultation in business policy decisions, the greater the likelihood of gaps occurring between what is provided and what the customer really wants.

Summary: customer satisfaction

To summarize, generally an organization will aim to consistently achieve certain standards or levels of quality as determined by business policy. The decision about the level of service to provide will be an economic one, and will be driven by what the competition is doing or is likely to do. The intention should be to define accurately what the customer wants, in terms of the basic requirements of specification, time and cost. Normally an organization will not be able completely to meet all the requirements of the customer and some trade-off will be possible. It is also wise to understand who the stakeholders are and what their concerns might be.

Where a strong organizational culture exists, the perception of service level can be enhanced by enthusiastic and helpful staff, at very little extra cost to the organization.

Dimensions of resource utilization

Given infinite resources any system, however badly managed, might provide adequate customer service. (Wild 1995: 10)

Many an organization has failed to survive despite the customers having been more than satisfied with what they have received. Thus customer satisfaction is not the only criterion by which an operations manager will be judged. Customer satisfaction must be provided *simultaneously* with an effective and efficient operation. The level of customer satisfaction offered must not only be *affordable* to the organization but it must also be *consistent* and *sustainable*.

Efficient use of resources

A prime concern of any operations manager is the efficient use of resources, and the elimination of non-effective (non-value-adding) activities.

In service industries the resources available will consist of a mix of the following:

- People.
- Information technology.
- Equipment and machines (display racks, checkout facilities, materials movement equipment, etc.).
- Vehicles.
- Space (offices, warehouses, display areas, etc.).
- Materials ('intermediate' materials such as wrapping and packing materials, stationery, etc.).
- Inventory (stock for sale).
- Time and information.

Obviously not all service industries will have, or need, all of these resources.

There will never be an unlimited amount of resource and often resources will be limited in quantity and quality. An increase of resources will be dependent on funds available. When funds are not an inhibitor there can be other constraints, for example we may need specialized packing materials which we order but it might be some weeks before delivery is made.

Prioritizing resources

The above list of resources may appear formidable, but generally it will be found that the list can be reduced or modified to show the three most *important* resources for the particular organization with which we are concerned. The important resources are those which are most necessary to satisfy the customers' essential requirements of specification, time and cost.

EXAMPLE

For a travel agent the three most important resources could well be people, information technology and space. Certainly stationery and other office supplies and equipment will be needed but these will be of only minor significance. Likewise the branch manager might see his car as an important resource, but it might have minor impact on the achievement of customer satisfaction.

Suppose that the travel agency have determined that they are valued by the customers for friendly service and useful advice on means of travel and accommodation, accurate bookings and ticketing, speedy service, and competitive prices and 'special' deals. This would enable the agency to say that 'our customers judge satisfaction by specification, time and cost'. *Specification* is advice and accurate ticketing, *time* equates to speedy service, and *cost* is competitive prices and special deals. To achieve customer satisfaction as defined in this manner the agency will need a reliable integrated computer system which gives on-line information, communication with airlines, hotels and so on, and confirmation of bookings, tickets and vouchers. The agency will need sufficient office space to accommodate several staff members and customers at any one time. Finally the agency will need reliable, systems-trained, well-presented and courteous staff.

Using the travel agency example we can now extend our matrix approach for customer satisfaction to include resource utilization:

Customer satisfaction			**Resource utilization**		
Spec	*Time*	*Cost*	*People*	*Information technology*	*Space*
3	2	1	2	3	1

Assume for this example that it has been established that customers rate advice and accurate ticketing as most important and that they are prepared to wait for information and for tickets, but they do not expect to wait more than five minutes before a consultant is available. Cost, although important, is of a lesser consideration to accuracy and to receiving speedy service. Having established this rating the next step is to determine the most vital resources needed to give the customers satisfaction. In this example it is found that a reliable integrated computerized information and ticketing system is essential. When the system is 'down' little can be achieved, information on prices, schedules and availability of seats cannot be provided, nor can bookings be made and tickets and vouchers issued. A back-up 'manual' system consisting of the telephone, bound books of pamphlets and handwritten tickets has proved in the past to be not only unwieldy and slow but expensive due to mistakes being made through information not being up-to-date and bookings being incorrectly recorded. Trained staff are important but of lesser importance than the system, for without the system the staff can do little. Space is an issue, but in our example generally has not proved too much of a problem. With a good system and well-trained staff, customers can be turned around quickly; when the system is slow or staff are inexperienced then the time taken to serve a customer is extended and space can become a problem.

EXAMPLE

Another example concerns a computer service bureau. The bureau writes specialized software to order. The customer satisfaction matrix showed that customers rated specification as important, time as not so important (they were prepared to wait to get exactly what they wanted), and were prepared to pay a reasonable amount. Thus:

	Specification	*Timing*	*Price*
Required	3	2	2

But the perception of the service actually received by customers showed a gap between expectations and performance.

	Specification	*Timing*	*Price*
Perception of service	2	1	1

It can be seen that customers were not satisfied. The software was not always to specification, time delays were unacceptable, and cost was too high (in comparison to what the competition were offering).

A self-analysis by the bureau found that the key resources were skilled people, own hardware and software used for developing new programs. Other resources such as office space, materials, stationery, etc. were of comparatively minor importance.

Resource analysis
Actual performance:

Hardware	*Software*	*People*
3	1	3

The analysis revealed that the hardware was adequate, the staff were well skilled, but there were problems with the in-house software. It had always been realized that there were problems with the software, but it was also thought that the time delays had been caused by not having enough trained people; indeed consideration was being given to increasing staff numbers. However, as pointed out by the accountants, an increase of staff would add to the costs. When the staff were asked for their opinion they advised that delays and costly rewrites were due to software problems.

The efficiency factor

The discussion above concerning resource utilization has been from the stance of customer satisfaction.

Traditional production and operation management texts tend to suggest that the role of the operations manager is primarily efficient use of resources in transforming inputs into outputs and that customer satisfaction is almost a subservient objective. While this might be so for certain types of capital-intensive operations where the customer is not an input into the system, such as a factory where goods can be produced irrespective of whether a customer order is held or not, we have concluded for service industries that resource utilization is *subservient* to customer satisfaction. That is not to say that efficient use of resources is unimportant; indeed efficiency is vitally important. However, total efficiency would mean making the optimum use of resources, i.e. elimination of all waste, no spare space, no idle time and minimum of time spent with clients, customer queues so that service staff are fully employed, and so on.

EXAMPLE

An example of where resource utilization takes precedence over customer satisfaction can be found with some airlines where the policy is to accept bookings for 440 passengers when the aircraft only has 400 seats. This strategy has evolved from past experience which shows that not all passengers arrive for flights, and consequently rather than having aircraft fly with empty seats, the policy is for some passengers to be offloaded and to be offered seats on a later flight.

Precedence of objectives

Some organizations will concentrate on customer satisfaction at an affordable and sustainable level as being the over-riding objective, and others will focus on efficient use of resource utilization ahead of customer satisfaction. This is not to suggest that the organization which is resource focused ignores customer satisfaction, and often resource utilization will be in harmony with customer satisfaction.

EXAMPLE

Aircraft passengers will value getting to their destination (specification) on time and will be prepared to pay a certain price. If the airline meets these criteria (specification, time and cost) customers will be basically satisfied, and if at the same time the airline has a full aircraft (no empty seats) and keeps its operating costs to a minimum then *simultaneously* efficient resource utilization and customer satisfaction will have been achieved.

In our first airline example it is only when pre-booked passengers are turned away that the objectives will conflict. Suffice to say that passengers travelling first class, those who have been prepared to pay for extra service, will not be the ones to be off-loaded. First-class passengers could well rate the service and all the personal attention that they get as being truly first class. Thus although some passengers will be less than happy (those who have been off-loaded) the airline company could still claim in its mission statement, and in its advertising, to provide world-class service, although the over-riding objective is clearly resource utilization.

YOUR TURN!

For your organization what limits the level of customer service provided? Also, is resource utilization the over-riding objective, or does customer satisfaction have first priority?

Balance of objectives: potential conflict

The two basic objectives for an operations manager are customer satisfaction and resource utilization. The examples given above show that having understood the key requirements of the customer then it is important to attempt a match with the resources available. It will not always be possible totally to gain a balance between what the customer wants and what the organization is able to do. For the operations manager the further restraint will be the objectives of the organization. If the objectives are driven primarily by the need for efficient use of resources then customer satisfaction will be more difficult to achieve. As stated in our opening sentence to this section, given infinite resources any system, no matter how badly managed, might provide adequate service. The truth will be that there will not be infinite resources, and often existing resources will not completely mesh with the achievement of total customer satisfaction. Nonetheless the operations manager will be expected to achieve adequate use of resources and a reasonable level of customer satisfaction.

Customer satisfaction matched with resource utilization

If the over-riding aim is to make the most efficient use of existing resources, it might mean that the service to be offered has to be rethought and repromoted. Thus the service will be altered to meet the competences of the organization, rather than extra resources being added to meet a higher-level service. Before any change to the specified service is contemplated it would be expected that the operations manager would seek improved methods of operating and better ways of doing things using existing resources. Rather than saying 'It cannot be done' the positive approach is to look for ways to make the impossible *possible* with existing resources.

CHAPTER SUMMARY

In this chapter we have determined that the prime objective of an organization is customer satisfaction through the achievement of a consistent and sustainable level of service. The determinant of the level of service to be provided will be driven by the competition and demands of customers and stakeholders. To provide the necessary *affordable* level of service the operations manager is vitally concerned with efficient and effective use of resources. We also noted that resources will generally be limited in quantity and quality. Therefore the operations manager must balance the two, potentially conflicting, objectives of customer satisfaction and efficient resource utilization.

CD ROM CASE STUDY

The CD ROM includes the Case Study Qormi Post Office (Malta). This case illustrates how the Qormi Post Office was able to improve customer satisfaction by better use of existing resources.

Part Two

In Part Two we consider the context of service operations management. As no man is an island unto himself, likewise no organization can isolate itself from the external environment, and within the organization no one department or function can stand alone. Every business is now competing on the world stage, and to survive must strive to reach world-class standards. National and geographic boundaries no longer afford a protective barrier for competitors. Customers today are well travelled and well informed and are quick to make value judgements on performance.

- In **Chapter 3** the link between the business policy and operations objectives are explained, and the importance of understanding the true mission is discussed. Factors which influence business policy, including external and internal influencers, are identified and explained. This chapter also establishes the importance of a good rapport between the operations and marketing functions.

- **Chapter 4** focuses on the efficient use of resources and takes a total value-chain approach, from supplier through to the ultimate customer. This chapter also expands on the need for co-operation between departmental functions within the organization if the overall corporate mission is to be achieved. Operational planning, implementation and the control process necessary to make the business policy happen is also discussed in this chapter; and the importance of communication and transfer of information in the control process is recognized.

- **Chapter 5** links back to the structure of organizations, and shows ways of establishing value-adding activities with a view to minimizing non-value-adding activities. It is seen that activities which are deemed to add value are those that are required to achieve customer satisfaction. It is accepted that some activities are essential to the overall operation but in themselves do not directly add value to the service, and thus these activities should be critically examined with a view to reducing the effort and cost incurred.

Chapter 3

Business policy

Objectives for this chapter

This chapter examines:

- How business policy is determined.
- Who the customer is, and how satisfaction is judged.
- Internal capability and feasibility (the competence of the organization).
- The external factors which influence policy.

In Chapter 1 we said that the role of the operations manager is to arrange and use resources efficiently and effectively to achieve the goals or *mission* of the organization. We also said that although operations managers may not always be involved in determining goals and objectives, nevertheless they are the people responsible for turning the goals and objectives into realities.

Ideally the operations manager will be involved in shaping the corporate policy and objectives of the organization, establishing and acquiring resources, and setting specific operational targets. But organizations seldom operate in an ideal fashion. The reality is that in many cases the operations manager will inherit an existing structure, and less than adequate or unsuitable resources will already be in place. More importantly the principal objective (be it customer satisfaction or efficient resource utilization) will not be clearly defined in the business policy. Indeed most organizations will have both customer satisfaction and resource utilization as twin and equal objectives without realizing that inherently there is a conflict between these objectives. The operations manager will then have the task of making the seemingly impossible possible. Operations managers need to be optimists and adept at employing structured thinking as well as unstructured or lateral thinking to problems to achieve the goals imposed on them. Various techniques and models to aid operational decision-making are given in subsequent chapters.

Business policy

The business policy sets for the organization:

- The objectives.
- The service to be provided.

- The market to be served.
- The way in which the service will be provided.
- Level of quality to be aimed for.
- The resources which will be employed.

Business policy does not happen by accident. It is a conscious attempt by organizations to provide long-term goals and to plan resources to achieve those goals. Business policy will start with the purpose of the organization – the very reason it exists. This is often referred to as the vision of the organization. As explained by Dulewicz, MacMillan and Herbert (1995)

> A vision depicts the aspirations of the company, a desired and attainable picture of how the company will appear in a few years' time, which can capture the imagination and motivate employees and others. The mission is to achieve the vision, expressing the commitment and will to do so. On the way, decisions will have to be made according to the values of the company, as indicated in the decision-making behaviour of the board – according to what the board believes is good or bad, right or wrong from the company's point of view.

Mission statement

The purpose of the business is often articulated in a mission statement. Frequently what the mission statement says may be at variance to the true mission of the organization. For example I know of no organization with a mission statement that says 'Our aim is survival and to survive we will reduce our workforce by 25 per cent', or 'We will aggressively advertise our service levels, but we will not spend any money on training our staff.' Such organizations are more likely to publish missions that proclaim 'We value and respect the importance of our highly trained and dedicated staff', and 'Our aim is to provide outstanding world-class service.' It is important for the operations manager to understand what the true mission is, irrespective of what might be stated in the published mission. For instance if survival is the mission, and this could well be a legitimate mission, this has to be understood and thus will shape the strategies to be employed.

Making the vision happen

The next stage in business policy is to determine what has to be done, and what can be done, to make the vision happen. If the vision cannot happen then it is no more than a dream. Determinants of whether the vision can happen, and of the consequent business policy decisions, are shown in Figure 3.1. The inter-relationships to policy are shown in Figure 3.2.

The customer

At the centre of Figure 3.1 is the customer. Without a customer the organization will cease to exist. But although the importance of satisfying the customer cannot be

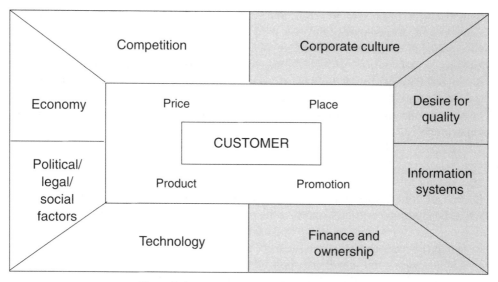

Figure 3.1: Determinants of business policy

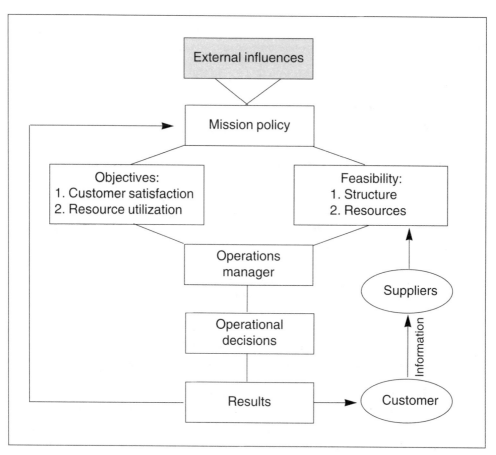

Figure 3.2: Inter-relationships to business policy

denied, it is important to appreciate that customer satisfaction is only one determinant of business policy. As Wild (1995: 10) points out 'many organizations have gone bankrupt despite having loyal and satisfied customers'. In short the level of customer satisfaction provided has to be *affordable* and *sustainable*. Most organizations can provide for a short period a high level of customer satisfaction, but the level offered has to be sustainable. In service industries customers will be very aware if service levels drop or are inconsistent with what they expect based on past experience.

Marketing mix

Before an organization can attempt to satisfy the customer it must first be known what the customer wants. Generally the marketing function has to establish:

- what the customer wants in terms of the service being offered (product);
- the price customers will be prepared to pay;
- where the service should be provided (place).

To complete the 'marketing mix' the marketing function will have the responsibility of promoting (advertising) the service. The marketing mix influence on policy is shown in Figure 3.1 in traditional marketing terms of product, price, place and promotion.

Service to be provided

Definition of the service to be provided is at several levels.

Specification of service (product)

The first and crucial level is the *specification. Unless the service is what the customer wants then it will not be used.* In Chapter 1 with reference to a commuter bus service we said if the bus is not going from 'A' to 'B' then we won't catch it. The service offered might include other 'nice to have' attributes, but unless the basic service is right, the extras, the 'nice to have' features, become irrelevant. In the case of a bus service no matter how clean, how comfortable, and how polite the driver, unless the essential service is right (the bus stops somewhere close to our home and gets us somewhere close to where we work) we will not be interested in all these 'nice' extras.

The second important issue is *consistency.* Customers expect the service to be at the same level, or better, each time it is experienced. With the bus service we would expect the bus to follow the same route each day and to keep to the published timetable.

Timing is also an important issue; unless the service is available when the customer wants it the bus company will more than likely lose the customer. With the bus service, not only is it important that it is going from 'A' to 'B', but *when* is important. If the bus does not get the potential customer to work on time, or if it does not connect with another service such as a train, then the service will not be used.

Time will be of lesser importance in some circumstances and for some services. For example we are conditioned to make appointments in advance for services such as consultancy services and often we are prepared to wait to get the person we consider will give us the best service (be it advice, the dentist, or the beauty salon).

Once the bus meets the basic requirements then all the other 'extras' such as cleanliness, comfort, plenty of seats, polite driver, waiting shelter, and perhaps even music interspersed with announcements from the driver, will add to the perception of quality and could provide the edge in a competitive environment.

Some specification issues are taken for granted by customers. Examples of this in the bus service are that the bus is roadworthy and the driver is licensed. Often, what the customer takes for granted will be crucial to the whole operation and will take a good deal of effort on behalf of the operations manager to achieve (such as keeping the fleet maintained and roadworthy).

Other 'requirements' of customers can be traced back to the marketing team 'selling' features that the customer had not previously considered important but which once 'sold' will come to be expected by the customer. Carlzon (1989) calls this the olive in the martini. In some service industries, for many customers, appearance and status will be every bit as important as the actual service received. Overall once a level of quality of service has been promoted or actually provided, customers will be quick to notice if it is not achieved or sustained. There is no point in setting a high standard of service if the operation cannot *consistently* meet the standard.

Price

Once the marketing team is satisfied that they know what the customer wants – the specification – then they will determine the price that can be charged. What can be charged depends, of course, on what the customer is prepared to pay. The issue for the operations manager will be 'Can the service be provided to the given specification (including all those fussy extras added by marketing) within the price set (marketing again) and still provide a profit?' Thus the operations manager in achieving a defined level of customer satisfaction will simultaneously be required to minimize the use of resources (cost) to an affordable level.

Where (place)

The location of the service is a marketing issue and the decision will be affected by where the customers are. Location issues are discussed in detail in Chapter 7. Location of services will have a great impact on operational decisions concerning supply and choice of suppliers, and distribution and logistic issues.

Promotion

Obviously marketing will advise on promotional strategies but the overall thrust and philosophy of the promotional drive is very much a business policy decision. No promotion activity should ever take place without the full involvement of the operations manager.

EXAMPLES

1. Recently a major TV campaign announced a special offer in aluminium ladders. Being a keen do-it-yourselfer (and the offer really was too good to miss), I hurried down next morning to the store only to be advised that the factory was behind schedule and the ladders would not be available for another month! I went to the competition and bought a ladder although the price was higher. Marketing had created a demand but lost a sale (I only needed one ladder and my needs had now been satisfied elsewhere).

2. A golf club advertised a free open day for prospective new members; the day chosen was a non-competition day when the course would be relatively free of club players. Noting that no play was scheduled for that day and unaware of the open day, the greenkeepers made an early start on coring and re-sowing the greens, and temporary rough greens were cut. The overall impression gained by the prospective new members was not good and the time and money spent on the promotion was to a large extent wasted effort.

Marketing mix and operational feasibility

It can be seen that the marketing team have a great influence on business policy. They determine who the customer is, what the service offered will be (specification, time, place and price) and they promote the service. The operations manager has to determine the overall feasibility; in other words, does the organization have the capacity to consistently provide the desired service and meet the expected demand and quality attributes within the price set, and return a profit? If not, what extra resources are required and what else could be done to make the impossible possible? In short: can the service, with all the desired features, actually be provided?

Feasibility and structure

Although we can accept from the outset that with less than adequate resources and overly ambitious targets, the operations manager is expected to, and frequently does, make the impossible happen, nonetheless it is helpful to know what is feasible – *what is the capability of the operation.*

Feasibility is limited by the structure, as discussed in Chapter 1, and understanding the limitations of the existing structure is essential for the operations manager.

EXAMPLE

If the structure is as shown in Figure 3.3, then it can be deduced that customer satisfaction (timing) is the prime objective and the organization operates with some spare capacity or a 'buffer' stock of resources. This structure also indicates that if customers cannot be served as they arrive,

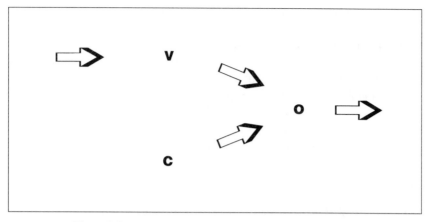

Figure 3.3: Customer satisfaction as the prime objective

the customer is likely to be lost to the system. The challenge for the operations manager, with this structure, will be to gauge the extent and timing of the demand and to have adequate resources on hand so as to meet the primary objective of customer satisfaction. The secondary objective will be to minimize the amount of time that capacity is unutilized, or to minimize the amount of buffer stock held. Thus the first concern will be to establish feasibility, that is how much capacity is available and what the limits are at which the organization can operate. The operations manager will be required to satisfy expected customer demand by making the *best use* of capacity so as to *prevent* customer queues and lost business. 'Best use' means that although the structure includes surplus, or stored (buffer) stocks of resources (spare capacity), it is incumbent on the operations manager to minimize idle capacity.

YOUR TURN!

At the end of Chapter 1 you were invited to consider the structure(s) that exist for your organization. Now analyse the structure(s) of your organization to determine challenges the operations manager faces as a result of the existing structure. Perhaps your structure implies that the primary objective is customer satisfaction; or is resource utilization the primary focus?

Feasibility and resources

As shown in Chapter 1, without input from the customer the function of providing service will not happen. Logically the operations manager plans ahead and has certain resources in place in anticipation of customer needs. In a service industry the major resource is likely to be people, and we need to know what their competences are, i.e. how skilled they are, their attitudes and dedication, and whether they are resourceful and capable of taking initiatives. Other resources include premises, information systems, time, equipment, materials and vehicles. The location of premises, the reliability of the information system and other necessary equipment, the reliability of suppliers, and most importantly the quality of the people of the organization will determine the overall capability or competence of the organization. Establishing a quality of culture, how to motivate people and continuous improvement are covered in Chapter 10.

Feasibility is one side of the equation. The other side of the equation is knowing what is required (demand), and anticipating what might be required. Demand issues and forecasting techniques are covered in Chapter 8.

To summarize: feasibility is the determination of how able or *competent* the organization is to achieve the business policy. Limitations of specific structures and what has to be done to change structures are discussed as we progress through the book and are further illustrated in the CD ROM case studies.

Policy influencers

Figure 3.1 has an outer band which includes on the left-hand side:

- Competition.
- Economy.
- Political, legal and social factors.
- Technology.

These are all factors external to the organization, but which affect customer expectations and also, at another dimension, limit what the organization is able to do. The other factors shown on the right-hand side of the outer band are:

- Corporate culture.
- Desire for quality.
- Information systems.
- Finance and ownership.

These are certainly influenced by external factors but they can be managed by actions of the organization. In a traditional SWOT analysis (strengths, weaknesses, opportunities and threats) the opportunities and threats are 'external' to the organization, and the strengths and weaknesses are 'internal' issues. Opportunities and threats are on the left side and strengths and weaknesses are shown on the right side of the model.

Knowing the organization's own strengths and weaknesses will help determine feasibility and will also indicate areas where corrective action should be taken. For the external factors, using the SWOT approach, the aim is to determine opportunities and threats, and to determine how the organization is, or might be, affected by these external factors.

Competition
In the determination of the service and the level of quality to be offered, at the very least the organization has to meet the service provided by the competition. Today the

competition is worldwide. No matter that we believe we are providing a service to a local market, people today are well travelled and very well informed, and our customers judge us by their perceptions of world-class standards. For any organization, competition, although not yet present, might soon present a challenge. Technology and innovation is no protection: technology can soon be copied and new methods and systems are readily available to anyone. Often customers are influenced by what the immediate competition says it can do, or will do (which may not be quite the same as what actually happens). Nonetheless it is the perception of what the competition is offering that sets the market standards. Knowing what the competition is offering is only possible if it is known who the competition is, and who the likely new (world-class) competition might be. For example, ten years ago insurance companies would not have appreciated that the banking profession would soon be their competitors for life insurance, and who would have expected that French companies could own or compete with British utilities? On the other side of the world many Australians still can't believe that one of their major breweries is owned by a New Zealand company, and New Zealanders in turn have recently been shocked to find that one of their major breweries is now owned by a Japanese company.

Economy

The economy, exchange rates, interest rates, population growth, house sales, building permits, the consumer price index, the average wage, unemployment and other statistics relevant to your service industry are all areas of vital information when considering business policy. The problem is to identify what is relevant to your industry, and to know where to find information.

Political, legal and social factors

In the home market laws and regulations might be seen as limitations, but laws and regulations also serve to protect an organization. Whatever the laws are, it is important that an organization is aware of how they will affect the operations of the organization. Laws could limit the number of hours drivers work, the amount of maternity leave people are entitled to, and so on. For our home market we will have a reasonable idea as to what is legally possible, and what our legal responsibilities (for example taxation, and health and safety issues) are. But when providing services in other countries it is essential that the organization makes the effort to find out what legal restraints exist and what is socially acceptable before commitment is made to any action. Generally, laws are for the benefit of the people as a whole, and are enacted as the result of pressure from the people to add a safeguard. Thus it is useful to be aware of popular issues and to make adjustments to operations so as to be seen to be a responsible organization within the pervading culture, rather than wait for legislators to take action as a result of public pressure. When a safeguard is made the subject of rules and regulations, it is likely to have more stringent conditions than when organizations or industries abide by their own self-imposed safeguards.

Technology

Customers will often be beguiled by technological promises as exaggerated in the popular press. On the other hand an organization will be limited by the technology that it has at its disposal. Keeping up-to-date with technology for the sake of keeping up is expensive. Often it is best to be aware of changes, be aware of what the competition is doing, and try to delay decisions to change until the new technology is tried and proven (and cheaper).

YOUR TURN !

What economic influences affect your organization and how do you keep abreast of what is happening?

Corporate culture

Corporate culture is the amalgam of beliefs, norms and values of individuals making up an organization ('the way we do things around here'). For a business policy to be successful it has to be accepted by the members of the organization and it has to mirror their goals and aspirations. The Chief Executive might be the one who articulates the vision but unless there is a cultural fit and the people of the organization buy into it, it won't happen. Culture and values are deep seated and may not always be obvious to members and to newcomers to the group. Culture and change of culture are discussed in greater detail in Chapter 10. Suffice to say that if the organization has a strong culture then each individual will instinctively know how things are done and what is expected. Conversely if the culture is weak, then the individual may not react in the manner that management would hope.

Desire for quality

The level of quality offered is very much a business policy decision. It has been said that quality is free. Certainly doing things right the first time and every time should cost us nothing apart from training our people to know what is right and what corrective actions they can take. But if we refer back to our earlier example of a bus service we will see that higher-level service and quality will cost. With the bus the aim was to run a regular service, keeping to a defined route, and to a set timetable. In addition the driver had to be licensed and the vehicle maintained to a roadworthy level. We could add the perception of extra quality at little if any additional cost by simply getting things right first time, and every time. For example if the bus kept to the timetable, the drivers took a pride in their appearance, were polite to customers, and the bus was kept clean, the perception of a quality service is enhanced at no appreciable extra cost to the organization. There might be a minor cost in providing uniforms, and in the cost of cleaning, and perhaps in training the driver in customer relations. If, however, we wished to increase the service by running a bus every ten minutes rather than one bus every half-hour, this would mean extra buses, more fuel, and extra drivers; thus to increase the service would now become very expensive. And yet this might be what the customers have asked for – a more frequent service. What determines our policy: the customer or economic considerations? No doubt we would consider how many extra passengers we would get and whether their extra fares would offset the extra costs. Then too, any change in policy would depend very much on whether we had competition on the route.

Quality: an economic decision
Quality is an economic consideration. At one level it is cheaper to do things right, and to do them only once, and it is also helpful to have happy and eager staff who will give customers friendly, helpful service. This shouldn't add to our costs, but extra quality above these levels will cost. Thus the level of quality we can afford and sustain is very much a business policy decision, and to a large extent it will be driven not by what the customer wants but by what the competition is doing or threatening to do.

Information systems
With the information technology available today there is no reason why every member of an organization cannot be kept up-to-date and understand what the policy of the organization is. Few of us do not have a personal computer on our desk with access to electronic mail systems. Two-way communication is now commonplace and many organizations go to great lengths with staff magazines, bulletin boards and so on to keep staff informed about company policy as well as social events.

The old method of management was for the bosses to do the thinking, set the goals, and to give directions. The workers were not paid to think; their job was to obey orders. With such an approach there is little wonder that many people were reluctant to show initiative and thus few really had the interests of the organization at heart. This is often referred to as 'Taylorism',[1] and is as relevant to service industries as it is to manufacturing organizations. Today, most of us work where we do because we understand the policies of the organization, believe in the product or service we are offering, and we enjoy being involved even in a small way in helping to shape the policy.

Financial ownership
Most organizations are limited by money. The necessary funding comes from the owners and from profits (equity or shareholders' funds) and from borrowing. Unless owners are getting a reasonable return on their investment they are going to ask questions.

Owners, investors, the share market and bankers will judge the organization on the bottom line in the accounts. If you work for a government department, or are funded by the government or the public, the return will be seen in terms of value for money, and the persistent question will be 'Can we get better value for our money by using private enterprise (out-sourcing)?'

Financial strength, being profitable, or getting value for money is a major shaper of business policy. More than anything else lack of funds will determine policy.

CHAPTER SUMMARY

The business policy is long term, takes an organization-wide perspective and is concerned with the setting of goals and targets for the whole enterprise and the best use of the available resources. Business policy must take into account several factors as shown in Figures 3.1 and 3.2. The effective operations manager will maintain a keen interest in all facets of the organization and be aware of, and study, external trends and factors that could influence the organization. We do not condone politics in organizations but the operations manager, to be effective, must be politically aware to the extent that policy changes should not come as a surprise; and ideally the operations manager should be sufficiently well informed of external pressures to make policy suggestions. In Chapter 4 we discuss ways in which all the functions of an organization can work together for the common good of the organization and to achieve the overall corporate mission.

Key points

- Business policy is not made in isolation. There are external and internal factors which influence the shaping of *policy*.
- The marketing function is the interface with the *market* and has the responsibility of advising: product (service specification), price, place (distribution), and for promoting the service. The market is influenced by the external factors of competition, technology, politics and the economy.
- In setting the business policy it is important to determine the capability of an organization so as to know what is *feasible*. Feasibility depends on structure and the availability and quality of resources. Internal factors are: culture, information, desire for quality and financial strength. Recognizing the competences of the organization is an important consideration when determining the business policy. The operational structure of the organization is a key element in determining what can or cannot happen.

CD ROM CASE STUDY

The Hua Hin Golf Tours Co. Ltd is set in Thailand, and illustrates how policy decisions are driven by outside influences.

Note

1. The American F. W. Taylor, known as the father of scientific management at the turn of the century. His philosophy was that management, by scientific means, should find the best way of doing a job (method and equipment), train the workers in the best way, and offer incentives to increase productivity. Supervisors were employed to maintain the best method. Workers were not expected to make suggestions; their job was to do what they were told while management did the thinking.

Chapter 4

Operations management and inter-relationships

Objectives for this chapter

This chapter will consider:

- The value-chain approach for total efficiency.
- The importance of suppliers.
- The benefits of being an open organization.
- The life cycle of services.
- Innovation and product development.
- Finance and accounting issues.

Introduction

The concern of the operations manager is with providing the goods and services, defined by the business policy, as efficiently as possible. A principal operations objective, although sometimes subservient to customer satisfaction, is the efficient use of resources.

Internally, efficiency means making the best use of resources and the elimination of any activity that is not adding value. It is not possible for an organization to rely on operations alone to be efficient; operations is only one part of the whole organization. World-class organizations are totally efficient, and each department or function meshes with the others to support the drive to achieve the common mission.

Value-chain approach

The value-chain approach transcends the traditional manner of departmentalizing stages of the business process. The value chain highlights the importance of the operations manager being involved in all aspects of the process, from suppliers right through to the customer. The 'old' approach was that one department or function would be responsible for purchasing goods and services, another for planning. Scheduling of activities was often a separate function, as was warehousing and distribution, and operations were just one step in the whole process of providing services. With the value-chain approach functional boundaries are ignored and in many organizations it is now accepted that the operations manager has to control the whole process from buying in goods and services to the final stage of satisfying the customer. Marketing, accounting, human resources and other support functions do not show up on the value chain as such but, as discussed below, operations managers must be vitally interested and involved in these internal functions of the organization. The value chain, shown in Figure 4.1, is derived from Porter (1990) and from Basu and Wright (1998).

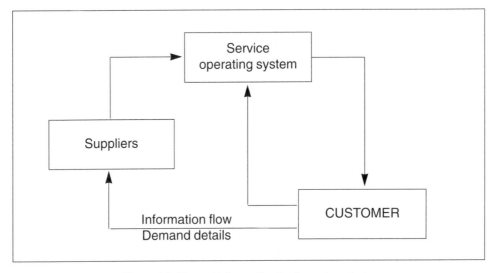

Figure 4.1: Flow of information for the value chain

External efficiency

External efficiency is measured by customer satisfaction and by market share. To achieve customer satisfaction the organization requires, and is dependent on, the timely receipt of goods and services to specification by external suppliers. The efficiency of suppliers to the organization is of as much concern to the operations manager as is the ultimate satisfaction of the customer. In this chapter we consider the importance of communication and teamwork within the organization between the various functions, and externally with suppliers at one end of the value chain and customers at the other.

As can be seen from Figure 4.1, the key to the whole process is information flow.

Suppliers

In some organizations suppliers are treated with distrust, and the business strategy adopted is to shop around and to get the best deal on each occasion. With this approach little loyalty is shown to any supplier, and the supplier is almost treated as an adversary. The value-chain approach is to treat the suppliers of those goods and services important to the smooth operation of the service system as part of the team. In some cases the supplier can become involved in the day-to-day operations of the organization and might be expected to advise and to assist. Cost no longer becomes the key issue. Instead suppliers will be judged on their loyalty and ability to deliver goods and services to the required standard and on time. Suppliers can also become part of the information-gathering arm of the organization; often suppliers have a different perspective as to what the competition are up to (changes in buying patterns, timetables, new packages, use of new materials and so on). Suppliers are also in a good position to offer technical advice regarding new technology and alternative materials.

The prudent operations manager, however, will always have a fall-back position. No matter how well intentioned your supplier, it is foolish to be in a position where you are so reliant on one supplier that you are seriously embarrassed if the supplier is unable to perform for some reason (a fire or an unfriendly takeover).

Operations and other functions

Generally organizations are divided into functional departments; and even if the organization has re-engineered, and no matter how flat the structure, some people's tasks will be primarily marketing, others will be primarily concerned with accounting, others will be purely administration, humane resource management and so on. We have already shown in our value-chain approach the importance of the operations manager having the responsibility for purchasing goods and services right through to delivery of service to the customer.

The customer and operations

As was shown in Chapter 3, Figure 3.1 the customer is the central focus for any organization, and the function responsible for knowing what the customer wants and what the competition is doing is the marketing department.

The total quality management approach of the 1980s propounded the philosophy of delivering a quality service in excess of customer expectations. 'Surprise the customer' was the catch-phrase. As we have discussed in preceding chapters, what is provided has to be within an organization's capability, sustainable and affordable. Shareholders, fund providers and financiers will measure performance in terms of return on investment and value for money. On the other hand, customers are becoming more and more sophisticated and expect continuous improvements in quality of services but always at no extra or even less cost.

Another of the many conflicts faced by an operations manager is *how to provide more for less!*

Polarization of marketing and operations

Chapter 3 described the essential job of marketing as being the definition (specification) of the service. Attributes may range from the essential down to the desirable and perhaps include extras that the customer does not even want.[1] As well as defining the service to be offered, marketing has to establish the price, forecast demand, and finally promote the service. Marketing also has to sell the product/service internally within the organization to the operations and other functions of the organization.

The responsibility of operations, using the value-chain approach, is to determine feasibility; do we have:

- the know-how;
- the skills;
- the specialized equipment;
- reliable sources of supplies and services?

Finally, taking into account existing priorities and workloads, can the service be provided for the customer to specification, within the time frame required and at the price set by marketing?

Thus arises the traditional polarization of marketing and operations. Marketing see themselves as the entrepreneurs, the go-getters, the trigger for making things happen. For them the bottle is always half full, whereas they believe that their colleagues in operations will see the same bottle as half empty! Operations see themselves as the realists, they are the ones who have to make things happen, and meet impossible demands with make-shift and insufficient resources. Marketing see the realistic, sometimes cautious approach of operations as negativity. They are apt to believe that operations are always looking for reasons why things can't happen instead of looking for ways that make things happen. Operations in their turn see marketing as going ahead with doing their own thing, making extravagant promises without bothering to determine the operational situation. They see marketing as having no appreciation of capacity or scheduling constraints and the time and effort required for the development and testing of new services.

Marketing is likely to ask questions such as 'Why are we always late?', or 'Why do we always keep customers waiting?', 'Why do we always seem to have insufficient capacity?', 'Why are our costs so high?', and then add that 'the xyz group (competitor) always out-performs us.' (Of course xyz has exactly the same problems but marketing listen avidly to what xyz are saying rather than noting what xyz are actually achieving). In this scenario operations is on the back-foot and is likely to reply: 'Forecasting was not accurate', 'Rush orders were taken', 'We were not consulted', 'Fancy extras, extra service, all cost time and money.' In other words 'It wasn't our fault.' The above examples, which at first might be seen as one department 'communicating' with another, are in fact no more useful than the pointless exchanges of two children along the lines 'You did so!' – 'No! I didn't', 'Yes you did' – 'Did not', 'Did' – 'Didn't'.

Bunker mentalities

Communication has to be two-way and has to be aimed to help rather than just to apportion blame or to criticize. With traditional hierarchical organizations a bunker mentality can develop whereby each function is walled off from the other, and any suggestion, no matter how helpful, is taken as a threat or a challenge. World-class organizations are noted by the manner in which the figurative fences that separated functions have been broken down, and by the teamwork that exists between all functions to achieve the common goal as determined by the business policy. This requires that everyone in the organization knows what the goals and objectives are and that the culture is conducive to the enthusiastic pursuit of the goals for the common good of the whole, rather than for the specific interests of one department. Information is open to all, and there are no secrets.

Benefits of being an open organization

With an open organization marketing will welcome any approach by operations to get closer to the customers. Operations managers will not be able to meet with all the customers, but a derivation of the Pareto principle[2] can be adopted whereby the operations manager asks to meet with the top ten customers, with a view to gaining first-hand information as to how operations can improve the service, and to gaining some appreciation of what the customer really values. This should not be seen by marketing as an attempt by operations to usurp 'their' authority but as a genuine effort by operations to serve the customer better. Most customers will be surprised and delighted to meet someone from the back room; they will find this far more meaningful then being asked to fill out a questionnaire which invariably doesn't give the customer the scope to say what they really want, or to express what really annoys them. Once the operations manager fully understands first hand from the customer what is really needed – and often this can only happen through visiting the customer's place of business and by first-hand observation as to how the customer is operating – it is more than likely that changes can be made which will benefit the customer and at the same time be more economical to provide.

From time to time, usually due to pressure from the competition, it will be necessary to offer new services, or to upgrade existing services. Before any new service is finalized, operations should be invited to meet and to discuss with the top customers so as to understand what they really want. However, for some new services, customers will not know what they want. For example it took many years before instant coffee became popular.

Life cycle of services

Service products have definite life cycles (see Figure 4.2).

- *Development* of a new idea. This stage requires research, market testing, no income is received and costs (often substantial) are incurred.
- *Launch* of the new service. This stage can include heavy marketing costs and small initial returns.
- *Growth* marked by rapid market acceptance and increasing profits.
- *Maturity:* income stabilizes as growth levels off.
- *Decline:* sales fall and eventually the service is phased out or updated and the cycle begins again.

For some service industries, the maturity stage for the essential service can last for many years; however, services are always changing and service providers find themselves constantly in new areas of endeavour.

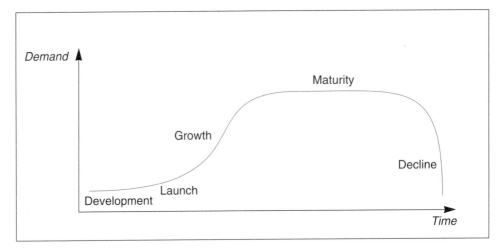

Figure 4.2: A service product life cycle

EXAMPLE

Once accounting firms kept the books and filled in the tax returns, but today accountants specialize in all sorts of areas and offer additional consulting services such as recruitment (head hunting), benchmarking, business brokering, and so on. Still other service providers have entered the 'boutique' market where they deal only in specialized niche areas, such as a law firm that only handles property title searches.

Different stages – different actions

Each stage of the life cycle will require different actions and decisions. The development stage will require operations to be involved in determining feasibility, acquiring necessary resources, training people and establishing a standard procedure. The introduction or launch stage will need the ability of operations to service fast-growing demand, and to be able to handle novel and unexpected problems. Procedures might have to be modified and people retrained to act in a standard fashion. With the growth phase, operations will likely be challenged by fluctuating and uncertain demands. By the time the maturity stage is reached, standard procedures should be in place, people will know instinctively how to react to problems, in short stability should have been achieved. This is the stage when there should be time to look for improvements to the service and to improve efficiency. Unfortunately when the pressure is off, sales are good and objectives are being comfortably achieved, the temptation will be not to look for changes (complacency sets in). Nonetheless there will always be room for improvements and ideally the culture of the organization will be to seek to make incremental improvements. The decline stage will bring another set of problems, either changes of a decisive nature will have to be made to the service to arrest the decline, or an entirely new service will have to be developed.

New initiatives

Changes to the service might include 'repackaging' – this would mean essentially the same service but promoted in a different manner and to a different target market.

EXAMPLE

Outdoor adventure tours (white water rafting, etc.), once for young backpackers, might now be tuned down (safer water) and repackaged as 'grey power adventure experiences' for the older market.

Other initiatives might mean the same basic service but with extra benefits, a reduced price, or at a different time. Whenever changes are being contemplated, the operations manager needs to be in a position to make suggestions and to be involved in the final decision.

In the public service, with the move to privatization of public sector management since the late 1980s, health services and utilities (such as water and sewage, and power generation and distribution) now find themselves operating in a totally different way and are surprising themselves with what they can offer commercially.

EXAMPLE

Water Boards, now privatized in the UK, have moved to establish and promote consultancy services for their customers and for new customers, and are finding themselves competing against organizations that once they would not have thought of as being in the same market.

Development process

The design process for a new service, or for the development of a variation to an existing service, has six distinct phases. They are:

- Concept – determination of a need.
- Systematic and rapid screening of various alternatives.
- Research, including market analysis and cost analysis.
- Development of the service.
- Testing the offerings developed.
- Launching on a commercial scale.

Speed is important

In today's fast-moving market, operations has to be able to react quickly to marketplace changes. Time is at a premium in gaining the initiative over the competition with a new service, or in catching up and reacting to a new service offered by a competitor. Customers are fickle and once lost are hard to regain.

Innovation and product development

There are several strategies available to the development of new services:

- Some organizations will position themselves as market leaders; this can be a high-risk strategy as time and money will be required to develop and set up the infrastructure needed. On the other hand, being first in the market can reap large benefits.
- Others will seek to imitate the innovations of other organizations and will attempt to join in the initial growth phase of a new service.
- Others will join in with adaptations before the market becomes saturated with suppliers or will endeavour to find a specialized niche market.
- Others will add nothing new except to rely on size and efficiency to enter the market at lower prices.

Whichever strategy is adopted, certain conditions have to be met:

1. Close links between operations, marketing, research and suppliers are essential.
2. Lead time, from concept to market, has to be minimized.

Overall it is essential to be continually monitoring the service product life cycle and to be aware of what the competition are doing.

Simultaneous development

Simultaneous development uses multi-functional project teams to design and develop the new service, and relies on strong two-way communication. Because service industries are reliant on customers as input for the service to happen, the design of the new service will mainly involve the process by which it will be delivered. It is difficult in service industries to produce a prototype 'product' although a new service can be tested in a small localized market. As customers must be involved, a flow process chart will be a useful tool for development and comparison of alternatives. The flow process chart will show, in detail, all the processes through which the customer will pass. In many services the customer will never come in contact with the back-office activities, such as exist for a post office, an insurance office, or a restaurant. However, such activities are essential to the provision of the service and it is crucial that these areas, and the suppliers to the system, are not ignored in the consideration of the feasibility of providing the new service. Therefore the flow process chart will need to cover the value chain from supplier to customer, and should consider the time taken for each activity. The technique of flow process charting, with examples, is given in Chapter 6.

Figures 4.3 and 4.4 show the advantages to be gained in lead time by simultaneous development of a new service.

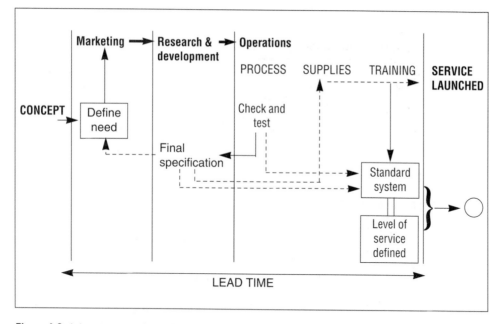

Figure 4.3: Advantages to be gained in lead time by simultaneous development of a new service

Finance and accounting issues

Many new businesses have a very short life span (over 70 per cent of small businesses fail within five years of beginning operations), and every month there are reports of medium and large businesses in financial difficulties. Like it or not, the continued success of any organization relies on financial stability. Often operations managers see the accountants as soulless people devoid of imagination, interested only in short-term returns on assets. However, unless there is a positive cash flow, long-term business plans for the future are meaningless. It is vital that any organization has a reliable accounting system in place to provide fast and accurate information. The minimum requirement is a budget and reliable feedback of actual results for comparison to the budget, in time for corrective action to be taken where required. In Chapter 11 we discuss key financial figures, and how the operations manager can make best use of financial information. Rather than the accountants pressing operations for returns and figures, it should be remembered that the accountants are a support function, and it should be the operations manager who is pressing the accountants to provide essential information!

Budgetary control is discussed in Chapter 5.

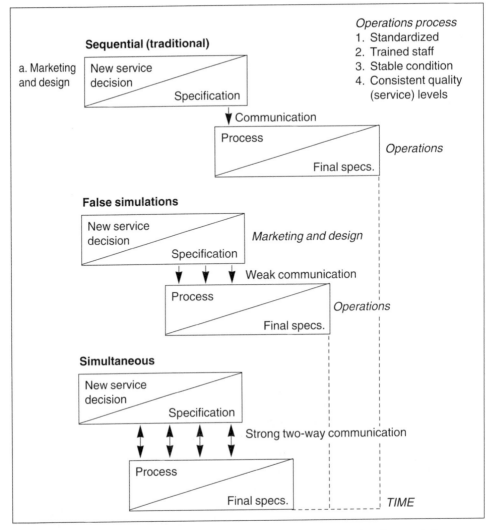

Figure 4.4: Advantages to be gained in lead time by simultaneous development of a new service. Source: adapted from Wild (1995).

CHAPTER SUMMARY

In this chapter we considered the direct inter-relationships of an operations manager with internal functions and with the external elements (suppliers and customers as part of the extended team) of the value chain. The need for understanding where a service is on its life cycle was discussed and the importance of speed in developing new services was stressed. It was concluded that accountants are not the enemy, but rather provide an important support service to the overall operation. It was recommended that operations should be pressing accountants to provide more information.

CD ROM CASE STUDY

The case study that adds value to this chapter is The Good Oil Company.

Notes

1. Why are some brands of golf balls wrapped in tissue paper? The paper is a nuisance when you are out on the course and decide to use a new ball (your last one having just disappeared into the river), and serves no useful purpose; after all, a golf ball is not fragile, indeed it is designed to be hit with some force by a lump of steel. The answer is that at some stage a marketing person decided that individually wrapped golf balls added to the prestige of the product. Another example is the way new shirts are presented. Why do they have so many pins stuck in them, and does the customer really want the pins? Both these examples illustrate the adding of cost, rather than value, to a product.

2. Wilfredo Pareto was a nineteenth-century Italian economist who concluded that 80 per cent of the wealth was held by 20 per cent of the population. The same phenomenon has often been found in businesses, where for example 80 per cent of the sales come from 20 per cent of the customers, or 20 per cent of the stock held accounts for 80 per cent of the inventory value. In other areas 80 per cent of road accidents occur in localized areas (20 per cent of the roads have 80 per cent of the total accidents). Lorenz, early in the twentieth century, produced a graph for demonstrating the cumulative dominance of the 20 per cent. Juran (1988) refers to the 80/20 phenomenon as the 'vital few and trivial many'.

Chapter 5

Planning, implementing and controlling

Objectives for this chapter

In this chapter we examine:

* The need to provide an operating surplus – the financial imperative.
* The need for long-range planning.
* The planning process.
* Implementation of plans.
* Control systems, including budgetary control.
* The importance of an effective information technology system.

Introduction

In Chapter 3 we considered external influences on business policy and in Chapter 4 we considered the importance of open communication between the various functions of an organization and externally with suppliers and customers. We used our derivative of the value chain to show the total process. In this chapter we begin by noting the financial imperative, and then consider the three stages of operations. These stages are planning, implementation and controlling. We also consider the benefits of information technology and the necessary steps to consider in introducing an effective information technology system.

The financial imperative

As stated in Chapter 1 the operations manager is the person who is responsible for using the resources of the organization as efficiently as possible to make goals and objectives happen. Central to the goals and objectives will be the need to make a profit, for without a profit a business will not survive. Apart from mere survival there will also be a need to satisfy fund providers (owners, shareholders, financiers) that their investment is secure and that they are receiving, or will receive, a satisfactory return on their investment. If an organization is a non-profit institution (such as government-funded) the central objective will be to show fund providers that *they* are getting value for money. The requirement to satisfy fund providers (value for money invested) can be considered as the *financial imperative*. In accountants' parlance this is known as 'the bottom line'.

Customer satisfaction

At the end of the value chain, as shown in Chapter 4 (Figure 4.1) is the customer and, as demonstrated in our study of structures in Chapter 1, without a customer no service industry is able to carry out its function. Thus to satisfy the financial imperative (value for money invested) a necessary requirement will be to satisfy the customer, for without customers there will be no income. To achieve these two complementary objectives – the financial imperative and the satisfaction of the customer – the operations manager is limited by the structure of the organization, the policies of the organization and the resources available (including the reliability of external suppliers).

Planning and control cycle

The overall planning and control cycle is depicted in Figure 5.1. It will be seen that the cycle is continuous and includes subsidiary cycles. It is recommended that you refer to Figure 5.1 as you progress through this chapter.

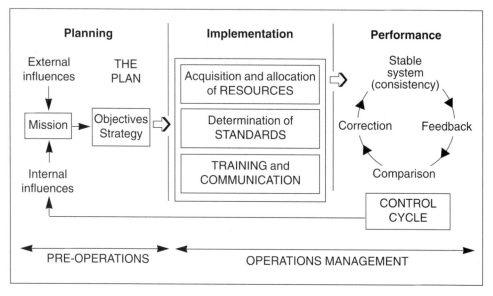

Figure 5.1: Planning and control cycle

The need for long-range planning

Planning takes place at several levels and can cover several different time frames. Thus an organization might have a ten-year plan, a five-year plan and will certainly have a twelve-month plan (e.g. 'the budget'). There will be a corporate-wide plan, business unit plans, department plans, and at the operations level the operations manager will have medium, short-term and daily plans.

Here we are concerned with the *corporate plan*. The corporate plan establishes the objectives of the organization which, as we said in Chapter 3, is made after consideration of external environmental factors balanced against the internal competences of the organization (see Figure 3.1). The overall thrust of the corporate plan is often articulated in a mission statement. The corporate or business plan however requires more than just the few well-chosen words of a mission statement. Generally the plan will need to be supported by sales figures which will include past trends, broken down into product group and market segments, and forecasts of future demand. The plan is also likely to include capital equipment budgets, cash flow forecasts, profit-and-loss forecasts, human resource and training requirements, property requirements and so on, and a budget will be produced every twelve months at least. Then some time after the end of a twelve-month accounting period (often months after balance date), an annual report with financial statements showing actual results will become available. The success of the plan and budgets could be compared and judged against these actual results, but seldom are.[1]

For the operations manager, annual reports are likely to be of historical interest only (unless there is a bonus payable which is tied to past results). Operations managers naturally will be more concerned with meeting immediate and short-term future demands rather than looking back to what happened last year; likewise with higher-level long-term planning which will often take on an unreal dimension as far as the operations manager is concerned. The cynic would say that each year much time and effort will go into the business plan, and each year before the plan is issued it will be out of date, and due to the dynamic nature of business there is a measure of truth in this. However, unless an organization has a long-range plan it will not be possible to develop appropriate capabilities as conditions change. Changes (or additions) to location, computer systems, recruitment and training of people, etc. cannot happen overnight. But once such decisions have been taken, and carried out, they cannot be undone in a hurry.

The operations manager, pressed with 'real', day-to-day operational problems, might be tempted to avoid involvement in what might be seen as esoteric long-term planning. If the operations manager is only marginally involved in long-term planning, business policies with important long-term operational ramifications will be made by strategic planners, accountants and marketing directors, and ratified by the board. Generally these people will not fully appreciate the time and effort needed to develop a distinctive operational competence. Indeed they might consider that the *real* work has been done in gathering the information and in making the plan, and that implementing the plan is by comparison a straightforward matter. Rather than trying to avoid involvement in long-term planning, the astute operations manager will press for inclusion in the planning process. Only by involvement in the long-range planning process can the operations manager hope to influence future operations.

The planning process

Establish goals and objectives

The first step in the planning process is to define the organization's goals and objectives, and to set priorities. This step will be built on the vision (the reason for being of the operation) and will likely be presented as a mission statement.

Competence of organization

The second step is to determine competences in relationship to the organization's market. As discussed in Chapter 3 this is done by reviewing external influences under the headings of political, economic, technology and competition, and by carrying out a SWOT analysis. Opportunities and threats are external to the business, and strengths and weakness are internal aspects. Examples of strengths might be financial stability and a particular operational competence; a weakness might be lack of skilled staff. An opportunity might be an emerging new market, and a threat will surely be new and emerging competition.

It is not sufficient merely to list strengths, weaknesses, opportunities and threats. The real purpose is to determine what *actions* have to be taken to capitalize on the strengths, eliminate weaknesses, to counter threats and to exploit opportunities. Often a threat, if considered in a positive manner, can be turned into an opportunity.

Strategy

The third step is to develop strategies to enable the business objectives to happen. In simple terms objectives/goals are *what* we want to do, and strategies are *how* we will do it, i.e. the necessary actions required to make the objectives happen.

In Figure 5.1 mission, objectives and strategy are shown as pre-operations planning.

EXAMPLE

Consider a new ambulance service. The objective as articulated in the mission statement might read:

To provide a quick response, first aid and transport service for the sick and injured in the Hillvale District.

The necessary strategies would include:

- purchase of a reliable vehicle and necessary first aid equipment;
- recruitment of trained staff;
- premises in a central location of Hillvale township;
- 24-hour on-call service/staffing;
- communication links with police and local hospital, and other ambulance services in nearby districts;
- maintenance of vehicle and equipment;
- ongoing training of staff.

Note the simplicity of the mission statement: no grand statements such as to be the best, to provide excellent service, or that people are our greatest resource, and so on.

Note also the brevity of the strategies, and how each is limited to supporting the mission. It could be said that ideally strategy is specific in the abstract, but not specific on detail. By not attempting to provide the specific details, plenty of scope is left for operational contingencies within the broad framework of the general strategy.

Implementation of plans

Action plans

Once the strategy is finalized then *action plans* can be made. In our ambulance example one action plan would be to locate suitable premises central to the area of operations (Hillvale District) large enough to house a vehicle and with room for offices, sleeping quarters and a communication centre. Once specific details are built into a plan it will be found that one strategic step will overlap with another. For example, before we can determine the amount of space required we first have to determine how many people have to be accommodated, and so on.

The ambulance example is a start-up scenario, but in day-to-day operations the resources, premises, people and equipment will already exist.

Implementation of the plan is an operational function. Operational plans will be based on forecasts of demand and the plan will consider systems, processes and resources to meet that demand. Invariably there will be several operational plans, at different stages of fulfilment, running at any one time.

For new projects such as the development of a new service as discussed in Chapter 4, in order to cut across functional boundaries and to streamline the process, a project team approach will be desirable.

For other projects, such as a move to new operational premises, then the operations manager will act as a co-ordinator and might take a project approach to the problem without actually setting up a team as such.

Network and/or critical path analysis is one technique commonly used by project managers to monitor the timely progress of projects. Chapter 8 includes a section on how to manage using a network analysis approach.

Performance control/control systems

Planning, it is said, creates standards of action, and controlling keeps the plans and actions in line.

The traditional approach to management is to control subordinates by supervision and measurement of performance to make sure that what is being done is what was intended. However, because the supervisory method of control relies on feedback of results, control tends to be in the past tense rather than in the present. That is, the manager checks after the event to see what has been done against what was intended. In this method of control the manager cannot control without a plan consisting of goals and targets. The more detailed the plan, the more control can be achieved.

The alternative method of control is to empower the worker, or a team of workers, so that control is exercised directly by the subordinates. The management responsibility in this model is to provide the workers with resources and support. Control, when exercised by the worker, can under certain circumstances be concurrent with carrying out the operation rather than retrospective.

It would seem logical that the earlier a variance to a standard is detected and corrected, the less cost will be incurred in subsequently correcting deviations.

Control elements

For any activity, no matter who exercises control, whether control is top-down (the manager's aim is to control the activities of subordinates) or a culture where control is exercised directly by the workers, the same four control elements apply. These elements are:

1. setting standards of performance;
2. feedback of actual performance;
3. measuring performance against the standards;
4. correcting deviation from the standards.

This is shown on the right-hand side of Figure 5.1, and is expanded upon in Figure 5.2.

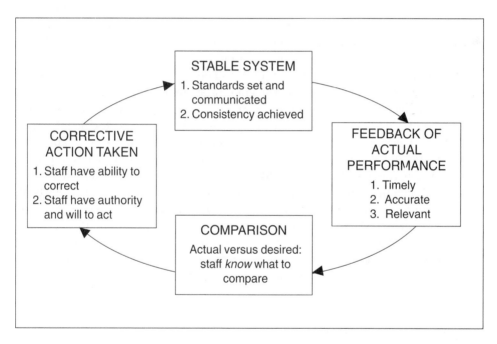

Figure 5.2: Performance control cycle

Stable system

An appropriate stable system exists when standards are known, and are consistently being met. The difficulty is in setting the standards, and then ensuring that deviations do not occur.

1. Setting standards of performance

Standards are usually expressed in terms of specification, time, quantity and cost, and include 'quality' elements. They can be imposed from above, or set by the workers themselves, either as individuals or as a team. If the workers are setting the standard, they have to know the overall limits (goals such as minimum outputs and quality levels). It is hoped that when the culture is right 'empowered' workers will voluntarily aim to exceed the minimum levels.

In a service industry it is often considered difficult to set quantifiable standards. How, for example, do you measure 'courteous service'? (Nevertheless, if customers *perceive* that there is a lack of courtesy then corrective action must be taken.) In other areas of service, standards can be set quite readily, i.e. How long do customers wait before being served? Did the customer get what was ordered? Was the service effective? and so on. Measurements that matter are covered in Chapter 10.

The only true way of knowing if a standard is being achieved is by 'hard' measurement criteria. Hard criteria are measurements such as quantity, size, number of failures, wrong deliveries, time taken to attend to a customer, down to the length of time taken to reply to a letter or an e-mail. Such measurements are quantifiable, are easily understood, and cannot be disputed. However, even when the hard criteria are met it is often the soft or intangible criteria that influence a customer to come back (or not), or encourage a customer to recommend your service to others. Word of mouth in service industries can be very telling for or against a service provider!

Aesthetics is an example of a soft criterion. Depending on the service provided, aesthetics can include the atmosphere of the office or showroom (cleanliness, fresh air, well-groomed people, situation in an appropriate part of town and so on), and of course will include the attitude of the people (are the people friendly and is advice given helpful?), and is there empathy, is the smile genuine and do the people really mean what they are saying? If the service offered is a product or the installation of a product, then other intangibles will become important such as evenness of colour, texture, finish, rough edges, flush fittings, etc. If the service includes a food product then smell, colour, taste, temperature of food when served and clean utensils all become important. When the culture of the organization is right and all the staff genuinely believe in the value of what they are doing, then a genuine enthusiasm and a desire to help will help overcome the adverse effect of a late delivery, or some other shortcoming. No manner of control imposed from above can substitute for people who want to get things right and who want to help the customer, provided that they are *empowered* to do so.

YOUR TURN!

Standards of performance

1. List hard measurements for your department.
2. Consider what soft measurements might be important to the 'customers' of your department.
3. Can service from your department be improved without extra cost?

2. Feedback of actual performance

The operating control system shown in Figure 5.2 includes a means of feedback of actual performance. Feedback needs to be reasonably precise, recognizable and timely. For example, budgetary control is virtually useless if actual results are achieved three months after the event. The importance of key measures cannot be emphasized enough. What should be measured is what really matters. Too often the desire for total accuracy and the detail of information provided takes too long to prepare and is so detailed as to be of little use to the recipient. Effective control requires a few key measurements that are sufficiently accurate to enable corrective action to be taken.

3. Comparison: actual to standard

As shown in Figure 5.2, the crucial issue at this stage of the control cycle is knowing what the feedback means and knowing how to compare results so as to be able to recognize deviations. This might seem obvious, but in reality how many people truly understand financial reports and know exactly what they should be looking for – or more importantly, why? In other areas, how many of us really understand what the computer is telling us when we get an error message, or for that matter what the red light means on the dashboard of the car? It is up to the operations manager to determine what information is required and to train staff in what to look for, and then what action they should take. Appropriate action might mean merely asking for help; staff who try to do too much when not sure can lead to interesting results. A willing and enthusiastic amateur can do irreparable damage!

4. Correcting deviations from standard

Once steps 1, 2 and 3 of the control cycle are in place, then whether in an office, a retail shop, a restaurant or a hospital, the output of the system can continually be compared with the plan or standard, and where necessary, corrections made to eliminate divergences. Ideally the level at which this is done is as low as possible. If a corrective action has to be reported up through five levels of management and down again before action can be taken, time is lost and often errors can be compounded; and if a customer is waiting for a decision to be made, customer satisfaction will diminish at a rapid rate. If a member of staff is facing a customer, that staff member needs to know the limits within which decisions can be made. The ability and knowledge of the staff member has to be taken into account when limits of authority are given. Some staff will welcome flexibility of action whereas others are afraid to make decisions.

Not everyone is comfortable with being empowered, and this also will need to be taken into account when limits of authority are being set. Members of the organization have to have mutual trust and confidence in each other. Management needs to be confident that staff are well trained and competent and that every person understands the goals. Staff have to be confident that they are empowered to take action and will be supported by management in difficult situations.

Budgetary control

Budgetary control is one example of a control system. With budgetary control the standard is the budget. Feedback of actual results after the event is provided by weekly or monthly reports. Often the report will show the actual, the budget, and the variance between budget and actual. Deviations from the budget will be investigated. Part of the investigation will be to determine if the report is correct – has there been a misposting? – and to correct the entry. If the deviation is not a result of a misposting then the question is: why has the deviation occurred? With budgetary control, the corrective action will be either passive or reactive; seldom will it be proactive. An example of passive action would be the correction of a misposting of an expense to a wrong account. As far as the end result (the bottom line) is concerned this might not make any difference if it merely transfers an expense from one category to another. Other actions are likely to be reactive.

EXAMPLE

If an expense category is above budget, the reactive corrective action could be to issue an edict that no more overtime will be worked without the direct permission of a senior manager. Rarely is action proactive. A proactive decision would be to note that sales are below budget, and rather than reducing expenses (reactive) to actually increase the advertising expense in an effort to attract more sales in the future.

Generally with budgetary control the thrust will be to control expenses.

Accuracy and timeliness are important. It is not much use learning three months after the event that expenses are above budget, when there are only four months of the year left. The result will usually be panic measures to reduce expenses and much writing of reports justifying why expenses are above budget. With budgetary control the danger is that managers will be judged on their ability to meet budget, and expertise in shifting expenses from one category to another. All this frenetic action is counterproductive, does not add value but does add to overhead costs.

Changes to standards

Where it is found that deviation from the required standard is consistently above or below the set level of performance, then the original conditions must be checked. If the level being achieved is *above* the set standard it could be that conditions have changed, such as new suppliers, improved technology, an improved process, or the workers themselves have found better ways to provide the service. Once the cause of the improved performance has been checked, and it is found to be legitimate and not a dangerous short cut, then it should be incorporated into the standard. If the level of performance has however *fallen* below the standard then it is important that action is taken to determine why this should be and what needs to be done to restore the system to stability.

Information technology

From the above we can see that control is exercised by comparison of actual results with intended results and with corrective actions taken when deviations occur. We have also noted that effective control relies on timely, accurate and relevant feedback of information.

A properly designed and integrated information system will provide prompt and accurate feedback of results and highlight deviations from plans. A further major advantage of a system that is well designed is that it will facilitate communication and the sharing of information between functional departments of an organization. In this section we consider the necessary actions to be taken, and areas that should be considered when installing a worthwhile information technology system.

Information technology (IT) is rapidly changing and becoming cheaper, more user-friendly and more powerful. Today, for most of us the personal computer on our desk has more computing power than most top organizations had ten years ago. International information networks (e-mail, Internet, high-speed data and video links, video conferencing and so on) have simplified global communication and operations. Electronic Data Interchange (EDI) technology has made possible extended supply chains between organizations and their suppliers. For example, cash register transactions will not only update accounting information, stock records and marketing statistics, but may also trigger automatic reordering from a supplier without the need to print and post an order to the supplier.

Problems

The rapid growth of information technology has not been without problems for the users. Most senior managers of organizations lack any detailed understanding of the complexity of information technology. They either don't want to know or try to believe that knowledge of the technology is not important. This attitude is fostered by computer salespeople who are adept at selling the idea of 'user-friendly' systems (i.e. 'You don't have to be an automotive engineer to drive a car, so why do you have to be a systems specialist to use a computer?'). After being told for over a decade about the amazing things that apparently low-cost computer technology can do, we can be pardoned for feeling let down when a systems specialist says 'It will take three years to develop and to install.' We will be even more upset when the installation project bogs down and there are overruns in cost and time budgets.

Another problem is that not all computers can easily communicate with each other, and in some cases not at all. Incompatible information systems usually result from looking at bits and pieces of systems to solve an immediate problem. For example, one distance-learning polytechnic in Australasia standardized on Apple Mac word processors for their production department (some twenty word-processing staff) and then provided the tutors and writers with IBM-compatible PCs. Another Australasian organization, with 32 wholesale stores, found that when the head office mainframe was updated (by the installation of an expensive 'new generation' machine) the printers in the branches were no longer compatible, and thus 100 new printers (not allowed for in the budget) had to be purchased.

Need for planning

Properly planned information technology provides tremendous benefits, but an unplanned piecemeal approach costs time and money, and is demoralizing. Technology is brilliant when it works but at least frustrating and at worst disastrous when it fails.

For example, the $60 million accounting system for a major bank in America had to be scrapped because it could not keep accurate accounts.

We are all aware that computer technology is constantly changing and genuinely becoming more user friendly and that versions of specific software and systems technology will continue to change. Therefore it is vital that any organization formulates a software strategy by careful planning.

The first step is to identify the areas of application. The software policy should be to include standard 'off-the-shelf' packages for the organization in specific areas of application. In the selection of software consideration should be given to:

- user requirements;
- reputation of the supplier;
- availability of software support.

The earlier examples of application software were relatively inflexible and the approach was for the user to conform to the system rather than to customize the system to fit the user. Many disillusioned users attempted to build their own software, which usually proved to be expensive and resulted in cumbersome systems. Today off-the-shelf software should be adequate for most organizations. We all believe that our organization is different and has different requirements from any other organization, but in essence, in areas that really matter, the differences are minor rather than radical. Bitter experience shows it is not prudent to let an enthusiastic IT manager attempt to develop or customize software. My earlier statement about the dangers of enthusiastic amateurs certainly applies in the area of information technology!

IT support
The supplier of hardware and software should be reputable and it is important that support should be available locally and on call. Every organization should also have its own IT support staff. These people should primarily be responsible for:

- first-level users' 'Help' desk service;
- user training;
- back-up and maintenance of the system;
- disaster recovery planning,

but not for developing new software and new systems.

IT systems: senior management support and project team
As for any company-wide programme, the implementation of a new IT system must have top management commitment. This should be reflected in setting up a project team comprising members from users (operations, marketing, sales, accounts, warehouse, human resources and, where appropriate, suppliers) and from the systems providers of hardware and software. Logically the project manager should

be chosen from the main user group. For example, if the application software is for supply-chain management then the project manager should ideally be selected from the operations function.

The project team should receive both basic technical training and operational training (functionality of the software). The project manager will then prepare a clearly stated action plan with target dates, and resources for key activities. The project will also have a budget. The plan must include review points, and senior management should be kept informed of progress in writing on a regular basis (maybe weekly but certainly not less than monthly).

Opportunity to increase operational effectiveness

It is essential that the existing procedures and processes are thoroughly and systematically reviewed before an IT system is changed. Various tools for analysing the flow and requirements of existing systems are included in Chapter 6.

The introduction of an IT system is an ideal opportunity to eliminate non-value-adding reports and activities and to break down barriers between departments. If this opportunity is not taken the new technology will only serve to speed up data collection, which in itself will not mean that information will be disseminated. It is important that all departments work together to achieve a common goal if the benefits of an investment in information technology is to be realized, otherwise the 'investment' could end up as an expensive addition to overheads with little benefit to operations.

User training

After the training of the project team the training programmes should be extended to all potential users of the system. The training features should contain both cultural education to establish acceptance by everyone concerned, and operational training to understand the functionality and operations of the new system.

Dry run

The next stage is the data input and 'dry run' of the new system in parallel with the existing system before the new system goes live. There are benefits of forming a users' group for exchanging experience with users drawn from both within and outside the company.

System maintenance

We have not discussed uninterrupted power supply, disaster recovery, the need to back up files, system security (log in, fire walls, etc.) and so on. All these issues are nuts and bolts and should be second nature to your IT manager. This section was not written for the professional IT manager, but to give the average manager an understanding of the strategy of IT implementation. However don't be afraid to ask the systems manager if there is a disaster recovery plan!

CHAPTER SUMMARY

In this chapter we discussed the planning and control cycle. We began with the mission (the reason for being for an organization), and we showed how the business plan is formulated to convert the mission into reality. Plans identify objectives, and strategy determines the steps that are needed to make the objectives happen. The operations manager is the person responsible for making the plan happen and for establishing a stable system that gives a consistent and reliable service in line with the standards set by the plan. The operations manager will control the situation by ensuring that staff at all levels:

- know what the standards are;
- get accurate and timely feedback of results;
- are capable of comparing results to standards;
- are empowered to take corrective action.

The lower the level of decision-making for corrective action, the quicker will be the response. An organizational culture that inspires staff at all levels requires mutual goodwill and trust by management and workers. However, not everyone wants to be empowered; some people prefer to be told what to do and not to take responsibility.

Communication and prompt and accurate feedback of information are essential if control is to be exercised. An information technology system that has been properly designed and installed is essential for any organization. The pitfalls of not properly planning an information system are legion. In this chapter we have detailed areas that should be considered when planning a new information technology system.

CD ROM CASE STUDY

The case study relevant to this chapter is based on McDonald's, and relates to how McDonald's establish partnerships with suppliers, set standards of performance for staff, and the importance of training staff in standard procedures. These are all key ingredients for McDonald's that have helped them achieve a high level of worldwide consistency.

Note

1. Sharemarket analysts generally make investment recommendations after consideration of published results, the 'strength' of the balance sheet, and the use of 'common size' benchmarks in the form of ratios (gearing, return on equity, stock-turn, and so on). Share prices are generally not calculated on how well the business performed against budget

(usually the past budget will not be shown in the published result); rather share prices change daily on the basis of interim announcements, rumours, speculation and sentiment. Calculations such as Profit/Earning Ratios and Dividend Covered, etc. as shown on financial pages of newspapers are by necessity based on the last published annual or interim accounts, which are by nature historical and often many months out of date.

Part Three

Parts One and Two tended to take a broad-brush or macro approach to management of service operations. In this part a micro approach is adopted and specific operational problems are considered. Issues that are discussed in **Chapter 6** include location of operations, layout of premises, workplace layout, method study and ergonomics. In **Chapter 7**, job enrichment, empowerment of workers and other motivational factors are considered.

- This Part begins in **Chapter 6** with location and then moves on to layout. It is maintained that it is generally necessary to understand the flow of work and the work relationships of people, before the layout of the premises is finalized. This is important when new premises are being contemplated, but these considerations are equally important when considering existing premises, as a changed layout can markedly improve efficiency. Chapter 6 also shows how the structured approach of method study will improve efficiency, including layout of premises, work flow and design of workplaces.

- From the worker's perspective, convenient and comfortable workplace location and layout, coupled with work flow and work methods designed to reduce unnecessary or complicated work are likely to have motivational aspects. Thus it was considered logical to include in this Part a chapter (**Chapter 7**) covering job enrichment and empowerment of workers.

Chapter 6

Facilities and work

Objectives for this chapter

In this chapter we consider:

- Location problems and decisions in relationship to customer service and to efficiency of operations.
- Layout of premises to gain the best use of space and efficient work flows.
- Layout of individual workplaces.
- Safety, health and ergonomics.
- Method study to improve the efficiency of staff.

Introduction

As discussed in Part Two, the operations function and day-to-day operational issues (problems and decisions) exist within the broader framework of the total organization and its external environment. It has been shown that business policy determines the services offered and the level (quality) of service that will be provided. It has also been seen that business policy will limit the resources available to operations and, to a large extent, establish the operating structure. We have seen that operations objectives include customer satisfaction and at the same time efficient use of resources. These, often conflicting, objectives have to be balanced by the operations manager within constraints of price, quality and overall feasibility as limited in the short to medium term by existing resources. The challenge for operations managers therefore is to make the best use of *existing* resources. A major resource, and a major constraint, will be the premises from which the business of the organization is carried out. In the long term new premises can be acquired but, in the short term, operations have to make do with what already exists.

Location of premises

The location problem applies to two basic situations, i.e. new premises and existing premises.

There are several factors to be considered when deciding on location:

1. Any business policy that requires speed of service to customers, or ease of access by customers, will lead to a choice of location near where the customers are. Example: the location of a corner shop.
2. Any policy that stresses efficient use of resources will lead to the question 'Can we make do with less?' Example: with the increasing popularity of automatic teller machines, telephone banking and the introduction of Internet banking, banks are tending to reduce the number of branches, and opting for smaller premises.
3. Any business policy which takes the value-chain approach, wherein the suppliers are dedicated and regarded as an extension of the whole organization, might well take into consideration proximity to suppliers as a criterion when determining location. Example: an advertising agency and a print shop.

For an existing location, operations managers will be accustomed to handling input and output relationships, and will have views on what can be achieved with the existing location. The operations manager will therefore wish to be closely involved in any business policy decision concerning a new location. Operational concerns will be either material related (access to suppliers) or market related (proximity and ease of access for customers).

Location – new operations
Wild (1995: 91) says 'The choice of location is vital for any new business; indeed there are numerous examples of new businesses which have had brief and troubled lives solely because of their disadvantageous location.' Poor location decisions are expensive and have long-lasting effects. A wrong initial location decision will lead to further expense and disruption if a subsequent move to a new location has to be made. If it is decided to stay with the existing unsuitable location, ongoing costs will continue and frustration is likely to escalate. Often the ongoing effects of a poor location decision are hidden as the costs will be in the form of lost opportunities.

Opportunity costs of a wrong location, such as lost sales and extra operating expense, cannot be separately accounted for (often they will not be known) and thus they are not shown in annual financial reports. This lack of exposure for scrutiny and comment generally means that only the operations manager will be truly aware of the extra effort required, the extra costs of transport, the cost of double handling and so on due to poor location. However, the marketing department may have some ideas on lost opportunities (sales) due to a poor location.

Location decisions – new and existing operations
Basic location questions are:

*   Why?
*   Where?
*   How much space (demand issue)?
*   Lease or buy?

- Cost/benefits?
- Evaluation of alternatives.
- And 'Why?' again!

Why?

A new operation will require premises

For a new operation the reason for acquiring premises is self-evident; premises and facilities will be needed to achieve the objectives of the organization. The decision to acquire premises will therefore be part of the overall consideration of the resources needed by the new organization.

Existing operation – why move?

When it is suggested that an existing operation move to new premises, the obvious question would seem to be 'Why move?' The answer, however, is not always obvious. Perhaps the question should be rephrased to ask 'How will the move to new premises improve the business operation, or improve customer service?' If a satisfactory answer can't be given, then why move?

Prestige versus operational efficiency

Many decisions to move to new premises (such as to build a new head office) are made for prestige purposes rather than to improve the efficiency of the operation or to give a better service to the customer. If the reason given for a planned move is nebulous (it cannot clearly be demonstrated that the move to new premises will improve operations or add to customer satisfaction) *but* the decision to move is still made, then the operations manager must clearly state what is required *to safeguard existing levels of operating effectiveness.*

To meet increased demand

If the reason for new premises for an existing business is to satisfy an increase in demand then the question must be 'Is it possible to expand the existing premises, (rather than relocate)?' It might even be found to be possible to rearrange the layout of the existing premises so as to make better use of what already exists. On the other hand, if a move is really necessary, then piecemeal additions or *ad hoc* solutions can result in facilities that will *always* be inefficient. Money thrown at an inadequate facility will be money wasted.

Long-term demand?

Many organizations, with enthusiasm fuelled by rapid initial growth or in periods of national economic growth, have committed themselves to costly new premises only to find that growth has not continued at the same initial meteoric rate. It has to be recognized that the economy is cyclical, and when there is an economic downturn expensive premises are hard to unload. Before committing to expensive premises it must be reasonably certain that the increase in demand is ongoing and not short term (i.e. based on a fashionable trend in the marketplace – yesterday's must-haves are tomorrow's junk).

Where?

Having determined that new premises are genuinely needed and demand will continue, then the next question is: 'Where?'

Service and transport industries have different criteria from each other. Service industries will generally evaluate location alternatives in terms of accessibility *by* customers (distance to be travelled by customers), and transportation (delivery system) industries will consider accessibility *to* customers (time to reach customers). In both cases, customer numbers and market density will be important, and in the case of supply services proximity of suppliers might also be important.

If the focus is on maximizing revenue the considerations will be market density and volume of business.

If the focus is on cost minimization, the considerations will be cheap premises, cheap labour, cheap energy, etc.

Manufacturing industries have a totally different set of criteria such as access to transport, deep sea ports, suppliers, cost of energy, reliable energy supplies, cheap/skilled labour supply, government and legal requirements, tax incentives, waste disposal and so on.

YOUR TURN!

What are the criteria that you would use in determining the optimum location for your department?

Fixed or delivered operations

Service industries can operate as a 'fixed' operation. With a fixed operation the customer comes to the location for the service. With a 'delivered' operation the service is taken to the customer. This applies to supply, service and transport industries. For example, a pizza shop might operate both ways: some customers come to the shop for service, and some customers phone in and the pizza is delivered to their homes.

For fixed operations high visibility is necessary, and accessibility to customers is essential. This can include adequate car parking, or a situation in a busy part of a town for foot traffic. Distance from customers and market density is obviously important in deciding on the location.

For delivered operations accessibility to the market, i.e. time taken to reach the customer, becomes important. Thus rather than being in the centre of town (if that is where the market is) the operation can be on the outskirts of town, which is likely to be cheaper in property costs, provided there is ready access into town to serve the customers. An example would be an insurance consultant/financial adviser working from a home office and visiting clients at their place of business.

How much space?

The amount of space is dependent on two issues, the first being demand and potential growth, and the second being how efficiently space is used. It is a truism that the more space is available, the more wasteful of space we will be, i.e. space requirements expand to use up the space available. It is also true that in a growing organization there never seems to be enough space. It could be argued that an organization can never have too much space, but on the other hand space costs money, and too much space, distance to travel between departments etc. will add to time taken/wasted in getting a job done. Use of space and space requirements is further covered in the sections on layout and method study.

Lease or buy?

Once land has been purchased and buildings erected, large amounts of money will have been spent. If subsequently it transpires that the location or the buildings themselves are not suitable, it is often found that a substantial loss will be made if a decision is made to sell. Accountants have a term 'borrowing short, lending long'. Large capital expenditure in land and buildings equates to large amounts of funds (own or borrowed funds) tied up in real estate (lending long) which reduces the amount of funds available for working capital for the business. Reduced working capital results in the business being forced to raise a series of short-term loans. If short-term borrowing cannot be serviced out of cash flow, or short-term loans cannot be repaid on due date, then although the business has large amounts of fixed assets on the balance sheet, it will face insolvency. Generally in a forced sale situation buildings will not realize their balance sheet value.

In the late 1980s, after a period of rapid growth in property values, and following the stock market debacle of October 1987 there were sudden and dramatic falls in property values and many organizations found themselves with 'negative equity'[1] for their property holdings. It is no wonder that even now, many years on, some organizations prefer to lease properties rather than to purchase. Leasing of property has two advantages: first it does not tie up working capital, and second if a poor decision has been made, leases are not for ever. Even with a long-term lease it is usually possible to negotiate out of the lease or to sub-let.

Although leasing is less final than building or buying, nonetheless the location decision must still be made just as carefully. If it later transpires that a leased property is in the wrong location, the disruption (internally to the smooth running of the operation, and externally to the customer), and the effort and money expended in finding new premises and moving, could have been avoided if the correct decision had been made initially.

Cost/benefits?

Break-even analysis can be a useful tool to determine location. Break-even analysis is a technique that shows the amount of sales revenue required in a given situation to cover the costs of the operation. For break-even purposes costs are divided into fixed costs, i.e. those costs which don't change no matter how many sales are made, and variable costs which are those costs which increase or decrease in proportion to sales activity.

EXAMPLE

Figure 6.1 shows a break-even chart which compares two possible retail locations. Location 1 is the centre of the town with a high pedestrian count and with a corresponding high cost for premises. Location 2 is one block away from the centre where premises are cheaper, but the pedestrian count is much lower. This particular business relies to some extent on attracting people off the street.

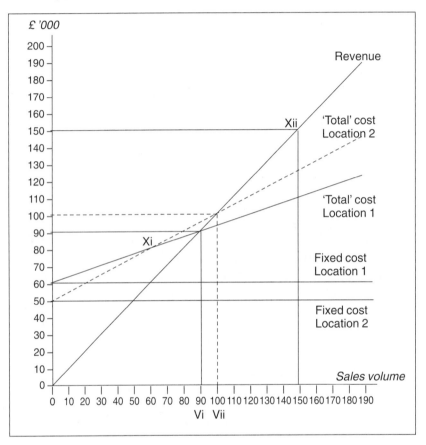

Figure 6.1: A location break-even chart

Explanation of Figure 6.1

Fixed costs do not change no matter how much is sold. In this example, fixed costs for both locations consist of any combination of: mortgage interest, interest forgone on money invested in the purchase of property, rent or lease of property, local government taxes/rates, insurance, any other property costs.

Variable costs for both locations include all costs which are directly attributable to making a sale. In this example variable costs would include purchase cost of goods sold, packing costs, advertising, and delivery costs. As sales increase so will variable costs.

Other costs not included in our break-even calculations are any costs that are the same irrespective of location. Such costs would include wages, electricity, etc.

In our example, Location 1 has the more expensive fixed costs, but less variable costs (less advertising and delivery costs). Location 2 is in a cheaper part of town, but with a lighter market density. By comparison more advertising will be necessary and more delivery costs will be required per sale made.

Sales price per unit will remain the same irrespective of the location, therefore only one revenue line is shown.

Vi (Location 1) and Vii (Location 2) show respective break-even points (where revenue equals respective total costs).

Xi shows the point where, with the same amount of sales, both locations make the same level of loss, i.e. at £60,000 of sales, Location 1 will give a loss of £20,000, likewise Location 2 with £60,000 of sales will also have a loss of £20,000. From this point on, the profit gap, that is the gap between the revenue line and 'total' costs, increases at a greater rate for Location 1 than it does for Location 2.

Clearly in this example Location 1 is the better choice: break-even is reached with fewer sales. A further factor, not shown in the break-even analysis, is that with the higher pedestrian count at Location 1 the potential for sales is greater than for Location 2, thus the shop at Location 1 is more likely to reach the £150,000 sales sooner than will Location 2.

Break-even can also be demonstrated in the form of a simple profit and loss statement as shown in Table 6.1.

	Location 1		**Location 2**	
Sales	90,000		100,000	
Variable cost	30,000	33.3%	50,000	50%
Gross profit	60,000	66.6%	50,000	50%
Fixed costs	60,000		50,000	
Profit	Nil		Nil	

Table 6.1: Profit and loss statement

In Figure 6.1, Xii shows the difference in profit for Location 1 and Location 2 when a certain level of sales revenue has been reached. This can also be demonstrated with profit and loss statements as shown in Table 6.2.

	Location 1		**Location 2**	
Sales	150,000		150,000	
Variable cost	50,000	33.3%	75,000	50%
Gross profit	100,000	66.6%	75,000	50%
Fixed costs	60,000		50,000	
Profit	40,000		25,000	

Table 6.2: Profit and loss statement

Evaluation of alternatives

Checklists

Given a choice of locations, perhaps the easiest method of evaluation is by a checklist of relevant requirements. In the checklist shown in Table 6.3 a point rating system has been incorporated. The importance of each criterion is given a weighting and then in the second column a further rating is given as to how well the criterion is met.

For example, the criteria might consist of :

	Weighting	×	Criteria met	=	Total
Customer access	9		7		63
Car parking	7		8		56

	Importance weighting (1 to 10) ×	Meets criteria (1 to 10) =	TOTAL
Access for customers			
Access to customers			
Parking space			
Proximity of suppliers			
Availability of transport			
Fixed costs of location			
Variable costs of location			
Labour supply			
Cost of labour			
Industrial relations			
Government: (local/national as appropriate)			
Zoning restrictions			
Capital restrictions			
Funds transfers			
Taxation rates			
Tax/other incentives			
Stability of government			
Reliability of sources: of energy			
of other utilities			
Cost of utilities			
Other factors			
TOTAL			

Table 6.3: Point rating system checklist

Overseas ventures

If overseas locations are being investigated, it is most important that the broader issues, such as political and economic stability, local customs and culture, tax structures and incentives, reliable communications, energy supplies and so on are considered. Obviously an overseas venture for an organization will require very detailed considerations. Often local problems do not emerge until the project is well under way. It is most sensible to solicit local assistance and knowledge from the outset when contemplating an overseas venture.

Transportation models

Transportation models are an iterative, mathematical approach to determining location and for solving transportation and distribution problems. However, transportation models are not only used for distribution problems; for example they can be adapted to determine whether to have few or many retail branches and where branches should be located so as to best serve (attract) customers. The transportation model approach can also be used to solve location problems in other service areas where cost or time of providing a service can be related to location. For example, a transportation model could be used to determine the location of appliances for a fire brigade service, or to determine where satellite (local) outpatient departments should be set up for a health service, and so on. Here we will provide a general method, based on the location of warehouses to supply known customer markets. As this is an iterative approach, a computer spreadsheet approach would help. There are 'off-the-shelf' transportation computer programs available. The example given is a simplified problem designed to give an understanding of the overall approach.

 EXAMPLE

A distributor has three warehouses:

Location	Capacity
Able	5,000
Baker	6,000
Charlie	2,500
TOTAL	13,500

Forecasts show that demand for four different regions will be:

North	6,000
South	4,000
East	2,000
West	1,500
TOTAL	13,500

Each region can be served by any one of the three warehouses.

We therefore have three warehouses to supply four markets, thus in total there are twelve possible routes. Each route will have a different cost of transport (if we were considering a fire brigade or ambulance service, then the 'cost' would be the 'time' taken to get to an incident). The aim of transportation problems is to minimize cost (or time).

For example transport costs are:

From: Supplier	To: North	South	East	West
Able	3	2	7	6
Baker	7	5	2	3
Charlie	2	5	4	5

Solution one: North–West Rule

A simple transportation allocation approach is known as the North–West Rule. With the North–West Rule a table is used to get an initial feasible solution. We begin by allocating as much as possible from the first supplier to the customer shown in the top left-hand (north-west) corner of the table. The cost of transportation is also shown on the table, in the right-hand corner of the cell for each of the twelve routes (see Table 6.4).

From	North	South	East	West	Supply
Able	3	2	7	6	5,000
Baker	7	5	2	3	6,000
Charlie	2	5	4	5	2,500
Required	6,000	4,000	2,000	1,500	13,500

Table 6.4: Table before any allocations

From	North	South	East	West	Supply
Able	5,000				–
Baker					6,000
Charlie					2,500
Required	1,000	4,000	2,000	1,500	

Table 6.5: Table after initial allocation of 5,000 units from Able to North

After the initial allocation (see Table 6.5), which totally depletes Able, North still requires 1,000 units which are allocated from Baker. The remainder of Baker's stock will go to South and East. North and South are now satisfied but East and West are still to be fully served. Charlie can be used to complete East's requirements and also to satisfy West's requirements. This allocation is shown in Table 6.6.

From	North	South	East	West	Supply
Able	5,000 ^{3}	2	7	6	5,000
Baker	1,000 ^{7}	4,000 ^{5}	1,000 ^{2}	3	6,000
Charlie	2	5	1,000 ^{4}	1,500 ^{5}	2,500
Required	6,000	4,000	2,000	1,500	13,500

Table 6.6: Allocation of remainder

We will call this **Solution one.** This approach gives a feasible solution, but ignores the costs, or time elements. If we apply the 'costs' to our solution we obtain the results shown in Table 6.7.

From	To	Volume	Unit 'cost'	Total 'cost'
Able	North	5,000	3	15,000
Baker	North	1,000	7	7,000
Baker	South	4,000	5	20,000
Charlie	East	1,000	4	4,000
Charlie	West	1,500	5	7,500
TOTAL				53,500

Table 6.7: Solution one

This is not likely to be the optimum solution! Actually the optimum is less than 40,000!

Solution two: An alternative approach begins with the largest supplier making the initial allocation, in this case Baker 2,000 to East, then stopping to re-evaluate to determine who is now the largest supplier. In this example Able still has 5,000 to dispose of and Baker has been left with 3,500. As Able is now the largest supplier, Able will allocate the maximum possible to the cheapest route – 4,000 to South. After this allocation Baker again becomes the largest supplier and would allocate 1,500 to West and so on. Carrying this method to its conclusion we have the allocation and costs shown in Table 6.8. Again not the optimum solution!

Another method is to begin with the cheapest route for the biggest supplier. In this case the biggest supplier is Baker with 6,000, and the cheapest route for Baker is to supply East. As East can only accept 2,000, Baker will still have 4,000 to dispose of, and using the cheapest routes Baker will give West 1,500 and South 2,500. Able is the second biggest supplier, and the best allocation still available for Able is 1,500 to South and 3,500 to North. Charlie will then deliver the balance required for North of 2,500. The result, **Solution three**, is shown in Table 6.9.

Able	1,000	×	3	=	3,000
Able	4,000	×	2	=	8,000
Baker	2,500	×	7	=	17,500
Baker	2,000	×	2	=	4,000
Baker	1,500	×	3	=	4,500
Charlie	2,500	×	2	=	5,000
TOTAL					42,000

From	North	South	East	West	Supply
Able	1,000 ³	4,000 ²	7	6	5,000
Baker	2,500 ⁷	5	2,000 ²	1,500 ³	6,000
Charlie	2,500 ²	5	4	5	2,500
Required	6,000	4,000	2,000	1,500	13,500

Table 6.8: Solution two

Able	3,500	×	3	=	10,500
Able	1,500	×	2	=	3,000
Baker	2,500	×	5	=	12,500
Baker	2,000	×	2	=	4,000
Baker	1,500	×	3	=	4,500
Charlie	2,500	×	2	=	5,000
TOTAL					39,500

From	North	South	East	West	Supply
Able	3,500 ³	1,500 ²	7	6	5,000
Baker	7	2,500 ⁵	2,000 ²	1,500 ³	6,000
Charlie	2,500 ²	5	4	5	2,500
Required	6,000	4,000	2,000	1,500	13,500

Table 6.9: Solution three

But is Solution three the best possible result?

Stepping-stone method

Another approach is to use any of the Tables as shown above and from any cell subtract one unit and follow through the resulting flow-on effects. Assume for our example using Table 6.9 that for the cell Baker–South one unit is added. The flow will be as shown in Table 6.10. The cost of making the adjustments is also shown. The net effect of this first set of steps is to reduce costs by 1. This shows that for every unit shipped from Baker to South there will be a cost benefit of 1. The process is then repeated cell by cell throughout the table. This approach is known as the stepping-stone method. Following through the stepping-stone method we find that the optimum solution is the same as Solution three, i.e. $39,500.

From	North	South	East	West	Change
Able	1,000 + 1 ^{3}	4,000 – 1 ^{2}			+ 3 – 2
Baker	2,500 – 1 ^{7}	+ 1 ^{5}			– 7 + 5
Charlie					
Required					– 1

Table 6.10: Stepping-stone method

As we said, this is a simple example. All assignment or transportation models are based on an iterative approach which is suitable for a computer package approach. For a more detailed study of algorithmic transportation and assignment models see Wild (1995: Appendix 1, Linear Programming).

Layout of premises

Having determined where our organization will be located, the next issue is to consider the layout with the overall objectives of facilitating efficient operations and first-class customer service. As in most areas of operations the first criterion is to establish the relative importance of customer satisfaction *vis-à-vis* efficient use of resources.

In most systems there will be a physical flow of people or materials. Layout planning aims to:

- optimize movement;
- reduce congestion;
- maximize use of space.

Optimize movement
In an office, or a backroom area, the aim will be to reduce movement. However in a retail store situation such as a supermarket, the aim might be to have a layout that will increase the distance to be travelled by the customer. For example, customers are channelled up and down aisles, and the actual distance travelled is maximized rather than minimized so that the customers are obliged to pass by brightly coloured and attractively presented goods and, hopefully, be tempted to buy up 'big time'.

Reduce congestion

The objective of operations management is to add value, and to eliminate non-value-adding activities. Seldom is value added by having customers waiting in queues. Time spent waiting does not add to sales, and merely adds to congestion. There is a limit to how long people will queue, no matter how good the service or product at the end of the queue. What can't be quantified is the number of sales lost by people who are put off by a queue. Recently there has been reported in Australia cases of 'supermarket rage' where shoppers have become extremely agitated by waiting in queues.

Maximize use of space

As we have seen in the section on location, space costs money; thus it is important to make the best use of space. For example, if there is spare space it can always be used for display purposes. Likewise, with the customers' interests at heart it follows that where possible more space per person should be allocated to customer areas (front office) and less space to backroom facilities. One large insurance company allocated the top floor of its new building as the staff cafeteria. Thus the floor with the best views was given to the staff who used it for about two hours a day (tea breaks and lunch). Two years later a new Chief Executive found space in the basement for the cafeteria, and leased out the top floor at a premium rate. We are not condoning relegating the staff to the dungeons, but on the other hand to be over-generous with premium space is not good economic sense. Sensible initial planning would have prevented staff subsequently becoming upset at losing 'their' cafeteria (what they hadn't had they wouldn't miss).

Types of layout

The basic types of layout are:

- Process.
- Product.
- Fixed position.
- Hybrid.

Process layout

With process layout all operations of a similar nature will be grouped together. Examples of process layout will be found in hotels, libraries, supermarkets and warehouses.

 EXAMPLE

In a library the reference section with computer terminals and indexes may be grouped together, the books will be grouped according to subject, journals and periodicals will be in another section, CD ROMS in another area, and the librarians' check-out department will be behind a counter near the exit. The customer goes to the section required and will bypass some sections.

Product layout
Here facilities are arranged according to the needs of the service.

EXAMPLE

Self-service fast-food outlet (without seating) (see Figure 6.2).

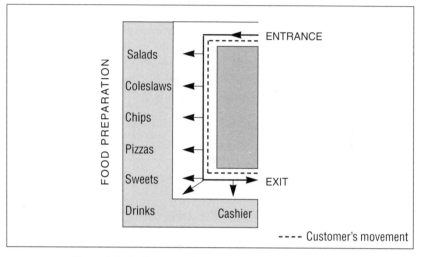

Figure 6.2: Self-service fast-food outlet without seating

EXAMPLE

Another example is the diagnostic department in a hospital where patients are given sequential tests, i.e. different types of specialized equipment are located adjacent to each other, and a mixture of specialized skills and tasks is required.

With product layout floor space is minimized, and ideally the process should be continuous with the person who is being 'served' moving from facility to facility.

Fixed-position layout
For process layout and product layout the customer moves past stationary service sections. In a fixed-position layout neither the customer nor the service provider moves, an example being the hairdresser or the dentist.

Hybrid layout
As the name suggests, this is a mixed form of layout. A restaurant is an example of a mixed product/process layout, where a buffet for self-service (product layout) and table service is also offered (process layout).

With some service operations the choice of layout will be limited by the service offered; in other cases it is often worth considering if a change from, say, a process-type layout to a product-type layout might improve flow of customers, or save space. There can be no hard and fast rules, but being aware of the different types of layout and daring to question, i.e. 'Can the customer become more involved in self service?' might well trigger a better use of space. Consider the old-style grocery store (before the advent of the supermarket) where customers stood still and the grocer and his staff 'picked' at the request of the customer. In today's supermarket customers do their own picking. Most supermarkets allow customers to travel up and down aisles, and customers can choose to bypass aisles, however other supermarkets are laid out in such a way that the customer can only travel one way and once the journey has started there are no short cuts – no aisle can be avoided as in essence there is only one long meandering route to follow (see Figure 6.3).

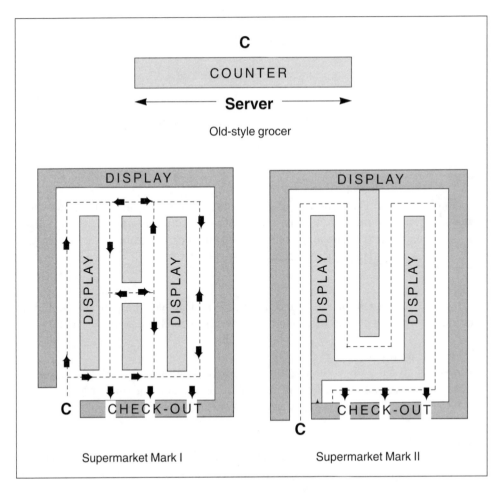

Figure 6.3: Possible grocery store layouts

Layout planning

Here we consider the layout of a new department. The approach will be the same irrespective of whether the decision is to remodel an existing area or to obtain new premises.

The two key issues for layout planning are *demand* and *capacity*. Demand will determine the capacity required, and the system structure will determine if storage space for goods is required where goods are being supplied so as to meet demand fluctuations. Thus detailed demand forecasting and capacity planning are required before layout planning can begin. Method study and the determination of a standard system (see the next section) coupled with capacity planning will lead us to establish the amount of resources that will need to be housed. Resources include people, equipment, furniture, fittings, display stands and so on. Other factors include customer waiting areas, rest rooms/toilets for staff and customers, additional services such as lunch-room facilities and so on. Health and safety regulations will also have to be considered. Once all the above has been agreed then layout planning can begin. It follows that every stakeholder should be invited to indicate requirements; no one person can hope to know it all!

Project approach

It is recommended that the layout of a new department should be treated as a project. Projects are defined as 'one-off' novel endeavours, and certainly a new layout meets this criterion. The intricacies of project management is discussed in Chapter 12.

Layout planning methods

The tendency today is to use computer simulation for layout planning, but in reality the same result can be achieved through the use of more mundane traditional methods. The methods we show here have stood the test of time and are simple to apply. The strong point with each method is that the planner must get personally involved and collect factual evidence.

Visual aids

Visual aids are an important element of layout planning. These include scale representations, including drawings, templates, three-dimensional models and movement patterns. One simple way of showing movement is to use coloured cottons on a scale plan to show the movement of materials, people, documents, or information. The power of this method lies in vividly highlighting inefficiency.

EXAMPLE

Figure 6.4 shows a 'before-and-after' string diagram. Imagine how much more graphic this would be with the use of different coloured cottons to indicate each person/department visited.

Note: With the string diagram the floor plan must be drawn to scale. Once the recording has been completed the string can be measured to determine the exact distance covered.

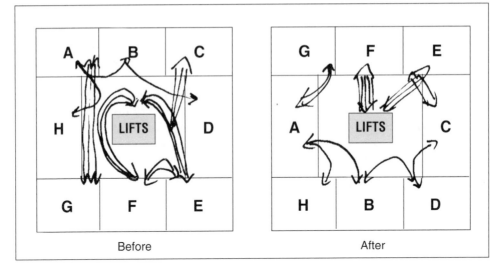

Figure 6.4: A 'before-and-after' string diagram

In a service industry the criterion may not always be to reduce the distance travelled. As discussed earlier, for a supermarket the criterion might be to make the most use of selling space by increasing the distance travelled by customers. Alternatively if space is at a premium then the criterion might be to reduce the amount of space needed. Before planning can begin the criteria for the layout have to be clearly established and agreed. It really comes back to the old conflict of operations: is the objective primarily customer satisfaction or resource utilization? For backroom operations resource utilization will generally be the objective, i.e. minimal movement and minimum space; for the front office the reverse could well be the objective.

Relationship diagrams
A relationship chart looks at movement and the need for one department to be near another; relationship diagrams also consider the underlying reasons for the relationships.

EXAMPLE

The following simplified example for a hospital shows the space requirements for each department.

Visitors' lounge*	1,500 square metres
Gift shop	1,500
Pharmacy	1,200
Autopsy	2,000
Morgue*	2,000
Accident and emergency department*	1,500
X-ray department	1,500
Toilets	1,000

Stairs and lifts	1,000
Routine admissions and Enquiries*	1,000
TOTAL	13,200

* Denotes external access to street required.

The first step in constructing a relationship diagram is to consider the importance of why one department should be close to another, or conversely why one department should not be next to another. A code is generally used, or a numeric scale, to determine the importance of adjacent locations. The code used in our example is:

Adjacency:
A = Absolutely essential
E = Extremely important
 I = Important
O = Ordinary
U = Unimportant
N = Not at all desirable

Figures 6.5, 6.6 and 6.7 demonstrate how the codes are used, and translated into a rough diagram from which a more precise layout can be determined.

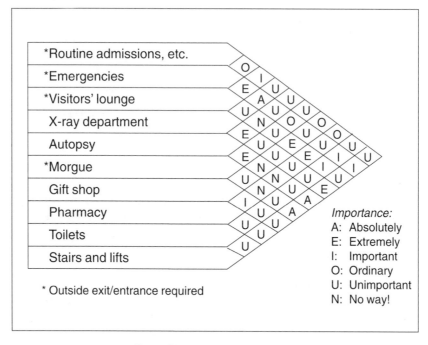

Figure 6.5: Relationship diagram

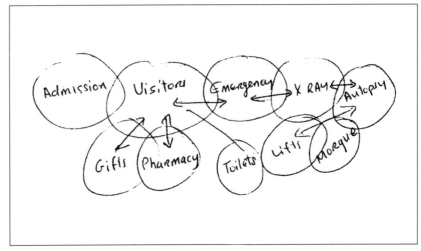

Figure 6.6: Rough diagram

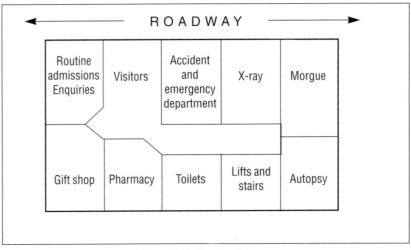

Figure 6.7: Precise layout

In all but the simplest of layouts, planning by hand can be a long and tedious process, and generally a computer-based approach can be used. The two basic methodologies in computer-based layout planning are proximity of departments or processes, and movement minimization of workers, customers, or flow of work.

Proximity maximization
The approach is to begin by placing the departments with the highest proximity rating together and working in descending order-of-closeness rating until all departments have been included. There will be other constraints such as space required and access and egress considerations. The programs work by assigning a value to closeness ratings, and the aim is to maximize the score.

Movement minimization

At first glance you could be pardoned for thinking that if proximity can be maximized then movement will automatically be minimized. However the closeness rating will often include other factors such as customer convenience or safety issues, and movement will be only one of the factors considered. Movement minimization, however, concentrates only on minimization of movement. Movement may be measured in the number of journeys, or in distance, or by cost of movement, and may be customer related, worker related, or related to movement of materials.

Proximity maximization is more general and some of the measures will be qualitative rather than quantitative. Movement minimization on the other hand uses factual information that can be quantified, i.e. metres travelled, cost of travel, number of journeys, volume of movement and so on.

A combination procedure allows an initial layout to be developed using one criterion, and then by adding other criteria changes will be made until the best 'mix' is achieved. The advantage of computer systems is the interactivity which enables the layout designer to change criteria and to try 'What if' scenarios.

Flexibility

Ideally layouts should be flexible and easily changed. To this extent movable and preferably free-standing partitions are recommended. Open-planned offices do make the most of floor space but generally staff, given the choice, prefer their own offices. Workstations which combine desk, filing cabinet, bookshelf and computer terminal, all ergonomically designed for the comfort and convenience of staff, can overcome the resistance to open planning to a large measure. Additionally a properly designed workstation will afford a measure of privacy and will have some acoustical properties to deaden extraneous office noise.

Safety, health and ergonomics

Occupational safety, health and ergonomics might be considered a moral issue, but even the Romans realized that well-maintained slaves were more efficient and more valuable. The average fully-employed adult will spend 25 per cent or more of his or her life at the workplace, and additional time in travelling to and from work. It could well be argued that employers have a moral obligation in addition to various legal obligations to provide a safe working environment, and that the worker who 'sells' his or her time has a right to a safe and healthy workplace. Sadly history shows that voluntary safety arrangements do not provide adequate standards, and thus legislation has been necessary. The fault has not always been with employers, as employees are often found to take short cuts. Statistics show that the home is still the most dangerous place for most people!

It is a fact that most health and safety requirements of workers are only common sense. It is common sense to have adequate light, correct temperatures, proper ventilation, noise controls and so on.

Ergonomics

Ergonomics is the science which seeks to improve the physical and mental well-being of workers by optimizing the function of human–machine environments. In today's office, workers are surrounded by machines, most of them electronic, and long hours are spent hunched over keyboards and in front of VDU screens. In particular ergonomics concentrates on:

- fitting the work demands to the efficiency of people, to reduce physical and mental stress;
- providing information for the design of machines, keyboards, etc. so that they can be operated efficiently;
- the development of adjustable workstations and chairs etc. so that individuals can self-adjust the workstation to meet their needs;
- providing information on correct body posture to reduce fatigue and to minimize OOS (occupational overuse syndrome – formerly known as RSI or repetitive stress injury);
- giving guidelines for lighting, air conditioning, noise limits and so on.

Figure 6.8 and Box 6.1 are examples of basic ergonomic information provided by the New Zealand Government. Most governments throughout the world have a department or agency which will happily provide (free of charge) ergonomic advice and information geared to local needs.

Method study

In service industries – no matter how automated the process, how clever the information technology – there will always be the need for people to interface with the customers, or by backroom endeavours to provide support for front-line staff. Method study aims to make the life of the workers easier and more rewarding by:

- providing an efficient layout (be it office, showroom, or warehouse);
- providing a well-designed workstation with adequate lighting, ventilation/heating/air conditioning;
- implementing standard work procedures;
- providing personal satisfaction – modern method study encourages workers to become involved in looking for improvements at the workplace.

Method study also considers the health and safety requirements for the workplace. The study of work, to streamline and to make work easier and more efficient (productive), will always be of importance.

The standard method study approach is through a *systematic* investigation of *all* factors that affect the efficiency of a particular work situation. Generally method study is applied to existing work situations and problem areas. The seven-step approach of method study is not limited to the workplace: it can be applied with equal effectiveness in the home, in the sports club, and indeed any situation where a problem is encountered.

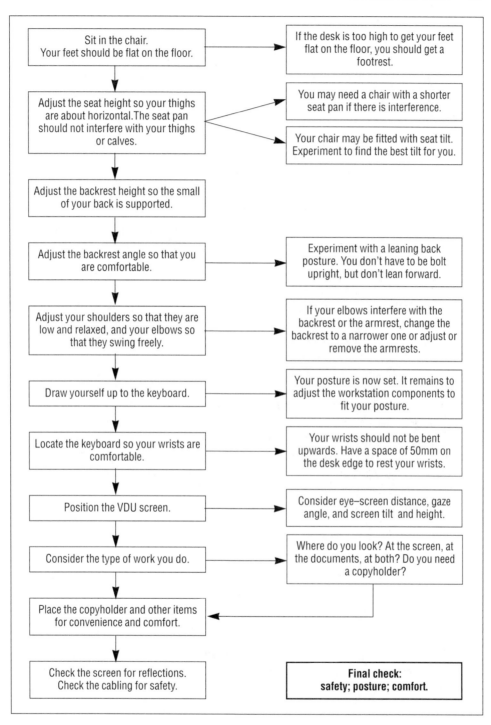

Figure 6.8: Getting comfortable at the workstation. Source: Frank Darby, Senior Occupational Health Scientist. Occupational Safety and Health Service. Department of Labour, PO Box 3705, Wellington, NZ.

FOOTRESTS

Footrests are an excellent way of making up deficencies in the workstation. Where people's legs would otherwise dangle, a footrest of the right shape, size and position, will be of great value.

Basically, the feet should be out in front of the body, slanting slightly to the vertical. This posture:

(a) counterbalances the body better;
(b) removes tension from the muscles of the back;
(c) relieves pressure in the intervertebral discs ;
(d) helps thrust the body onto the backrest.

You can't get these advantages if the feet dangle or have to bend at the knee to rest on the chair legs.

- The footrest needs to slant slightly (10 to 15 degrees) and to be at the correct height for the person.
- The height of the footrest may be found by sitting the person with their feet flat on the floor and their thighs horizontal. Measure the distance between the bottom edge of the desk and the top of the thighs. Subtract 25mm (for clearance) to get the height of the front of the footrest.
- The footrest should be at least 450×300 mm in size, to allow for variation in foot posture.
- Where feet must operate foot pedals (such as on a dictaphone machine), these should be built in to the footrest, so that the feet (and toes) don't have to hover above them. Constant muscle tension will be required in the muscles down the front of the legs if the toes have to be held up. This can lead rapidly to fatigue. If possible, the foot pedal should be relocatable so that it can be used by either foot. Even better, consider replacing the foot pedal with a knee paddle, if the complexity of the controls allows it.
- The footrest should not slide on the floor. The foot surface of the footrest should not be slippery – the feet should not have to be held in place.
- Several types of footrest available have the ability to be adjusted for angle by foot action alone. The principle of being adjustable while in the seated position is good for two reasons:

    1. It is easy find the best/most comfortable posture.
    2. It is a good principle to change the posture (of any part of the body) regularly.

- The footrest should be adjustable from the seated position, preferably with the feet.
- The footrest should be easy to move around – it should not weigh more than a few kilograms.

Box 6.1: Footrests. Source: Frank Darby, Senior Occupational Health Scientist. Occupational Safety and Health Service. Department of Labour, PO Box 3705, Wellington, NZ.

Seven steps of method study

The systematic method study approach consists of the following seven steps (some steps can be combined depending on circumstances).

1. Select.
2. Record.
3. Examine.
4. Develop.
5. Define.
6. Install.
7. Maintain.

1. Select

The select stage of method study includes *recognizing* that there is a problem and then *defining* the problem. Before the study proper is commenced it is advisable to determine the *aim* (e.g. to increase the number of customers served per staff member), the standards by which the results of the study can be judged (such as savings in cost or time) and the boundaries or scope of the study.

2. Record

This stage requires the recording of all the *facts* relating to the existing way the work is carried out. Much of the success of the whole method study procedure relies on the accuracy with which the facts are recorded. How the recording will be done depends on the nature of the study, e.g. a localized process or of a functional procedure which accounts for the activities of an entire section, department or branch.

Information recorded will include existing data, such as outputs, specifications, job descriptions, methods, hours worked, time sheets, and so on. However it is important that all information used is tested to see if it is current and accurate.

The best information is that which is gathered from *direct observation.* Flow charts can be used to chart the job process for people, machines, or combined person/machine. For example a person/machine process chart might show: worker accesses computer (worker and machine involved), worker leaves machine to answer phone – computer idle. Alternatively the computer system prints a report while the worker has cup of coffee (worker idle). Flow charts can be used to show the flow of work, materials, people or information.

The symbols used are:

Operation (value added)	O
Transportation (movement of people or material)	⇨
Inspection (checking of work)	I
Storage (e.g. filing of paper records, goods on display, items in warehouse)	V
Delay (idle time)	D

In all the above activities the only time where value is added is when an operation takes place. All other activities add time and cost to the overall process. A simple example of a flow process chart is given below.

Person		*Inwards goods*	
To inwards goods	⇨	Goods held in arrival dock	D
Locates paperwork	O		D
Matches paperwork to parcel	O		D
Carries parcel to desk	⇨		⇨
Unwraps parcel	O		O
Checks against specification	I		D
Records receipt of goods	O		D
Goods taken to store	⇨		⇨
Goods placed on storage rack	O		V
Returns to desk	⇦		

To the above could be added distance travelled and time taken.

The amount of detail recorded depends on the nature of the study. For some studies an overview is sufficient to gain an appreciation of what is causing a problem, or where a bottleneck is, and only two symbols are used: O and I.

3. Examine

The traditional method study approach is a step-by-step critical examination of each element of the job or process. The main question is 'Why?' The first question being 'Why is this job or element of a job done at all, and what would the ramifications be if this job or element was not done?' If the answer is 'If it wasn't done it would make no difference', then the study is over, i.e. eliminate that job or element. This means of course being absolutely sure that the job can be eliminated; on the other hand, if the only answer is along the lines 'We have always done it this way', this is in itself a very good reason for not doing it that way again!

There are six sets of questions and they are used in the sequence shown below.

1. What is being done, why, what else could be done, and what should be done?
2. Where does it happen, why there, where else, and where should it be done?
3. When is it done, why then, when else, and when should it be done?
4. Who does it, why that person, who else, and who should do it?
5. Who checks it, why that person, who else could, and who should?
6. How is it done, why that way, how else could it be done, and how should it be done?

Asking the above questions requires tact, otherwise resentment or defensive reactions are possible. It is also important to distinguish between facts and opinions. Opinions can be argued, facts can only lead to valid conclusions. The analyst must have an open mind and not have preconceived ideas. In considering what else, where else, when else, who else, and how else, lateral thinking will be needed. Although the method might appear to be a pedestrian step-by-step approach, the aim is to find a *creative* solution which will ease work and increase efficiency. It is also important to determine the cause of a given condition rather than its effect.

The Japanese approach is to ask 'Why?' five times.

EXAMPLE

An invoice for an important customer is wrong, and the customer complains and in doing so claims that 'your invoices are always wrong'. Using the five-'Why?' approach the questions will be:

- Why was the invoice wrong? Answer: The discount amount allowed by Accounts differed from that quoted by Sales.
- Why was a different rate quoted? Answer: Sales had been sent a memo from Marketing with a new rate. Accounts did not use this rate.
- Why did Accounts not use the new rate? Answer: Because they did not receive advice of the new rate.
- Why was Accounts not advised of the new rate? Answer: Because Marketing thought it was Sales' responsibility to advise rates to Accounts, and Sales thought that the responsibility was Marketing's.
- Why did this confusion exist? Answer: The procedure had changed but the administration manual had not been updated.

Solution: Update the manual, and in future Marketing will send a copy of rate changes to both Accounts and Sales (previously rates had been set by Sales and not by Marketing, the policy had changed so that Marketing and not Sales set rates).

In the above example if the effect alone had been addressed, Accounts would have checked with Sales, as per the standard procedure in the manual, and asked what the rate was. Sales would have given Accounts the new rate, and Accounts could have been excused in thinking that the problem was a one-off oversight by Sales. In this scenario Marketing would not have been aware of their responsibility. As rates only change every six months or so, the same problem would therefore re-occur, and the customer again would get several wrong invoices before a further correction was made.

4. Develop

Answers to the questions in the Examine stage furnish clues to improvement. If it is found that a particular task or an element of a task is unnecessary it should be eliminated or modified. Wherever possible, related tasks should be combined to reduce movement of people or paper, i.e. if a clerk is properly trained and given responsibility, then a check of work by a supervisor may not be necessary. Likewise delays can be cut to reduce time and expense. Changing the sequence of activities is another possibility for developing a better work pattern.

Once a new method has been developed then it should be subject to the same questioning technique before final installation. Quite often an initial solution can be adopted with existing resources and layouts, as an interim measure until more radical improvements can be made. Sometimes a radical improvement will take time to develop and to implement, but there is no reason why a lesser improvement could not be adopted as an interim measure, if only to get people used to working with the proposed overall changes.

The input of all stakeholders to any proposed changes should be sought throughout the method study. The biggest problem with method study is resistance to change; this can be overcome if people are won over through being involved in developing the new method. If they take 'ownership' the chances of successful implementation will be enhanced. Unless people wholeheartedly support a new method it is suggested that sometimes it might be wise to settle for a less than optimum solution, if it is more acceptable to the workers.

5. Define
Once the new method has been developed, it is important that it is defined in writing. It should be described in sufficient detail for others to be able to install it and for it to be used in training and instruction.

6. Install
This is the ultimate goal of the preceding stages – the effective application of the improvement. If this stage fails the earlier stages will be wasted effort. Installation needs careful planning, communication and training. Often modifications might be needed; however, a careful watch should be made to ensure that modifications are really necessary and are not just the result of people slipping back to old systems or misunderstanding new systems. When computer terminals were introduced it was not unusual for mistrusting people to secretly keep the old manual system running in parallel, and then blame the computer for creating extra work and bottlenecks.

7. Maintain
Although an improved process has been installed it does not follow that the benefits will automatically be maintained. Reasons for variations need to be examined and corrective action taken to return to the standard system.

EXAMPLE

A building society was taking over three weeks to approve home mortgage applications. This delay was causing problems for clients and often a client would 'miss out' on a house. The reason given was that time was needed to arrange a qualified survey for any house before a mortgage could be approved. On examination, using flow process charting with times shown for each activity, it was found that on average surveyors took less than half an hour to inspect a property and the entering of a survey report on a standard format in the computer system took no more than fifteen minutes. All the rest of the three weeks' delay in giving approval to the client was in the 'processing' of paper from desk to desk, and to the regional office for approval of recommendations. It was quite possible that, if the building society had streamlined its paperwork and communication lines, and given branch offices some authority with clear guidelines, mortgage approvals could be given within 24 hours of application, and certainly within 48 hours. Although a report was made and accepted, the same building society two years later is still taking ten days to approve mortgages, and clients are going elsewhere for their mortgages!

CHAPTER SUMMARY

This chapter has covered the practical aspects of location, layout and method study. All of these areas are intertwined. It is obvious that a method study could likely recommend changes to a layout, and in itself layout will be limited by the size and shape of the space available.

Location, layout and method study are very much operational issues, and exist in the broader strategic context of the organization.

Location decisions are essentially to do with where a service operation is best placed to serve the market. The alternatives are speed to customer, or ease of access by customer. Although a location decision will not ignore the extended supply chain, nonetheless generally the supplier will be of lesser importance in the determination of service locations.

Business policy will to a large extent determine location; it will not be so evident on layout decisions, but will not be entirely absent. The nature of the product or service will likely affect the system structure which in turn will influence the layout.

Method study deals with increasing efficiency down to the smallest element of the operation, and it can be carried out irrespective of the business policy. Method study can be done with the express aim of making the most efficient use of existing resources with no need for increased capital expenditure. Method study, however, is not limited to just increasing efficiency, but also includes making work more enjoyable for staff by involving them in improvements, and considering and improving aspects of the working environment such as noise, ventilation, lighting, ergonomically designed workstations and so on.

CD ROM CASE STUDY

This is a large chapter and many important issues have been covered. The case studies which add value to the chapter are the Sahil Tea Garden (Turkey) and the Bedfordshire Fire Brigade (United Kingdom).

Note

1. In the late 1980s and early 1990s many home-owners in the UK and other parts of the world found themselves in a position of negative equity. That is, the price they could sell their home for did not cover the amount still owing on the mortgages. The same applied to business houses. With the Asian economic crisis of the late 1990s the same problems have again emerged in Australia and New Zealand, just ten years after the last property 'crash'.

Chapter 7

People power:
the most valuable resource?

Objectives for this chapter

Although much has been written about motivation, and many theories have been developed, the reality is that few organizations have a staff of high-performing, self-motivated people.

In this chapter we consider the importance of the human resource to a service industry and how the operations manager can make the best use of this resource. In particular we look at:

- The importance of motivated people.
- Motivation theories.
- How to create a culture for self-motivation.
- The need for continuous learning.

Introduction

As most of us will have read, or heard in the chairperson's annual address, an organization's most 'valuable' resource is its people. The chairperson could also probably have added 'the most expensive'.

In service industries the level of service provided to customers, and the internal efficiency of the organization, depend heavily on people – *the human resource* – and their consistent performance. The operations manager has to manage this valuable *and* expensive resource just as carefully as any other resource. But the difference between managing non-human and human resources is that actions taken with inventory, equipment and machines will lead to predictable results (if the input into a computer is correct the output is predictable), whereas people are not predictable. In a given set of circumstances people will react one way and in similar circumstances, for no apparent reason, they may react in a different way.

Motivated people will provide high levels of service for the customer at no extra cost to the organization and at the same time they will constantly be looking for the most efficient way of using the other resources. Although much has been written about motivation, and many theories have been developed, the reality is that few organizations have a staff of high-performing, self-motivated people.

Basic requirements leading to self-motivation
Getting the best out of the human resource will be achieved partly by:

* making sure that the people of the organization have all the necessary materials and equipment to do the job;
* making sure that staff know what to do and how to do it;
* encouraging self-motivation and development.

In Chapter 6 we looked at the physical aspects of working conditions with a view to increasing efficiency. These physical aspects included location and layout, safety and health, ergonomic issues and methods of simplifying work. If the physical aspects are not right, that is if the layout does not make it easy to be efficient, if conditions are uncomfortable, and if the work includes unnecessary steps, then it is not likely that staff will be motivated to extend themselves. Indeed much of their energy will be used up in combating, or adapting to, the difficult conditions in which they are expected to work. In this chapter it is assumed that the physical aspects are right, and the non-physical or intangible aspects which will encourage self-motivation are considered.

The importance of motivated people
The importance of motivated staff can perhaps best be shown by example.

 EXAMPLE

In Chapter 2 we discussed what customers expect from a commuter bus service. We said that achieving specification, cost and timing would meet a customer's basic needs (safe journey from 'A' to 'B' at the right time and at a reasonable price). We also said that meeting basic expectations would not in itself be considered to be a 'quality' service. We said that on top of basic requirements customers would appreciate punctuality, a clean bus, a friendly, well-presented driver, and consistency of service. We agreed that cleaning the bus, issuing the driver with a smart uniform, and training the driver to be courteous and well groomed would incur some minimal costs, but that the overall perception to the customer would be an improved, or perhaps even a 'quality' service.

If drivers can be sufficiently motivated to think of the bus as being 'their' bus, then it is possible that much of what management would like – bus kept clean, timetable adhered to, friendly helpful service to customers and so on – can be gained at no extra ongoing cost to the organization. The only cost will be the investment in the time to change the *culture* of the organization. Once the culture is right no longer will the drivers think of their job as just a means to get a weekly pay packet; they will be proud of what they are doing, believe that their actions can make a difference, and will constantly surprise management with their helpful suggestions.

An organization with motivated staff does not need service question-naires filled out by customers. Unsolicited feedback from customers will all be positive.

Sounds too good to be true, doesn't it!

YOUR TURN!

Consider the staff in your section. Do they arrive on time (just), and are they prompt (very prompt) to leave at the end of the day? Do they do what they are told (more or less) but lack the initiative to make changes or suggest improvements? Or are they at work early, then work on through their lunch hours and even past 'going home' time until the job is done, and without any thought of extra pay?

No doubt the answer will be that some of the staff – you for instance – do go the extra distance, but many don't.

'Front-line' staff motivated by desire to serve

Many front-line staff in service industries enjoy customer contact, and generally prefer to be cheerful and helpful. They do their best to give good service. This attitude will often exist despite poor pay, indifferent working conditions and bad management. Social workers, teachers and nurses are obvious examples of people who have a desire to serve (even when their pay and conditions may be less than satisfactory). People who have a desire to serve are able, in their minds, to separate the employing organization from the customer. Thus good service is provided in some cases despite lack of resources, poor organization, or poor pay and working conditions, not for the benefit of the employer or to please management, but purely from the personal satisfaction gained from meeting the needs of the customer.

Other front-line workers, such as restaurant waiting staff, might provide good service irrespective of poor pay and conditions, in the expectation that the customer will leave a reward (a tip) – the suggestion being that it is the expectation of a reward that encourages the serving staff to provide higher-level service. However in some countries, such as Australia and New Zealand, tipping is not common and it is noticeable that restaurant service is every bit as good, if slightly less formal ('there yer go mate') than in countries where tipping is expected. This suggests that people who are drawn to front-line service genuinely like working with people and given the opportunity or encouragement prefer to give good friendly service, and that an extra reward is not necessary to motivate these people to give better service. But where a tip or other reward has become the custom it is not likely that people would remain motivated for long if tips suddenly stopped coming, and indeed the tip is regarded as part of their remuneration.

'Back-office' workers

Back-office service workers, such as clerical and administration support people, seldom come face to face with external customers and thus to a large extent lack the incentive of seeing or interacting with satisfied 'end user' customers, or conversely of having to field the complaints of dissatisfied customers. Back-office staff therefore are less likely to be motivated by management pleas that customer satisfaction is important. Of course all workers, front and back office, will pay lip service to a credo of customer satisfaction; after all no one is going to say that customer satisfaction is anything but important.

To a large extent it is on the efforts of back-office people that the overall efficiency and eventual customer satisfaction will rest. For example in a restaurant, no matter how friendly the waiting staff, if the food is badly cooked the customer will rate the service as poor.

Thus front-line staff might provide reasonable service to customers, despite poor conditions and poor management, simply because they are people-oriented and like positive relations with the people whom they are serving; these types of people do not need management to tell them that the customer is important. On the other hand, back-office staff lacking direct customer contact are less likely to be motivated by a plea to provide customer satisfaction, even when management tries to promote the concept of internal customers. The internal customer theory is that within the organization the next person in the process is the customer. For example, a writer giving a manuscript to a word processor would, in theory, consider the word processor as the customer. Human nature being what it is, although the writer might even buy into this concept, the writer is still going to be irritated when work is not completed on time. Therefore, in reality, the writer will never truly consider the word processor to be the customer.

Motivation theories

As indicated in our introduction to this chapter an operations manager needs to have at least an understanding of the various motivational theories. However it has to be remembered that theories are just that – and what will work for one person will not necessarily work for another.

Sometimes management does not understand that motivation is up to the individual. People motivate themselves; all management can do is to provide the environment to encourage self-motivation.

Economic man and scientific management

Scottish economist Adam Smith in 1776 (*The Wealth of Nations*) and F. W. Taylor, the late nineteenth-century American industrialist, both said that people are primarily motivated by money. This is known as the economic man principle. Both Smith and Taylor also studied the conditions necessary to allow workers to be efficient.

Adam Smith in a famous study on pin-making showed how division of labour (standard procedures and specialized work in a team situation) would dramatically increase productivity. His study showed that one man working on his own could scarcely make 20 pins a day whereas ten people working together, each with specialist tasks (division of labour) would make up to 48,000 pins a day! Of course the team would not make any pins at all unless it was worth their while (economic man principle).

Taylor is known as the father of scientific management. Taylor's approach to motivating people was to find by 'scientific' means the best way of doing a job. The best way included finding the right tools and the most efficient process. Once the best way was established it became the standard method. People were trained in the standard method and supervised to see that the method was kept to. To encourage above-average performance bonus payments were offered (economic man approach). In one celebrated case, 'the Bethlehem Steel Works', Taylor reported he was able to reduce the workforce from 400/600 people to 140 and to increase profits by over 100 per cent. He also reported that each worker earned far more and that 'they were almost all saving money, living better, happier, they are the most contented set of (workers) seen anywhere'. Taylor's approach was for management to develop the best method with little, if any, input from the workers. (Management did the thinking and workers did what they were told, and were rewarded if they performed above a set standard.)

Today, 200 years after Adam Smith, it is evident that productivity will increase if work processes are simplified and if people are trained to follow a standard process. To this extent the approaches of Smith and Taylor cannot be disputed, and neither can it be argued that people work for money. What can be questioned is that if people are encouraged to make suggestions and given a measure of autonomy will they take 'ownership' of a job and become more productive? It can also be questioned whether people can be motivated to be more efficient and customer-focused without being paid extra to do so.

Before these questions are answered it is necessary to discuss the importance of money.

Money: a necessity and a means of keeping the score

My belief is that, depending on their circumstances, some people are motivated by money more than by anything else (people with children and mortgages need money – lots of it). Money is also a method of keeping the score – it is the one sure way of knowing if our efforts are appreciated. A pat on the back is nice, and so are kind words, but money is tangible – it is a certain measure of the value given to our efforts. There is also the question of equity. If we are being paid a certain amount for doing a job, even if initially we thought the pay was good, we would be less than human if we didn't get upset if we found a colleague was being paid substantially more. *My belief is that money is important, and it is more important for some people than it is for others.*

Money is only one factor

I believe that if people are being paid a reasonable amount then it is possible to increase motivation without paying extra amounts *but* conversely, simply by paying more money increased productivity cannot be taken for granted. Money is important, but money alone is not the answer. All we can be certain of is that the amount paid must be reasonable, and must be equitable.

Need theories

Motivational theorists fall into two broad schools: those that state people are motivated by the desire to satisfy internal needs, and those that state people react to external stimuli.

Hierarchy of needs

Abraham Maslow (1943), a clinical psychologist, claimed that people have five levels of needs and that each level has to be covered before the next level can be addressed.

- Level 1 (the lowest) is physiological and includes food, water, shelter, and so on.
- Level 2 is safety needs which include a desire to feel secure and free from threats to existence.
- Level 3 is the need to belong, which includes being accepted in a group of people.
- Level 4 is self-esteem – this includes feeling positive about yourself and being recognized by others for our achievements.
- Level 5 (the highest) is self-actualization, which roughly translated means development of our capabilities so that we reach our full potential.

Maslow accepted that each level did not have to be completely fulfilled before people moved on to the next level, but that until a level had been *substantially* covered it was unlikely that people would address a higher level in the hierarchy of needs. In prosaic terms, if you are grubbing around in the gutter for fag-ends, wondering when the soup kitchen will open, you are not interested that the ballet company is offering free tickets to the first twenty people who arrive.

It should be noted that Maslow's hierarchy-of-needs model was developed from a very small sample. (He observed fourteen close friends and studied the lives of nine famous people – including Lincoln, Jefferson, Eleanor Roosevelt, Einstein and Sweitzer.) His theory has often been questioned because of this lack of depth in his research.

Two-factor theory

Following Maslow's line of reasoning, Herzberg (1966) and (1968) developed a two-factor theory based on satisfiers and dissatisfiers (or motivation and hygiene factors). Herzberg's theory (like Maslow's) is that until the lower-level needs – the hygiene factors – are covered then the higher-level satisfier factors will not motivate. Roughly translated hygiene factors include:

- adequate wages;
- safe working conditions;
- job security;
- non-threatening supervision and control.

Motivators are the higher-level needs and include:

- recognition;
- responsibility;
- the importance of the work;
- prospects for growth and advancement.

Herzberg's initial study was based on questioning 200 accountants and engineers in the United States. The study was therefore not based on the typical worker (accountants and engineers would of course have been well above the national average for wages and working conditions).

Nonetheless the theory does merit consideration. For example, using Herzberg's approach it might be considered that spending money on improving the staff cafeteria in itself will not motivate people to work harder if they have little responsibility. (The cafeteria would be considered a hygiene factor, and increased responsibility would be seen as a motivational factor.) On the other hand, responsibility and recognition of achievements might not motivate if people feel that their pay is inadequate or if there are threats of redundancies. Thus being asked to accept extra responsibility without extra benefits might only be seen as an attempt by management to give the recipient extra work (job enlargement rather than job enrichment).

Expectancy theory

Victor Vroom (Vroom *et al.*, 1973, 1988) argued that people are motivated by expectations, and performance is linked to the assessment of the probability that increased performance will lead to increased rewards; rewards may be extrinsic, that is money and promotion; or intrinsic, that is sense of achievement. Bateman and Zeithaml (1993) added that the assessment of whether the rewards will be sufficient to induce increased performance depends on self-evaluation of own abilities and the availability of necessary resources.

In other words, unless the chances of success, and consequent rewards, are reasonable, people will not be motivated to make an extra effort. (It won't be worth their while.)

All the above theories are cognitive theories, that is they are concerned with people's thought processes an as an explanation of behaviour.

Reinforcement theory

The other broad school of thought is that people's behaviour can be conditioned by external stimulus and there is no need to seek cognitive explanations. B. F. Skinner (1971) claimed that if good behaviour is rewarded and poor behaviour punished people will be conditioned to act in a positive rather than a negative manner. An example would be if a worker stayed until midnight to complete some urgent work and was subsequently given favourable recognition. It is likely that that person would be encouraged to act in this way again. If, however, the worker was criticized for some minor error then the worker might feel that the effect of staying on late resulted in a negative outcome and consequently would be less willing to put in extra effort on a future occasion.

Skinner's theories were based on tests with rats and pigeons. One experiment included rats in a maze; if the rat took the right option it received a reward in the form of food, if it took the wrong action it received an electric shock. It was found that it did not take long for the rats to learn the correct route, and rewards and shocks were no longer necessary. This approach, reward and punishment, is also known as reinforcement theory.

The one common thread that all these theories have is that people's behaviour is goal-directed.

Combined approach

It is probable that most people have many needs:

- To have a job that pays enough to meet personal commitments (family, mortgage, social activities).
- To be in a job they like.
- To feel they belong.
- To have the opportunity of increasing self-esteem (important job, status, and responsibility).
- To feel comfortable that they can do the job.
- To have job security.
- To have sufficient leisure time to enjoy/follow personal interests.

Work a necessity?

For most people work is not the be-all and end-all but a necessity. To achieve personal needs people need adequate wages and job security, and it seems obvious that ideally if they have to work, people would prefer to do something they enjoy, and to be given some authority (sense of belonging) and recognition for skill and above-average effort (esteem factor). It would be reasonable to suppose that people will not be motivated to make an extra effort if they think the job is beyond their scope or if the chances of success are limited. It would also seem that people can be conditioned to act in certain ways by reward or punishment. I would suggest however that people, rather than acting as robots as a result of conditioning, are aware (cognizant) of likely outcomes (rewards/punishments) and consider likely consequences before they act. I know that I do, and I am sure that you do!

The above would seem to cover the reasons why people work and what they would like in a job, but it does not necessarily follow, given the individuality of people, that even if all the above factors are taken into consideration, people will necessarily be motivated to be more efficient, to make suggestions or to go out of their way to provide extra service for customers. I could give plenty of examples of well-rewarded middle managers with autonomy to make decisions who do not appear to be overly motivated. To achieve a situation where every worker in the organization is excited about what the organization is doing and willingly puts in extra effort, requires a special type of organizational culture.

YOUR TURN!

Why do you go to work?

If you won or inherited a large amount of money would you still go to work?

What do you think encourages staff to come to work? Is it job satisfaction, or is it *only* for the money?

Culture

Organizational culture is the amalgam of beliefs, norms and values of the individuals making up the organization ('the way we do things around here'). Organizations are made up of many individuals, each with their own set of values. The culture of the organization is how people react or do things confronted with the need to make a decision. If the organization has a strong culture then each individual will know instinctively how things are done and what is expected. Conversely, if the culture is weak, people may not react in the manner in which management would hope.

The value to an organization of a dedicated, enthusiastic workforce cannot be underestimated. Such a culture begins with everyone in the organization, from the chief to the cleaner, believing in what the organization is trying to achieve. This means that not only is every person customer-focused, but each person is determined to eliminate any cost that is not adding value. For this culture to exist there are several prerequisites, and these prerequisites apply to everyone in the organization. As already discussed in this chapter:

* Working conditions have to be right (location, layout and process).
* Wages and rewards have to be equitable.
* There has to be job security.
* Staff must have a chance for self-development (self-esteem).
* Staff must feel 'good' about the job: it has to be meaningful.

And as discussed in earlier chapters:

* Everyone in the organization has to know *who* the customer is and ideally know *what* the customer values.
* The level of service which the organization is aiming to provide must be known by all.
* Service has to be affordable and sustainable.
* Service has to be consistent, and standards need to be set and communicated to maintain a consistent level.
* Controls have to be in place to ensure that the standards are being met.
* People must know how to make corrections.
* People must know their individual level (limit) of authority for taking action.

Finally, but importantly, everyone must feel free to make suggestions, and management must listen and treat suggestions with respect. Management must give more than lip-service to the above; they must passionately believe in the capabilities of their staff, and show this by their actions. This does not mean that management abdicates responsibility. Far from it! Management still has to make the important decisions and set the policy. Staff will be expected and encouraged to contribute to policy, but once a policy decision has been made, workers have to conform to the policy. Policy cannot be changed at the whim of individual people! Such actions would lead to chaos. In summary:

- Objectives must be clearly communicated.
- Management sets policy and guidelines.
- Staff have freedom to act within the guidelines.
- People are encouraged to make suggestions to change policy.

Bureaucratic culture
In a bureaucratic culture, some people (management) do the thinking, and workers do what they are told. In this type of culture the bigger the organization, the more rules and procedures will be required and control will be achieved by supervision and reports. In this type of culture communication is one way, top down. Such a culture is sterile, and foments a nine-to-five attitude (sign on at nine in the morning and leave promptly at five in the afternoon). Staff will pay lip-service to service and customer satisfaction, but will not have the authority, let alone the motivation, to actually provide above-average service, for to do so will result in breaking rules, and the possibility of a reprimand.

Open culture
An open culture is where management is highly visible and approachable, there are few rules and procedures, the staff know instinctively what is right and what has to be done to correct a situation. The 'way we do things around here' is second nature, not just a slogan or a mission statement. People have authority to act and are self-motivated. Chapter 12 discusses how to engineer a quality culture.

Mission statements

Where the culture has been bureaucratic, and staff have a nine-to-five mentality then to change the culture will require a major effort. Research (Wright, 1996) has found that a major change can begin with the issuing of a mission statement. The mission statement however must be more than mere words or clichés such as 'People are our most valuable resource, we will provide excellent world-class service'. The sentiments cannot be argued, but like any platitude they are only words – 'full of sound and fury signifying nothing'.

The fad over recent years has been for new chief executives to feel it is mandatory to issue a new mission statement with the ostensible reason of communicating a change of direction. In this sense, the mission is given as a statement of where we are going (the vision) and how (the strategy) we are going to get there. But often the real reason for the new statement is for the new chief executive to establish authority, (the 'I'm the new boss, and things are going to change around here' syndrome). Sadly, from a study of over 1,000 mission statements, I have come to the conclusion that most mission statements are mere rhetoric, full of sound and fury, and signify nothing.

To be meaningful a mission statement has to give the 'vision' – where we are going; and the strategy – how we are going to get there. To be successful the mission statement has to be in tune with what the staff believe and want to do. The mission has to reflect 'the way we do things around here'.

YOUR TURN!

Write a mission statement for an ambulance service.

A mission statement for an ambulance service might read 'To provide a quick response, first aid and transport service for the sick and injured' – this is the central *vision* of the mission. The statement might continue to include a strategic element along the lines of 'To operate from a central location, to be on call 24 hours a day, to have well-maintained vehicles and equipment, to have well-trained staff, to network with hospitals, police and the fire service'.

Thus, as shown in this example, the mission statement shows what is going to be done and who it is being done for (the central vision) and outlines how it will be done (the strategy). There is no need for the words such as 'To be the world's best', or 'We value our staff'. This will be embodied in the culture of the organization and does not need to be put into words.

Mission – only the beginning

A well-written mission statement gives a clear statement of vision and strategy which will give the people of the organization a focus, and give the reason-for-being for the organization. The mission statement is, however, only the beginning – albeit an important beginning.

Having established the mission the chief executive must show a real desire to involve all levels of staff in the decision-making of the organization. As previously stated, this does not mean an abdication of responsibility; the chief executive will always be the person who is accountable for the success or otherwise of the organization.

Leadership

Getting effective decision-making down to the lower levels of the organization requires the creation of the right structure so that people can get involved, can become committed and are able to make things happen. This can never happen with a centralized bureaucratic structure. The flatter the structure, the closer the leader will be to the real workers; that is, the people who are actually involved in adding value in the process, rather than those who are administering and regulating. A true leader creates leaders, whereas a manager tries to retain control and in doing so creates or perpetuates a culture of compliance and conformance. To become a leader, rather than a manager, requires a major paradigm change. 'Real leaders communicate face to face not by memos.'

Organization structure and change management are further developed in Chapter 12.

Accepting responsibility

For an organization to change from a top-down bureaucratic culture to an open culture requires managers to trust the workers. For some managers the giving up of 'power' will be extremely difficult to handle. But it is just as difficult for those who have been used to receiving orders and being told what to do to accept responsibility. It has to be accepted that some people prefer to be told what to do and are not comfortable with making decisions and accepting responsibility. Empowerment is a two-way street; managers have to be prepared to let go and trust, and workers have to be prepared to accept responsibility. As Schein (1988, 1991) points out, any change process involves not only *learning* something new, but *unlearning* something that is already present. Chapter 12 is our 'change' chapter and discusses the management of change.

Learning programmes

Human resource management can create real strategic advantage by proper planning for people with the right skills and calibre to suit the corporate strategy. If it is recognized that 'people make things happen', then there will be a continuous need for recruitment, training and development of the workforce at all levels. Schonberger (1986) describes training as the catalyst for change programmes such as total quality management – TQM (the TQM philosophy is explained in Chapter 10). Related to this, education and training are critical components of an empowered work environment.

Basu and Wright (1998) discuss a status distinction between the terms 'training' and 'education'. For example, training is associated with imparting skills (how to do) and education with imparting knowledge (why it should be done). Training is thought of as being needed by people at a lower level to yourself, and education is for your level and above (also see Tompkins, 1989). To overcome this implied snobbishness, many prefer to use the term 'learning' to cover both training and education. Learning includes the development of people in their career progression.

Learning programmes of a leading-edge organization should comprise five elements:

1. Continuous recruitment and development.
2. Annual appraisals.
3. Learning for a company-wide change programme.
4. Learning resources.
5. Learning performance.

1. Continuous recruitment and development

The development of people starts at the recruitment stage. Organizations, in the drive for efficiency and capitalizing on the benefits of technology today, require fewer people than previously but the people required do need greater knowledge and flexibility. The ability to attract high-calibre people is an indication of the future of an organization. A recognized world-class organization will attract high-calibre people. The recruitment policy of a leading organization will seek high qualifications at the entry level. For example, as a minimum requirement a management trainee should have a degree, with above-average grades, from a reputable university. All other staff should have a polytechnic or equivalent diploma in a suitable discipline.

2. Annual appraisals

World-class organizations take time to consider development plans each year so as to respond to changing needs.

The learning programmes for staff should include appraisal procedures. Key people should be given the opportunity to move to higher levels, provided that they have the skills, experience and performance requirements. A well-administered and fair appraisal system which includes a personal development plan will help an organization to gain a competitive edge. An ineffective appraisal scheme will lead to dissatisfaction and cynicism, and will do more harm than good. On the other hand, when the scheme contains agreed objectives based on measurable parameters and the appraiser is impartial, the scheme can be effective for identifying the development needs of the staff member. The appraisal system loses its credibility when the agreed action points are not followed.

Any learning scheme should be well publicized, and available to all staff.

3. Learning for a company-wide change programme

Change management and the need for change are covered in Chapter 12. Learning is an essential component of a company-wide change programme, whether it is TQM or a change of structure to empowered teams. Staff require learning opportunities in work process and analysis skills as well as so-called soft skills such as inter-relating with team members. Managers need to learn how to make the transition from an out-of-date autocratic management role to that of coach and mentor. The learning for all employees and managers must extend beyond skills and include learning about the need for 'cultural' change. It is essential to generate trust between all members by following the same learning process.

4. Learning resources

The investment made by an organization in continuous learning includes money, time, key personnel and facilities.

A learning organization will allow for the time required for both on-the-job and off-the-job learning of each employee. The total time will be variable depending on the change programmes of a particular company.

EXAMPLE

Bell Canada allocate for each person fifteen days per year for training, and budget accordingly (Ruth Wright, 1995).

Consideration should be given to a budget for learning programmes, and the measurable cost of training and education should be expressed as a percentage of annual sales. Basu and Wright (1998) say 'The amount allowed should be no less than 0.5 per cent of sales and in some companies it is reported to be 2.0 per cent of sales'.

The use of a third party for specialist learning is usually successful. Each manager, supervisor and team leader should have responsibilities for the learning of their own personnel. In addition a senior manager should have the responsibility of co-ordinating the continuous learning programmes of an organization. (For smaller organizations this responsibility might be coupled with other responsibilities.)

Ideally an organization will have dedicated learning facilities including a learning centre, equipped with personal computers, appropriate training videos, presentation facilities and a library of relevant management books, periodicals and internal reports as a source of self-education and information.

5. Learning performance

The effectiveness of education and training programmes of a company is usually assessed in terms of input as it is not easy to measure their output. The input measures are often expressed as:

- Number of learning hours per employee.
- Learning expenditures as percentage of annual sales (as discussed above up to 2.0 per cent of sales).
- Number of courses and seminars conducted.

Staff turnover is an indirect output measure of learning performance. A well-structured management development programme, and a reputation as an organization which provides good learning opportunities, will attract high-calibre candidates to an organization. A learning programme must be integrated with career development. If the management approach to human resources is well defined and considered, then most staff will repay their learning with longer service to the company. When a company loses people soon after they have been trained, then it may have got its training right but everything else is wrong.

Another assessment of learning performance involves the accreditation of learning programme against national standards. One such scheme is 'Investor in People' in the UK. The scheme comprises four principles of employee development standards set by the Department of Education and Employment:

1. A commitment from the top to develop all employees.
2. Regular reviews of learning and development needs.
3. Actions to train and develop individuals throughout their employment.
4. Evaluation of achievement in learning and development.

The assessment indicators stem directly from the standard. If a company measures up to the National Standard as assessed by Training and Enterprise Councils (TECs), then it receives an accreditation certificate of 'Investor in People'.

The drive to continuously acquire new knowledge and transfer it into skilled people to achieve its business objective is the fundamental spirit of a learning organization. A learning organization is a leading organization.

CHAPTER SUMMARY

In this chapter we began by saying that people are an important resource, and like all resources the operations manager must manage people so as to get the most out of them. We showed that if people can be motivated, then they will be an extremely valuable resource; but it was stressed that management cannot motivate – people are self-motivated. All management can do is provide the correct environment for self-motivation. Such an environment includes getting the physical aspects of location, layout and process 'right', and of having known standards and known levels of individual authority. The importance of money was discussed and it was suggested that provided that the money paid is sufficient and equitable, people can be self-motivated if the culture of the organization is positive. A positive culture is where the members of the organization, from the most senior person to the most junior person, believe in what the organization is doing, there is open communication, and every day each person strives to do the best for the organization. The importance of a mission statement was discussed, especially where a change in culture is required. Finally the need for annual appraisals aimed at the development of people, and the need for continuous learning, was stressed.

CD ROM CASE STUDY

The case study used to illustrate the importance of setting standards, enthusing people, and the provision of learning programmes, is McDonald's. The setting is initially Hong Kong but then moves to London.

Part Four

This part considers the four key operational issues of:

- capacity management;
- scheduling of activities and flow processing;
- materials management and the extended supply chain;
- time management.

The objective of capacity management is to have sufficient capacity to meet the organization's needs as determined in the business policy. The business policy determines what level of service will be provided to the customer. The business policy might well be full utilization of resources and to accept that, on some occasions, customers will queue and some customers may be lost to the system; thus customers' needs may not always totally coincide with the business policy. Part of the responsibility of the operations manager will be to determine:

- what resources are needed overall;
- what can be achieved with existing resources (feasibility);
- the allocation of resources on a day-to-day basis in the most efficient way possible to achieve the policy of the organization.

Knowing what the capacity is – feasibility – is one side of the equation; the other side is knowing what is required – demand. Forecasting demand is therefore an important element of capacity management. **Chapter 8** begins this part with an introduction to methods of forecasting demand and examines capacity management – a critical area for the operations manager.

Equally critical is the planning and timing of activities (scheduling) which is considered in **Chapter 9**. Likewise, what is feasible and what is desirable influences how activities are scheduled. Scheduling feasibility is mainly limited by the system structure, and influenced by what is desired by business policy and operational objectives.

Much of what is identified in the strategy of scheduling also applies to materials management and to the control of the extended supply chain. The supply chain introduced in **Chapter 9** encompasses the flow of processing of inputs through the system to the delivery of service to the customer. The flow of information is shown to be a crucial issue in supply-chain management.

Chapter 8

Capacity management

Objectives for this chapter

This chapter considers:

- Establishing demand and forecasting techniques.
- Types of forecasts.
- Capacity management and capacity management strategies.
- Practical day-to-day capacity management techniques.

Establishing demand and forecasting techniques

Events as important as numbers

Forecasting is used by various functions, for example the marketing function forecasts sales (the annual marketing plan), accountants forecast expenses (the budget) and the meteorological department forecasts the weather. Funny how none of them ever get it quite right!

The reason why it is so difficult for forecasts to be totally accurate is that although expected trends can be factored into the calculations, the basic information used is drawn from what has happened in the past. In considering the past, numbers alone are not sufficient, as the numbers will merely be a reflection of a variety of circumstances that influenced or determined the outcome. Establishing circumstances, or events that shaped past demand, will not always be easy as there can be no guarantee that all the circumstances of the past will be remembered or that they will occur in exactly the same way again in the future. The danger for statisticians and researchers is to concentrate on the numbers and to ignore the circumstances.

For some types of demand forecasting, seasonal trends and so on might well be sufficient to provide a reasonably accurate forecast. In other cases, and this is especially relevant to service industries, demand will often depend on a myriad of circumstances and events.

Capacity forecasts

Capacity decisions use forecasts at several different levels. Long-range capacity planning requires forecasts to be made several years ahead; this would include forecasts of capacity requirements for facilities. Short- to medium-term forecasts usually span two to three years, and are typically used to determine personnel and training needs, renting of premises and equipment, and details of service and products. In the immediate short term, forecasts are needed to plan, order and allocate resources on a monthly, weekly and daily basis. The shorter the time frame, the more accurate the forecast has to be.

Types of forecasts

There are three ways of looking at forecasts: the qualitative approach, the mathematical or time series approach, and the causal approach. In reality all three are interlinked and should be taken into account when determining a forecasted demand figure.

Qualitative forecasting

Qualitative forecasting uses judgement, past experience, and existing past and present data. Due to the implicit nature of qualitative forecasting, two seemingly equally knowledgeable people given the same information are likely to arrive at different results. Because much forecasting is based on the past we must accept that to predict the future will require a certain amount of judgement of what the circumstances will be, and which circumstances from the past are relevant to the present. If forecasting on past results and based on current conditions was easy, the book-makers would soon be out of business!

 ## Examples

Past statistics show that our local football team has always won on its home ground. This does not prove that it will win next time they play at home.

Last spring our sales were twice that of the winter period. Further examination of the figures might show that this has been the trend for the last three years, i.e. spring sales double that of winter sales. However, the circumstances existing each spring might well have affected the results. For example, in the spring of the first year we launched a new service or product which had a short-lived success. In the second year our main competitor went out of business towards the end of the winter and our sales increased by default. In the third year, due to tough new competition, we were forced to cut prices and to advertise heavily to get the sales. The figures on their own could be misleading if we were not aware of all the other relevant factors. Knowing which of the factors to include and which to discount in forecasting the future requires knowledge of what happened and judgement as to what is relevant.

The best-known methods of qualitative forecast are:

* Expert opinion.
* Market surveys.
* Life cycle analysis.
* Time series forecasting.

Expert opinion
Delphi method
The Delphi method is considered by many to be the most successful of the qualitative methods. It is time-consuming and costly, and best used by large organizations. (The Delphi method was developed by the Rand Corporation and is named after the ancient Greek oracle.) The method uses a set of questions to a group of managers or 'experts' who, working without collusion, give their individual opinions. The opinions are then tabulated by a co-ordinator, and if individual results differ significantly, the results are fed back (names are not revealed) to the panel with a further set of questions. The process is repeated until consensus is reached. Questions and feedback generally continue for four rounds with the questions becoming more specific with each round. The benefit of the method is that a group opinion can be achieved without the team meeting together. The weakness of a face-to-face group meeting is that members might be swayed (group dynamics and team-think) by a dominant member, or perhaps an 'expert' member may be embarrassed to back down from a publicly stated opinion.

The Delphi method has also been unkindly described as 'pooled ignorance' as the tendency is for the feedback questions to force a convergence towards the group centre.

Sales force, and 'jury of executives'
Two other 'expert' methods are:

* to invite the sales force to give their opinions;
* the 'jury of executives' approach.

The problem with sales force opinions is that they are likely to be influenced by recent events (memory and sometimes experience is short) and, as would be expected from salespeople, their forecasts tend to be optimistic (nobody hires negative salespeople – do they?).

The 'jury of executives' approach involves the averaging of independent estimates from a panel of company experts and sometimes from people from outside the organization. The danger of any panel approach is that a dominant person, or one who is best able to present their ideas, is likely to sway the other members of the panel.

The advantage of all the expert-opinion approaches is the use of experience and judgement of several experts and the obtaining of various points of view.

Market surveys
Surveys can be carried out by phone, personal interview and by mail. Market surveys use two approaches: a structured approach and an unstructured approach. With the

structured approach the survey uses a formal list of questions; the unstructured approach lets the interviewer probe and perhaps guide the respondent.

The framing of questions is an art. The key is to establish from the outset exactly what information is wanted, and then to design questions which will give the information required. Questions which are not relevant to the issue are a waste of time and money. Other problems are that sometimes people are unable to answer survey questions because they have never thought about what they do and why; or they may be unwilling to answer questions that they consider personal. Others might feel obliged to give an answer rather than appear uninformed even when they don't know or don't understand the question; or they might even try and help the interviewer by giving what they think are the required answers.

Kotler (1997: 120) gives the following advice when creating questionnaires: 'carefully choose the questions and their form, wording and sequence. A common error is including questions that cannot, would not, or need not be answered and omitting questions that should be answered. Questions that are merely interesting should be dropped because they exhaust the respondent's patience'.

Additionally the form of question asked can influence the response, and Kotler goes on to distinguish between open-ended and closed questions. Open-ended questions allow respondents to answer in their own words, whereas closed questions ask respondents to select an answer from a given list of answers.

An easy form of market survey includes group interviewing or focus groups. With the focus-group approach six to ten people are invited from a market target group to a meeting. They are sometimes paid a small fee, the conditions are relaxed with refreshments and so on, and after the interviewer has set the scene it is hoped that group dynamics will bring out actual feelings and thoughts. At the same time the interviewer attempts to keep the discussion focused on the subject of the research. The concern with this approach is that too much can be read into the opinions of a small and non-random sample. To some extent this can be overcome by holding several focus-group meetings on the same subject and then pooling the results.

Market surveys are generally *not* used for forecasting demand for capacity management; they are perhaps more appropriate to determine the shape or style of a new service, or to find out why an existing service is not performing as well as expected.

Life cycle analysis

The classic life cycle S curve is shown in Figure 8.1. It is generally accepted that products and services have a time-based life cycle. The launch stage has few sales, the growth stage shows a rapid increase in customers, and at the maturity stage the demand will be relatively stable. For most types of services life cycles are readily predictable and the rate of growth/decline will not be dramatic. For services such as medical, educational, legal, commuter transport and so on, it is a moot point whether a life cycle exists; and if it does the extended length of the cycle and in particular the decline phase will be sufficiently obvious for demand forecasts to be adjusted. However, for retailers of some fast-moving consumer goods or fashion items, growth can be explosive and decline equally rapid. Other fast-moving consumables such as toothpaste, soap or baked beans only reach the decline stage if there is a dramatic

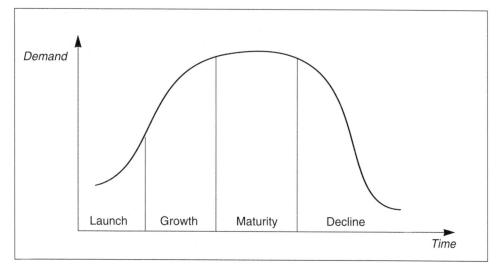

Figure 8.1: A product/service life cycle

change in technology, such as canned peas being replaced by frozen peas; but even then once the decline has settled there is still a demand (easily forecast) for canned peas. Experienced managers who have been involved with the introduction of new products can, often with a high degree of accuracy, forecast how long a fashion item will stay in each stage of the life cycle. If an organization is in a market with a defined life cycle then knowing where a product is on a life cycle will enable decisions to be made, such as stockpiling items in anticipation of a high demand in the growth stage.

Time series forecasting

Time series forecasting uses mathematical analysis of past demand trends to forecast future demand. The accuracy of a forecast will not be known until after the event. However, a particular method of forecasting can always be tested for past accuracy. Accuracy is usually monitored by the deviation of the actual result from the forecast result. Calculation of standard deviation, total absolute deviation, and deviation spread is explained later in this section.

Short-term forecasting involves taking historical data of demand patterns from a few past periods and projecting these patterns into the future. The simplest method is to take the last period's actual demand and use it for the next period's forecast, as shown in Table 8.1.

Period	Actual	Forecast	Deviation
Spring	20	–	–
Summer	22	20	–2
Autumn	23	22	–1
Winter	18	23	–5

Table 8.1: Forecast from last period's actual

The method gives a quick response to a trend; if the trend is upwards then the forecast will be upwards but lagging behind. If, however, there are marked seasonal fluctuations then this method would, following a buoyant autumn, forecast high winter sales, when in fact past history shows that winter sales will always be lower than autumn sales. In the above example, based on autumn sales actual results, the forecast for winter sales is 23 although past history shows that winter sales are always about 25 per cent below autumn sales.

Forecasting by past average
This method is to average the past results. The accuracy of the method is tested by the deviation from the actual (see Table 8.2).

Period	Actual demand	Forecast (average of *all* past actual)	Deviation (forecast to actual)
1	20	nil	–
2	18	20	+2
3	22	19	–3
4	23	20	–3
5	21	21	0
6	19	21	+2
7	24	21	–3
8	25	21	–4
9	22	22	0
10	23	22	–1
11	25	22	–3
12	26	22	–4
13		22	

Total Absolute Deviation 25 (pluses or minuses are ignored)
Mean Absolute Deviation 2.3

Table 8.2: Forecasting by past average

Total Absolute Deviation (TAD) is the sum of all the deviations ignoring plus or minus signs. Mean Absolute Deviation is the average of the deviations. In this example although there are twelve forecasts, there are only eleven deviations. 25/11 = 2.3 which is the Mean Absolute Deviation (MAD).

Periods 8 and 12 show large deviations from forecast to actual. If capacity had been arranged to meet the forecast demand of 21 then there would have been a shortfall for Period 8 of 16 per cent ($4/25 \times 100$ =16 per cent) and for Period 12 a shortfall of 15 per cent ($4/26 \times 100$ = 15 per cent). Clearly in this case past average is not sufficiently reliable with this pattern of demand.

This method 'dampens' rapid responses when there are fluctuations, but it is slow to respond when there is a definite trend, either up or down. In the example, after Period 8 the trend is up but the forecast remains steady.

Forecasting by moving average

This method provides a reasonable response to trends, and also dampens fluctuations (see Table 8.3).

Period	Actual	Forecast	Deviation
1	20	–	–
2	18	–	–
3	22	–	–
4	23	20	–3
5	21	21	0
6	19	22	+3
7	24	21	–3
8	25	21	–4
9	22	23	+1
10	23	24	+1
11	25	23	–2
12	26	23	–3
13		25	
Total Absolute Deviation 20			
Mean Absolute Deviation 2.2			

Table 8.3: Forecasting by moving average

Calculations for the forecasts in this example were made by taking the previous *three* periods and dividing by three, e.g. the forecast for Period 10 is the sum of the three previous periods divided by three, $24 + 25 + 22 = 71$, $71/3 = 23.7$, which rounds up to 24.

The number of periods used for averaging is a matter of judgement. If there are definite cycles the number of periods in the cycle can be used to determine the number of periods used for averaging. In our example the last two periods in each group of four have the higher demands (in the first four periods, 3 and 4 are the highest, in the next group of four, 7 and 8 are the highest, and likewise so are 11 and 12 in the next group of four), thus a four-period average might prove to be more accurate. We will test this theory in Table 8.4.

The discerning reader will have noted that we have used the same 'actuals' for each of the last three methods of forecasting. If we compare the MADs we will see that the last method proved to be the more accurate for this set of figures.

However, for a true comparison, as there are only eight forecasts in the last method we should only compare MADs calculated on the last eight forecasts for each method.

Method 1: Past average will now show a MAD of $17/8 = 2.1$
Method 2: Three-period moving average, MAD $17/8 = 2.1$
Method 3: Four-period moving average, MAD $11/8 = 1.4$

This shows that, for this example, the four-period moving average has given the most accurate forecasts.

Period	Actual	Forecast (four-period average)	Deviation (forecast to actual)
1	20	–	–
2	18	–	–
3	22	–	–
4	23	–	–
5	21	21	0
6	19	21	+2
7	24	21	–3
8	25	22	–3
9	22	22	+0
10	23	23	+0
11	25	24	–1
12	26	24	–2
13		24	

Total Absolute Deviation   11
Mean Absolute Deviation   1.4

Table 8.4: Four-period moving average

	Actual	Average for year	Seasonal factor (Percentage of average)
Year 1998			
Qtr One	20		96.4 (20 is 96.4% of 20.75)
Qtr Two	18		86.75
Qtr Three	22		106.0
Qtr Four	23		110.85
	83	83/4 = 20.75	400
Year 1999			
Qtr One	21		94.3
Qtr Two	19		85.4
Qtr Three	24		107.9
Qtr Four	25		112.4
	89	89/4 = 22.25	400
Year 2000			
Qtr One	22		91.7
Qtr Two	23		95.8
Qtr Three	25		104.2
Qtr Four	26		108.3
	96	96/4 = 24	400

Table 8.5: Seasonal factors

Year 01	Forecast	
Quarter One	24 × 94.1%	23
Quarter Two	24 × 89.3%	21
Quarter Three	24 × 106%	25
Quarter Four	24 × 110.5%	27
		96

Table 8.6: Forecast for 2001

Seasonal adjustments

Where there are distinct seasonal trends then the forecast can be further refined by adjusting for seasonality.

Let us assume that Period 1 is the first quarter of a year and Period 2 the second quarter and so on. We can then recalculate our forecasts as in Table 8.5. The next step is to average the seasonal factor for each season:

Year	1998		1999		2000				
Qtr One	96.40	+	94.3	+	91.7	=	282.40/3	=	94.1
Qtr Two	86.75	+	85.4	+	95.8	=	267.95/3	=	89.3
Qtr Three	106.00	+	107.9	+	104.2	=	318.10/3	=	106.0
Qtr Four	110.85	+	112.4	+	108.3	=	331.55/3	=	110.5

By taking the four-period moving average for the last four actual results, which is 24, (96/4 = 24) and applying the seasonal factors, the next four quarters can be forecast as in Table 8.6. This gives us the same total (96) for Year 01 as for Year 00. As there is an obvious upwards trend, this is *not* logical. We therefore add a trend factor to our calculations.

Trend factor

The trend factor is obtained by calculating a time lag factor. The formula for the trend factor is (Number of periods of moving average –1) / 2 +1. In our example:

$$(4 - 1) \quad = \quad 3$$
$$3/2 \quad = \quad 1.5$$
$$1.5 + 1 \quad = \quad 2.5$$

Therefore our time lag factor will be 2.5.

We now return to our four-period moving averages, calculate the trend between successive moving averages and multiply each trend by the time lag factor (Table 8.7).

98.125 / 4 gives an adjusted average quarter of 24.5. Using the adjusted average plus the seasonal fluctuations we can forecast for Year 01 as shown in Table 8.8.

Actual (a)	Moving average (b) × 2.5	Successive trend × 2.5	Time lag factor (c)	Adjusted average (a + c)
20				
18				
22				
23				
21	20.75			
19	21.00	+0.25		
24	21.25	+0.25		
25	21.75	+0.50		
22	22.25	+0.50		
23	22.50	+0.25	2.5	0.625	23.125
25	23.50	+1.00	2.5	2.500	26.000
26	23.75	+0.25	2.5	0.625	24.375
—	24.00	+0.25	2.5	0.625	24.625
				98.125

Table 8.7: Adjusted average

Quarter One	98.125 /4 =	24.5	× 94.1% =	23
Quarter Two		24.5	× 89.3% =	22
Quarter Three		24.5	× 106.0% =	26
Quarter Four		24.5	× 110.5% =	27
				98

Table 8.8: Adjusted forecast 2001

We now have a forecast for the next twelve months (four quarters) which is seasonally adjusted and which has allowed for growth based on the past trend. Naturally as each new 'actual' comes to hand we recalculate our moving forecast.

The main weakness of the moving average method is that equal weight is given to each of the historical figures used, and it is also necessary to have, or to build up, a history of information to test against and to forecast from.

Another disadvantage is the number of calculations involved, although with a computer spreadsheet once the formula is entered (and proved) this is not as onerous as it once would have been.

A method known as exponential smoothing (see Table 8.9) overcomes some of these problems without losing any of the accuracy.

Exponential smoothing

Exponential smoothing requires only the previous forecast figure and the latest actual figure. It allows the forecast to respond to fluctuations but at the same time it maintains a level of stability.

We begin by calculating a smoothing constant. The formula for the smoothing constant is:

$$\frac{2}{N + 1}$$

N is the number of periods we wish to smooth. For example, if six was the number of periods the smoothing constant will be:

$$\frac{2}{6 + 1} \quad = \quad \frac{2}{7} \quad = 0.28$$

For our example (see Table 8.9), we will use an exponential smoothing constant based on four periods:

$$\frac{2}{4 + 1} \quad = \quad \frac{2}{5} = \quad 0.4 \text{ exponential smoothing factor}$$

The actual demand for the last period is multiplied by the factor, and the forecast for the last period is multiplied by the sum of 1 – the factor. In our case using a factor of 0.4 the actual for the last period is multiplied by 0.4 and the last forecast is multiplied by 0.6, (that is 1 – 0.4 = 0.6). Forecast calculations for each period use the *previous* period's actual and exponential smoothed figure.

Starting with Period 5: (For Period 6)	Actual 21 and forecast 21. As there is a Nil Deviation no smoothing is required, and thus for Period 6 the forecast will be 21.
For Period 7:	The actual was 19 and the forecast was 21. Using exponential smoothing for Period 7 the forecast is: 0.4 (19) + 0.6 (21) = 7.6 + 12.6 = 20.0
For Period 8:	0.4 (24) + 0.6 (20) = 9.6 + 12.0 = 21.6
For Period 9:	0.4 (25) + 0.6 (22) = 10.0+ 13.2 = 23.2
Period 10:	0.4 (22) + 0.6 (23) = 8.8 + 13.8 = 22.6
Period 11:	as no deviation to actual for Period 10, forecast is 23
Period 12:	0.4(25) + 0.6 (23) = 10.0 + 13.8 = 23.8
Period 13:	0.4(26) + 0.6 (24) = 10.4 + 14.4 = 24.8

This example is given to demonstrate the mechanics of exponential smoothing. The next steps are to add a trend factor and a seasonal factor to update the exponentially smoothed average. In a four-seasonal forecast, the factor for Period 5 when the actual is known will be upgraded to provide a new seasonal factor for Period 9 and so on; it is in effect a closed loop based on the past. The problem is in deciding values for the smoothing constants. Such decisions are often arbitrary, based on past experience, and tested against past information. Computer programs exist which will do this systematic-ally and are found in cash-flow forecasting programs and in inventory control programs.

Period	Actual	Forecast (four-period average)	Deviation (forecast to actual)	Exponential smoothed average	Deviation
1	20	–	–		
2	18	–	–		
3	22	–	–		
4	23	–	–		
5	21	21	–		
6	19	21	+ 2	21	+2
7	24	21	–3	20	–4
8	25	22	–3	22	–3
9	22	22	–	23	+1
10	23	23	–	23	–
11	25	24	–1	23	–2
12	26	24	–2	24	–2
13		24		25	
Total Absolute Deviation			11		14
Mean Absolute Deviation			1.4		2

Table 8.9: Exponential smoothed average

Finding trends

When looking at a column of figures it is difficult to visualize if there is an increasing or decreasing trend. A simple method of determining if there is a trend is to calculate a mean and then to calculate the variation from the mean for each period (see Table 8.10).

In our example the first four periods total 20 + 18 + 22 + 23 = 83, and

$$\frac{83}{4} \quad = \quad \text{a mean of 21.}$$

Period	Actual	Cumulative difference from mean	
1	20	–1	$(20 - 21) = -1$
2	18	–4	$(18 - 21) = (-3) + (-1) = -4$
3	22	–3	$(22 - 21) = (+1) + (-4) = -3$
4	23	–1	$(23 - 21) = (+2) + (-3) = -1$
5	21	–1	$(21 - 21) = (0) + (-1) = -1$
6	19	–3	$(19 - 21) = (-2) + (-1) = -3$
7	24	0	$(24 - 21) = (+3) + (-3) = 0$
8	25	+4	$(25 - 21) = (+4) + (0) = +4$
9	22	+5	$(22 - 21) = (+1) + (+4) = 5$
10	23	+7	$(23 - 21) = (+2) + (+5) = 7$
11	25	+11	$(25 - 21) = (+4) + (+7) = 11$
12	26	+15	$(26 - 21) = (+5) + (+11) = 16$
13			

Table 8.10: Trends

We can now clearly see that from Period 8 onwards there is a marked upwards trend.

Causal

In forecasting it is easy to get caught up with the method of calculating and to overlook the purpose. The purpose is to get the best possible forecast of what might happen in the future. Therefore forecasts (calculated on past events) must be carefully considered against all the known facts of what is happening or is likely to happen. The state of the economy and key indicators such as interest rates, inflation rates, currency exchange rates, employment rates, and factors such as the entrance of new competitors, new technology and materials, fashion changes, and planned marketing drives will all have causal effects on future results, irrespective of carefully calculated results based on the past. Likewise past results should be examined to determine how they were affected (caused) by similar events. Knowing the *causes* for changes in demand is important.

Common sense

The commonsense approach with forecasted figures is to test them by asking 'Are these figures sensible, what happened before and what is likely to happen in the future?' Once the future demand forecast has been agreed then the operations manager must determine the future capacity of the organization, and anticipate what changes might be needed to meet the level of forecasted demand.

Capacity management

Capacity management is a key planning responsibility of operations managers. As defined by Wild (1995) 'capacity management is concerned with the matching of the capacity of the operating system and the demand placed on that system'.

Capacity management involves the study of likely demand patterns for the medium to long term, and the organizing of resources to meet the demand pattern. The organizing of resources includes acquiring resources, training people, and the development of strategies for meeting changes in demand.

Capacity planning and management

Figure 8.2 shows the relationship between the various stages in capacity planning and capacity management.

Measuring capacity

An organization has capacity if it has some of *each* of the resources required to carry out its function. For example a bus service has capacity to transport a passenger if it has a bus with some empty seats, a driver, fuel etc., but it must have some of *each* of the necessary resources (bus, seats, driver, fuel). In measuring capacity we concentrate on the key resource. The key resource is the most crucial resource for the provision of a service, and it may be determined by factors such as being the most costly, the most used, or the most in demand. Table 8.11 shows resources which are likely to be considered key resources.

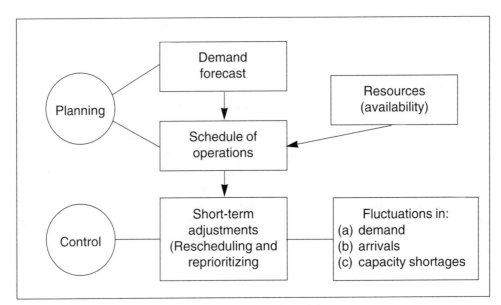

Figure 8.2 Capacity management

Service	Key resource
School	Number of classrooms = limits number of students
Hospital	Number of beds = limits number of admitted patients
Professional practice:	
Dental, medical, legal, accounting, etc.	Number of professionals, dentists, lawyers, etc. and hours available
Hairdresser	Number of chairs
Restaurant	Number of tables
Theatre/sports:	
Arena	Number of seats
Petrol station	Number of pumps
Tele-sales	Number of phones
Passenger service:	
Airline/bus/train	Number of seats
Retail shop	Shelf space
Ice cream vendor	Capacity of refrigerator
Accommodation:	
Motel/hotel	Number of beds

Table 8.11 Measurement of capacity

 YOUR TURN!

What is the key resource for your organization as a whole?
What is the key resource for your department?

Can service be stored?

In many service industries if capacity is not used when available, then that capacity is lost to the system. For example, aircraft seats cannot be stored; once an aircraft takes off with only half the seats occupied, although major costs have been incurred in providing the capacity, the empty seats have been lost to the system. The same applies for the theatre and sports events, professional consultants, hairdressers, restaurants, taxis, hotels and so on; service cannot be stored, without a customer the service capacity has been lost. In retail services the situation may be different; goods not sold today could well be sold tomorrow, the sale is not necessarily lost to the system (a customer might buy groceries only once a week and if the customer doesn't buy on their normal shopping day, then they will buy the next day, thus the supermarket's sales have not suffered for the week).

Controlling capacity

There are two basic approaches to controlling capacity: one is to manipulate capacity, the other is to manipulate demand. Most organizations will seek to match capacity and demand by a combination of both approaches.

Manipulating capacity

With the first approach capacity is planned ahead to meet the expected demand, and if or when demand changes capacity is juggled to meet the new demand. If there is insufficient capacity, customers must either wait for service or customers will not wait and thus be lost to the system. If there is too much capacity, then resources will be under-utilized (the aircraft flies with empty seats). For many service organizations under-utilization might be considered more profitable than the loss of customers.

Manipulating demand

With the second approach capacity is fixed and demand is manipulated to match the available capacity. Common methods of manipulating demand are advertising, promotions, cheaper fares/rates in the off season, cheaper meals for early diners, happy hours (half-price drinks) in bars, and so on. Where demand exceeds capacity prices can be raised, or customers might be allowed or even encouraged to go elsewhere.

Uncertainty of demand

If demand is known in advance and is stable, the operations manager's job is to plan and make the best use of resources to meet the demand. Minor fluctuations cause only minor problems. Where demand cannot be accurately predicted then, although the aim has not changed, operations management problems can become extremely complex. Uncertainty of demand has three dimensions:

1. The number of customers and their arrival times (a steady, even flow is obviously easier to cope with than peaks and troughs).
2. The length of time each customer will need (if the service is of exactly the same duration each time, or can be planned, such as half-hour appointments in the dentist's chair, planning is easier than when it is not known how long each service encounter will require).
3. The amount of resources and the scheduling (timing) of resources.

Capacity management strategies

Faced with uncertain and fluctuating demand there are two basic strategies which can be used:

- Efficient use of resources and the variation or adjustment of capacity.
- Eliminating/reducing the need to adjust capacity (Wild, 1995).

Strategy 1: adjustment or variation of capacity

Generally system capacity can be changed to some extent. Staff can work overtime, unskilled people can be employed in busy periods to free up skilled staff, staff can be re-allocated from their normal duties to help in the front office and so on.

 EXAMPLE

In busy periods a small supermarket will open up extra check-out counters, and office staff including the manager will help with processing customers. In quiet periods counters are closed, some check-out staff are re-assigned to stocking shelves, and the office staff go back to their normal duties.

Table 8.12 summarizes ways of adjusting capacity.

Resources	Capacity additions	Capacity reductions
People	Add permanent staff	Reduce staff
	Train staff (multi skilled)	Re-assign staff
	Strong culture (willing staff)	Retrieve subcontracted work
	Add temporary staff	Retrain staff
	Work overtime	Work short weeks
	Re-assign duties	
	Delay (batch) paperwork	
	Subcontract.	
Space	Rent or purchase	Sub-lease or sell
	Reorganize layout	
Machines/equipment	New machines/systems	Dispose of
Information systems	Buy, hire or rent	Cancel contract
	Subcontract	
Materials/goods deliveries	Add substitutes	Aim for just-in-time
	Increase suppliers	

Table 8.12: Strategy 1 – capacity management

Strategy 2: reduce the need to adjust

If the policy is never to keep the customer waiting, then it follows that there must be a surplus of capacity for most of the time. The aim will be to avoid adjusting capacity by having available surplus capacity.

It is more likely, however, that it will not always be possible to have sufficient capacity to meet every demand. Thus if the policy is not to adjust capacity then it has to be accepted that from time to time customers will have to queue, or customers will be lost to the system. In some service situations it might be possible to hold stocks of resources, such as in a retail situation, a restaurant, or a fast-food shop and the customer is buffered from waiting by being supplied from stock.

EXAMPLE

A fast-food store will anticipate when customers are due and have a stock of made-up hamburgers. To maintain quality of food the store policy is that hamburgers will be only held for four minutes before being discarded. Thus the aim is to prevent customers waiting by having a buffer of stock, and the store accepts that some stock might be wasted. The holding of output stocks, even where it is possible, will not in itself prevent queues if there are insufficient staff to serve the customer. Strategy 2, avoiding adjustment of capacity, therefore has several sub-strategies which for convenience we will label 2a, 2b, 2bi and 2bii. Also see Wild (1995).

2a: Surplus capacity at all times.

2b: Sufficient capacity for most situations, but

2bi: It is accepted that customers might have to queue and that it is likely some business will be lost.

2bii: Output stocks are held (only where possible) to absorb demand fluctuations.

Structure and capacity

In Chapter 1 we identified three service system structures. To a large extent the system structure will determine the capacity strategy which can be adopted (Figure 8.3).

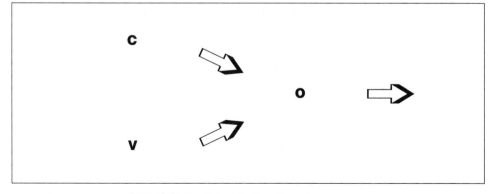

Figure 8.3: Surplus capacity, nil customer queue

In the above example Strategy 1 applies; that is, the system can be adjusted to increase efficiency. This structure requires surplus capacity and does not allow for customer queues. Strategy 2a would also be applicable, and to a limited extent 2bi, that is loss of customers, but *no* customer queues (Figure 8.4).

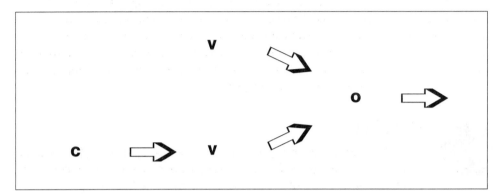

Figure 8.4: Output from stock and customer queue

Again Strategy 1 applies, this structure also enables Strategy 2bi and 2bii (loss of trade and customer queues are both feasible).

Practical capacity management techniques

As we have already seen, service systems cannot serve customers until the customer arrives. Therefore when demand falls short of capacity the result is idle capacity. Day-to-day management of capacity concerns attempting to alter demand and capacity levels so that they are in balance while still responding to random customer demands.

Planned and random demand

In the supply of most services demand can be separated into two separate perspectives, planned and random demand. It is useful in day-to-day management of capacity to know the pattern and proportion of demand which can be reasonably predicted and therefore planned for, and the proportion which is random. Once this pattern is known it is likely that planned demand can be used to fill the troughs as much as possible and thus smooth the overall demand for a given period.

Due to the fluctuating nature of demand many service organizations could sell more capacity than they are able to accommodate in peak times and have a large amount of excess capacity in off-peak demand times. We are all aware of how the tourist industry promotes off-season specials (air fares, hotel rates, package deals and so on) and increases fares in the 'high' season to try and smooth demand. Other examples are variable phone-call rates, early-bird specials in restaurants, and so on. Additional measures include offering complementary services to make waiting more palatable, such as a lounge bar for customers waiting for a restaurant table; and at airports, coffee bars, bookshops and souvenir shopping are provided for customers.

Where possible, capacity can be managed by encouraging customers to book in advance or to make reservations. The appointment book for doctors, dentists and hairdressers is in effect a queue of customers. Ideally the dentist would hope to be fully employed with no spare capacity and with patients arriving at pre-arranged times. The problem is that not all dental work takes exactly the same amount of time, and where half an hour might normally be adequate for an extraction, a complicated dental problem will take longer. Thus the service itself is variable in the time required. This variability of service time applies to most services.

Capacity management in service industries also includes doing as much of the work as possible in advance of the customer arriving. For example, the hotel will have rooms prepared before the customer arrives, the chef in the restaurant will have salads made up in advance and other food partly prepared before patrons arrive. Identification of core work which can be done in advance will speed up the actual service when the customer arrives. Another method of overcoming demand fluctuations is to increase customer participation.

EXAMPLE

Auditors have peak periods at annual balance times. A method of overcoming the pressure is to provide customers with checklists and proformas of information required, so that when audit staff arrive the customer has much of the required information at hand and set out in a manner that makes checking straightforward. Another method is to carry out interim audits in advance, so that only a sample audit is required at balance time.

To overcome heavy demand periods, once the pattern has been established, if work cannot be delayed (paperwork held and completed after hours) or otherwise smoothed, then a bank of pre-trained temporary or part-time staff can be used (the demand anticipated and temporary staff trained in advance). In addition, in really busy periods, as discussed earlier (the supermarket example) back-office staff can be switched to front-office duties and so on.

Addition of people to increase capacity – learning curve

The addition of extra people, no matter how good the induction training, will not necessarily provide a fixed level of capacity. As discussed in Chapter 7, service industries rely heavily on people, and a strong corporate culture will help overcome some short-term increases in demand. Additionally, the longer that people have been with an organization, the greater their ability to respond to sudden changes. The 'learning curve' effect is shown in Figure 8.5. Thus experienced staff and a strong corporate culture will increase the capacity of a given number of human resources.

Queuing theory

Due to the random nature of customer arrivals (even when there is an arrival pattern) and due to the variability in time taken to satisfy each customer, no matter how good the planning of resources is, queues will build up, disappear when there is a lull, and then reappear.

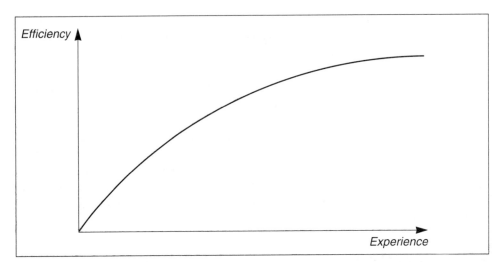

Figure 8.5: The learning curve

YOUR TURN!

Some questions which you could consider for your department are:
How long should a customer wait, what is 'reasonable', and how long on average will customers be prepared to wait?
How much idle time is acceptable for service staff?
What is the cost of having unused capacity?
What is the cost of not being able to provide a service?

Variability of arrivals

It is often not possible, unless an appointment book or reservation system is used, to control the actual moment of arrival of a customer. The number of arrivals and the length of time between subsequent arrivals is not constant. By recording the number of arrivals a histogram can be used to show a frequency distribution, as in the example in Figure 8.6.

When the number of potential customers is large the probability of the next arrival does not depend on how many customers are already in the system. On the other hand, when the number of customers is finite and also small the probability of the next arrival will depend on how many customers have already arrived (supposing there are known to be eight customers then the probability of the next arrival will depend on how many have already been served).

The assumption in most queuing systems is that arrivals occur singly, and therefore the concern is with the probability of a customer arriving or no customer arriving at any point in time or period of time.

Service units

The service mechanism for customers is probably the most controllable part of a queuing system. The simplest form is a single facility through which all customers must enter if they are to be served; more complicated systems will have several serving units which may not all be the same. Multiple serving units can be arranged in

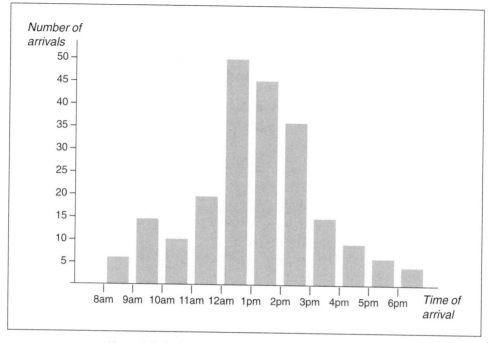

Figure 8.6: Example of a frequency distribution graph

parallel, so that a customer might enter any of the units. A single queue may form and a customer will go to the first unit that becomes available, or alternatively a queue may form for each unit.

Queue discipline

Customers might form orderly queues where newcomers go to the back of the queue and wait their turn (first in, first out), or the system might be that the last one to arrive is served first (last in, first out), for example when processing inward mail, the last letter received goes to the top of the pile and is processed first. Other methods might be to have a priority system for serving customers, to have no system at all with customers being selected or selecting themselves for service at random. Discipline or lack of discipline is not likely to affect the speed at which the service unit operates, but will affect the waiting time for customers.

Service times

Some customers might take longer to serve than others, or all customers might need exactly the same amount of time to process. Nonetheless, as in the case of measuring the variability of arrivals, so too can the variability of service times be measured and averaged. It might be observed that as the queue lengthens, the average throughput increases, with the serving staff allowing themselves less time per customer. If customers are being rushed through the system they might believe that the level of service is below standard, or if they are kept waiting they might become dissatisfied and leave the queue.

Queuing formulae

An important measure for a simple queue is customer intensity, where:

$$\text{Customer intensity} = \frac{\text{Mean (average) rate of service}}{\text{Mean rate of arrival}}$$

For example if the inter-arrival time is on average eight minutes and the service time is on average six minutes, then customer intensity will be:

$$\frac{6}{8} = 0.75$$

Thus 0.75 is the probability (p) of a customer having to wait for service. If p (customer intensity) is more than 1 then the queue will get longer and longer (assuming that the service does not speed up but remains constant).

The question now is how long do customers have to wait for service, and how long will the service unit be idle?

EXAMPLE

Where   p = Probability of customer waiting in queue
         a = Mean service time
         b = Mean arrival time

For a single queue with a customer intensity of less than 1:

Probability of customer waiting for service   = p

Average number of customers in the system $\dfrac{p}{1-p}$

Average number of customers in queue $\dfrac{1}{1-p}$

Average time a customer is in the system $\dfrac{1}{1-p} \times \dfrac{1}{a}$

Average time a customer is in the queue $\dfrac{p}{1-p} \times \dfrac{1}{a}$

With the use of these formulae it is easy to calculate the length of time a customer has to wait or the length of time a service unit is idle.

EXAMPLES

Example 1

What is the average number of customers in a simple queue system if the customer density is 0.5, 0.75, 0.9 or 0.95?

p	1 − p	p/1 − p = average number of customers in the system
0.5	0.5	1
0.75	0.25	3
0.9	0.1	9
0.95	0.05	19

Example 2

If the average service rate is six minutes (ten customers per hour) what is the average time a customer is in the queue with customer densities of 0.5, 0.75, 0.9 and 0.95?

$$p \qquad \frac{p}{1-p} \qquad \frac{p}{1-p} \times \frac{1}{a} = \text{average time for customer in queue}$$

$$0.5 \qquad 1 \qquad \frac{0.5}{1-0.5} \times \frac{1}{10} = 0.1 \text{ hour} = 6 \text{ minutes}$$

$$0.75 \qquad 3 \qquad \frac{0.75}{1-0.75} \times \frac{1}{10} = 0.3 \text{ hour} = 18 \text{ minutes}$$

$$0.9 \qquad 9 \qquad 9 \times 0.1 = 0.9 \text{ hour} = 54 \text{ minutes}$$

$$0.95 \qquad 19 \qquad 19 \times 0.1 = 1.9 \text{ hours} = 1 \text{ hour } 54 \text{ minutes}$$

Thus if customer density is 0.95, and serving time is six minutes, on average customers will wait two hours to be served (1 hour 54 minutes in the queue and six minutes for processing).

CHAPTER SUMMARY

Capacity management is a key responsibility for the operations manager. Capacity management has two aspects: demand and capability.

Demand

In service industries demand is likely to be uncertain and to fluctuate. In this chapter several forecasting techniques were introduced. It was stressed that any forecast must be tested against past experience and the causes established (the commonsense approach).

Having established a forecasted demand the next uncertainty is the arrival times of customers and the duration of each service occurrence.

Capability

Establishing the capability of existing resources and knowing how resources can be manipulated and managed to adjust the level of capacity (up or down) is a key role of the operations manager. The major resource in service industries is usually people, thus training and motivation of people is important.

Strategies

Strategies for capacity management were identified and discussed. It was noted that systems structures to an extent limit the strategy that can be adopted.

In addition measures of capacity were considered and practical day-to-day capacity techniques were suggested, including an introduction to queuing theory.

 CD ROM CASE STUDY

The case study that is used to highlight some of the issues addressed in this chapter is San Lodovico Palio, based in Italy.

Chapter 9

Scheduling, inventory and time management

Objectives for this chapter

This chapter considers:

- Scheduling issues and techniques.
- Inventory issues and stock management.
- Time management.

Introduction

In this chapter we identify the various types of scheduling problems which may be encountered in various service operations and we consider some techniques for their solution. We also consider inventory management issues, and we use retail services to illustrate the main concerns of inventory management.

Although inventory of stocks may not be an issue for some service operations managers, the management of time, and the timing of activities are of concern to all managers; both are discussed here.

Scheduling

Scheduling is a key issue for the operations manager. Scheduling is the art of:

- listing activities;
- deciding the order of completing activities;
- arranging the necessary resources, including inventory, to complete each activity;
- timing the activities.

In the service system scheduling, like capacity management (Chapter 8) is a key area for the operations manager. And like capacity management the task is to *minimize* the cost of having resources of people, equipment, goods and materials available to meet the customer's service requirements, and at the same time to provide adequate customer satisfaction. The two major elements of scheduling are: *when* (timing) and *how much* resource is required to fulfil planned activities.

Theoretically it is possible to have just sufficient resources available, and just at the right time, to meet demand. In practice demand forecasts, as shown in Chapter 8, generally are inexact, and arrival of customers can seldom be exactly known; thus it is not possible to know precisely what resources will be required, and when.

Customers pre-booked

For some service systems customers have been conditioned to book in advance (restaurants, doctors, transport etc.) and the service provider makes the booking to coincide with availability of capacity. In these cases the system controls the time of service delivery, and the scheduling of the necessary amounts of resources can be fairly exact. Efficiency is dependent on arrival of the customer at the prearranged time; if the customer is late service will be delayed, or if not delayed (the train leaves on time) the customer will miss out. In either case, resource utilization will be inefficient. Nonetheless if customers keep to the prearranged booked times a high degree of accuracy and efficiency in the scheduling of resources will be possible. In some areas of service, to overcome non-arrival of pre-booked customers, service operators will deliberately over-book.

 ## EXAMPLE

In the international air travel service, based on past experience of the non-arrival of passengers, an airline may frequently accept bookings for, say, 440 passengers although the scheduled aircraft only has 400 seats. When, as often happens, more than 400 customers arrive on time, then the front-line staff have the problem of placating customers who cannot be seated, or offering inducements for passengers to take a later flight. In this example the airline has placed the efficiency of the operation as its first objective, and scheduling of resources can be fairly precise.

Scheduling for forecasted demand

For most service systems the arrival of customers cannot be precisely determined and scheduling relies on the accuracy of forecasted demand. In such cases, if it is the policy *not* to keep customers waiting, then surplus capacity will need to be held. The problems are, as seen in the section on queuing in Chapter 8, the random nature of arrival of customers, and the variability of the amount of time required for each service activity.

 ## EXAMPLE

No matter how experienced the general practitioner, time required for a routine treatment will vary from patient to patient. If the doctor is determined that no customer is ever to be kept waiting in the ante room then the doctor might schedule perhaps only one patient per hour. This might mean that for a good deal of the time the doctor would be idle.

The dilemma faced by the doctor – either the doctor waits for customers or the customer waits for the doctor – is compounded for many other types of service operations. The doctor can at least make appointments in advance and therefore know with some degree of accuracy the time of arrival of customers, whereas for many service operators arrival times will be random.

This generally means that a third approach to scheduling has to be adopted – to try and have sufficient capacity most of the time but to accept that queues will sometimes form and that there could well be some loss of business. The two basic strategies of capacity management discussed in Chapter 8, of either avoiding adjustment of capacity, or providing for efficient adjustment of capacity, equally apply to scheduling decisions.

The relevant systems structures covering the three distinct scheduling approaches are shown in Figure 9.1.

Scheduling: feasibility versus desirable

The broad approach to scheduling activities is influenced by business policy and, as shown in Figure 9.1, by system structure. Operations scheduling is thus limited by

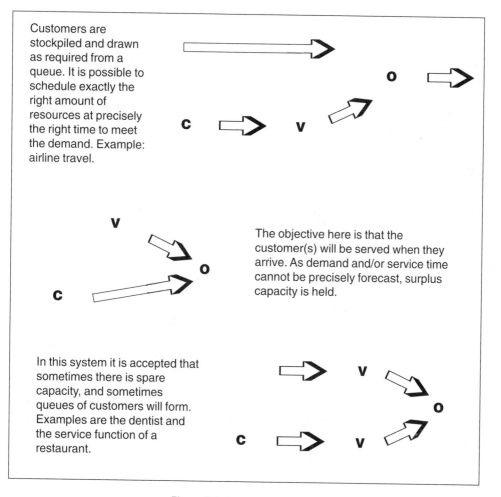

Figure 9.1: System structures

what is feasible given the resources (capacity) available and the limitations of the system structure, coupled with what is desirable in terms of customer satisfaction.

In considering the subject of scheduling it is necessary to understand two perspectives: those of the customer and those of the organization. The operations manager must know what these perspectives are; that is, what the customer expects, and what the organization is prepared and *able* to provide. These areas of conflict are likely to centre on timing or speed of delivery of service, cost of service, flexibility and responsiveness.

Timing of service

Customers may not expect to queue for service, and if the organization's policy is to avoid queues then there will not be a conflict. If, however, the operations manager does not have sufficient resources available, or fails to schedule sufficient resources, then there will be a conflict. If the organization's policy is to accept that sometimes queues will form, but if the customer has been led to believe, or has assumed, that prompt service will be provided, then when a queue does form customers will regard the service as less than adequate.

Where queues are accepted as almost the norm, such as at the supermarket checkout or at the post office, then customers will be aware that they might have to queue. In these cases, provided the queue is seen to be moving and service is equitable (no queue-jumping), then customers will be reasonably satisfied. If a new competitor arrives in the market and offers the same specified service but with no queues, then the queue disappears! The operations manager's job is to manage the scheduling of resources to prevent or at least minimize queues.

Scheduling techniques

Gantt chart, also a control mechanism

The Gantt chart or bar chart is the simplest method to schedule activities, being first developed towards the end of the nineteenth century by Henry Gantt, a colleague of Frederick Taylor. In essence it is a bar graph with time shown on the horizontal axis and activities on the vertical. A variation is shown in the example in Figure 9.2, where it can be seen that some activities overlap; for example applications can be sorted and screened/checked as they arrive, although the position is still being advertised.

As activities are completed they are colour coded; thus not only is the Gantt chart a scheduling aid but it is also a means of control to show which activities have been completed, which still have to be completed, and if the time frame is being kept to.

Load charts

Load charts are another variation of the Gantt chart. Instead of listing activities the Load chart shows departments or individual people on the vertical axis, and the operations manager can then see which resources are available for scheduling. If all resources are fully utilized then further work might be declined or steps taken to temporarily increase capacity as discussed in Chapter 8. Table 9.1 gives an example of a Load chart.

A similar approach is used when timetables (such as a school timetable) are being constructed.

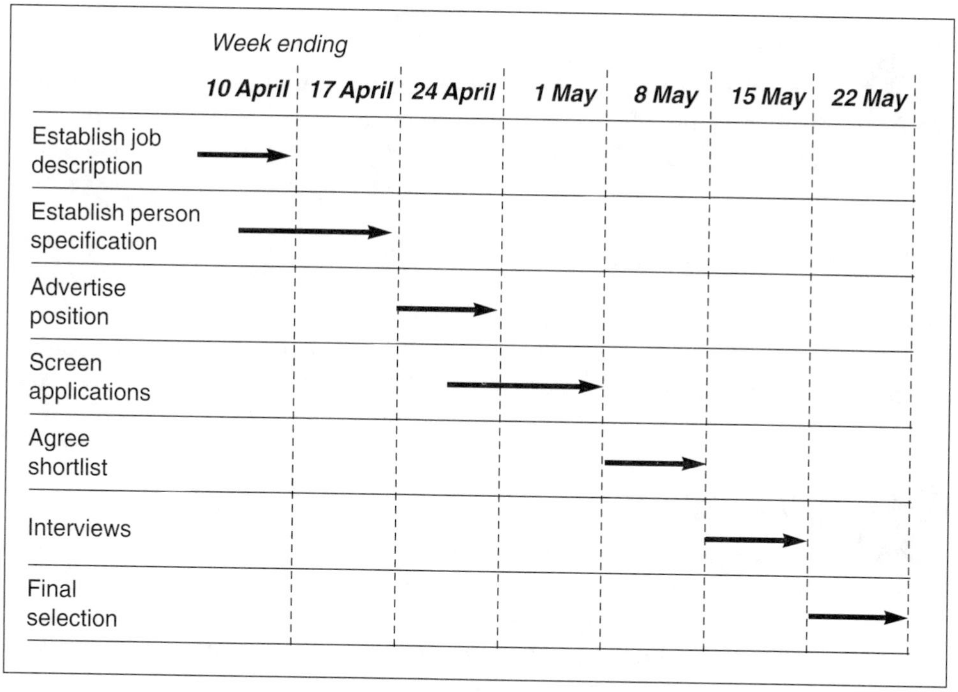

Figure 9.2: Schedule for recruitment of new staff member

Sales reps	Monday	Tuesday	Wednesday	Thursday	Friday
John	Holiday	Paris	London (exhibition)	Reading	Oxford
Jill	Bristol	Cardiff	Swansea	London (exhibition)	Hamburg
Harry	London (set up exhibition)	London (exhibition	London ⟶	London	London final day)
Hannah	Edinburgh	Glasgow	Ayr/Carlisle	Sunderland	Scarborough

Table 9.1: Example of load chart

Forward scheduling

Forward scheduling begins as soon as the demand is known. Service is performed to customer order and delivery is required as soon as possible. Orders are usually accepted on a first come, first served basis even if the service provider knows that customers are going to have to wait. Often customer queues form. Examples are hospitals and restaurants.

EXAMPLE

Customers arrive (not pre-booked) at a restaurant and if possible are taken to a table where they wait for service. If no table is available they are shown to the bar, and will be called when a table is ready.

Backward scheduling

Backward scheduling begins with the due date. By working back from the due date activities and resources are scheduled one at a time so as to arrive at a start time. With backward or reverse scheduling it might be found that the organization does not have all the necessary resources and thus the operations manager has the task of hiring equipment, arranging subcontractors, temporary labour etc. to meet the requirements.

EXAMPLE

The due date for a wedding will be the day the bride and groom have booked the church. Working back from this date the other arrangements include hiring of a marquee, erection of the marquee, hiring of caterers, making of the bride's and bridesmaids' dresses with various intermediate fittings, booking hairdressers and photographers, the two mothers arranging their outfits, the timing of the hen and stag parties, the booking of entertainment, the hiring of cars, and so on. On top of all this the poor bride and groom have to find time to occasionally see each other.

Assignment method

The assignment method of scheduling resources uses a linear programme model and follows the transportation models demonstrated in Chapter 6. The objective is to minimize the total costs or the time required. Examples include assigning salespeople to areas and people to tasks or projects. With the assignment method a limitation is that only one activity or person can be allocated to one area or activity at a time. The assignment method uses a tabular approach as demonstrated in Table 9.1.

EXAMPLE

A business has three staff members: Andreas, Jacob and Stefan, and there are three tasks to be completed. Each employee has different skills, and each employee has a different hourly wage rate. The estimated cost for completing each job per employee is as follows:

	Task A	Task B	Task C
Andreas	£33	£42	£18
Jacob	24	30	33
Stefan	27	36	21

Stage 1

Begin by subtracting the smallest number in each row from each number in that row. The table will now be:

	Task A	Task B	Task C
Andreas	15	24	0
Jacob	0	6	9
Stefan	6	15	0

Now subtract the smallest number remaining in each column from every number in that column.

	Task A	Task B	Task C
Andreas	15	18	0
Jacob	0	0	9
Stefan	6	9	0

The next step is to draw a straight line passing through each zero. In our example there will be two straight lines as shown above, along the Jacob row and down the Task C column. If there are fewer straight lines than there are numbers of rows a further stage is needed to find the optimum solution. In our example, as there are only two straight lines and there are three columns, we will move to the next stage.

Stage 2

In this stage we take the smallest uncovered number, in our case Stefan and Task A:

	Task A	Task B	Task C
Andreas	15	18	0
Jacob	0	0	9
Stefan	[6]	9	0

Subtract the smallest uncovered number from every other uncovered number, which in our case is Andreas Task A (15) and Task B (18), and Stefan Tasks A (6) and B (9), and *add* it to the number where the two lines intersect.

Stage 3

We now have:

	Task A	Task B	Task C
Andreas	9	12	0
Jacob	0	0	15
Stefan	0	3	0

In Stage 3 we draw sufficient straight lines to cover all the zeros. If, as our example shows, the number of lines is equal to the number of columns, we have arrived at an optimum solution. In this case we will assign Task C to Andreas, Task B to Jacob, and Task A to Stefan. Note as Andreas has only one zero he must get Task C, which leaves Stefan with only Task A. The optimum cost is:

Task A	Stefan	27	
Task B	Jacob	30	
Task C	Andreas	18	= 75

This was a simple example with only six possibilities $(3 \times 2 \times 1)$ which no doubt some of our readers could have solved in their heads without going through all the three stages. If there had been four staff members and four tasks the possibilities total 24 $(4 \times 3 \times 2 \times 1)$, and if there were nine staff and nine tasks the possibilities are 362,880 $(9 \times 8 \times 7 \times 6 \times 5 \times 4 \times 3 \times 2 \times 1)$ i.e. not quite so easy to solve in your head!

Dummy tasks

Earlier it was said that the assignment model requires only one task for each person, or an equal number of columns and rows. How then do we cope if there were an uneven number of rows and columns (three tasks and four workers)? This is overcome by creating a dummy task with a row which only has zeros in it. When the assignment is complete the employee who is assigned the dummy task is in effect unassigned as there is no task to be done.

The transportation model and its uses

The basic transportation approach allows for the allocation of people to tasks and projects, people to sales territories, contracts to bidders. The aim is to minimize costs and/or time, or to maximize profits or effectiveness. In our example another approach would have been to consider opportunity costs by subtracting every number in the first table from the largest single number (rather than the smallest number), thus converting our maximization exercise into a minimization result.

Bottlenecks

Bottlenecks are where the whole process is held up because one particular task takes longer than the subsequent task. For example, invoices are held up for mailing out due to the checking clerk being away sick, or mortgage approvals are held up due to the need for approval from the district office. Bottlenecks can be overcome by adding resources, by re-routing work, by method study at pressure points, or by rearrangement of layouts as discussed in Chapter 6.

YOUR TURN!

Do bottlenecks occur in your workplace? If so what actions are taken, or could be taken to ease the bottleneck?

Network analysis

Network analysis is a key tool of project managers and there are many computer programs available. There are many names given to this basic process, such as Critical Path Method (CPM) and Program Evaluation Review Technique (PERT). The approach for network analysis is:

- list all the activities needed to complete the project;
- allow sufficient time for each activity;
- monitor progress against the plan.

In the simple example given below the project is to shift an office to a new location.

EXAMPLE

Activity		Duration	Preceding activity
Sign new lease	A–B	One day	None
Agree layout plan	B–C	Five	A–B
Pack for move	B–D	Three	A–B
Re-decorate	C–D	Seven	B–C, B–D
Wire for computers	C–E	Three	B–C
Move and install	D–F	Two	B–D, C–D, C–E
Staff move in	F–G	One	D–F

Until the lease is signed little else can be done. We assume that the new office is in the right location, the rent is acceptable, and the floor space is no less than what we need (see Chapter 6). Thus signing the lease is the first step. However, before we move in it has to be decided where each department will be and where each person will sit. This has to be done before we can establish where the telephones will be and where the computer wiring will run to and so on. The time taken for wiring, installation of telephones and computers, and the redecoration will determine the date that staff can be moved. Once that date is known then packers and removal people can be arranged and staff advised.

The network will first be drawn to show the sequence of events, and it will be found that some events can occur simultaneously. For example, packing can begin while the layout plan is being decided, and packing can continue while re-decorating and wiring is taking place. But the actual move cannot take place until the wiring, the re-decoration and the packing are completed. The final step in this simple example is for the staff to move in, and if everything has gone to schedule, within sixteen days from the beginning of the project to the end, they will be fully operational.

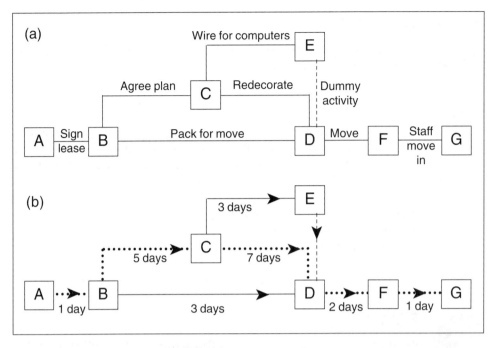

Figures 9.3a & b: Precedence diagrams

Figure 9.3a is a simple precedence diagram which depicts the order in which activities must occur. The logic of drawing a network is to have all the arrows moving from left to right across the page, with no backtracking. The convention of networks also allows for a dummy activity to enable the sequence of events to be maintained. In our example if we had drawn the arrow for wiring computers from C to D then we would have two activities for C–D, i.e. redecorating and wiring, which clearly would be confusing; thus wiring has been designated C–E. As activity D–F cannot start until B–D, C–D and C–E are completed it is necessary to show these preceding activities in the diagram; this has been overcome by adding the 'dummy' activity E–D.

Time frames and critical paths
By adding the time required for each activity it is then possible to calculate the time required to complete the project. This is shown in Figure 9.3b.

If we follow along the path A–B, B–D, D–F, F–G we can calculate that this sequence of activities will take seven days, and for the path A–B, B–C, C–D, D–F, F–G, this sequence of activities takes sixteen days, and for the third path of A–B, B–C, C–E, E–D, D–F, F–G the sequence is twelve days.

Thus the longest path is sixteen days and the earliest the project will be completed is sixteen days. It follows that if any activity on this path does not keep to schedule, say re-decorating takes ten days rather than the scheduled seven days, the complete project will be extended by three days to nineteen days. If time is important, then it is *critical* that no activity on the longest path, i.e. the *critical path*, is allowed to extend beyond its allotted time. To make this obvious on the diagram the critical path will be colour coded and, like the Gantt chart, as each activity is completed it will also be colour coded so that the operations manager can see at a glance the progress of the project and the importance of activities in the overall time frame. Activities not on the critical path can, however, be delayed provided that the delay does not exceed the *slack* existing in that path. For example, the first path of A–B, B–D, D–F, F–G takes seven days, so overall for this path there is a *slack* or *float* of nine days. But as activities A–B, D–F, and F–G are also on the critical path, only activity B–D can be delayed, and provided everything else keeps to schedule, B–D has a slack of nine days, or can take up to twelve days without delaying the overall project beyond the scheduled sixteen days.

The only other activity that could be delayed is C–E. As this activity is on a path that takes twelve days the slack here is only four days (16 – 12 = 4), and if all other activities keep to time then C–E can be delayed by four days without affecting the finish date.

Of course if the total amount of slack is used up for an activity then that activity becomes critical to the project.

Our example is a very simple one designed to give you the rudiments of the network approach. Many standard computer packages exist for critical path analysis. Built into the software will be the ability to have a minimum of three estimates of time for each activity, e.g. the expected time (most likely), the most pessimistic and the most optimistic. The software will also show the earliest start time, the latest start time and the most probable start time, and will calculate various critical paths and provide for printouts, on an exception basis, of a list of activities that are falling behind schedule, thus enabling the operations manager to take action to correct the situation. Correction might include adding extra resources or delaying one activity and transferring resources to another activity and so on.

Added resources means more cost, and a trade-off will have to be made along the continuum of accepting a delay to a project and the cost of adding extra resources to complete a project on time.

Inventory issues and stock management

For some service operations stock control and management is not an issue, for others it is a major issue. As any retailer knows, a stock out generally results in a lost sale. On the other hand, surplus stock leads to all sorts of problems such as losses due to:

- fashion changes (style, colour, texture);
- past 'Use-by date' for foods;
- deterioration;
- obsolescence due to model changes or new products (the cassette replacing the record, the CD replacing the cassette);
- damage;

- pilfering;
- storage;
- handling;
- finance costs including interest and insurance.

Finance costs

Accountants do not like high amounts of stock, and they have a means of measure for stock efficiency known as stock turn (what is a 'good' stock turn will vary from industry to industry). The calculation of stock turn for a retailer is quite straightforward. The formula is:

$$\frac{\text{Annual cost of goods sold}}{\text{Value of stock on hand at balance date}}$$

EXAMPLE

If the cost of the goods sold in a year is £6,000,000, and at balance date £2,000,000 is on hand, then the stock turn is 3 (6/2 = 3. Note: to simplify the calculation remove all the noughts). This means that the stock on hand turns three times a year. Expressed in months this shows at balance date that the retailer is holding four months of stock based on past sales (12 months divided by 3 = 4 months). To calculate how many days of stock are on hand divide the cost of sales by 365 (the usual number of days in a year); i.e. £6,000,000/365 = 16,438.36; as the amount of stock on hand is £2,000,000 then £2,000,000/16,438.36 = 121 days or four months.

If it is assumed that the retailer is paying for goods within a month of them being received into store, it follows that the retailer is carrying the cost of holding the stock for three months or 91 days. If this is a cash business (that is the retailer does not sell on credit – goods paid for when the sale is made), and assuming an interest rate of 12.5% p.a., the retailer will be either paying the bank if the account is overdrawn or forgoing a return on investment of close to £62,500. (£2,000,000 × 12.5% pa = £250,000 and 250,00/365 × 91 = £ 62,329).

On top of the interest cost, or interest forgone, there will be a cost of insurance and the cost of storage space. The true cost, taking all factors into account, will be between 15% and 40% p.a.

Traditional stock management

In traditional stock management there are two basic approaches: the pull system and the push system.

Pull system

With a pull system (Figure 9.4) a warehouse is viewed as independent of the supply chain, and inventory is replenished with order sizes based on a predetermined stock

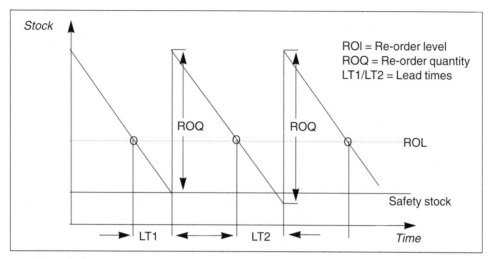

Figure 9.4: A basic 'ROL/ROQ' model' for a pull system. Source: Basu *et al.*, 1998.

level for each warehouse. The stock management system usually operates with a re-order level and a re-order quantity. As Figure 9.4 shows, when the stock drops to a certain level, a re-order is triggered for a predetermined amount. This system takes into account past usage and the lead time needed for a re-order to be satisfied. The aim is to have as small an amount of inventory on hand as possible at any one time and likewise the re-order quantity will be as small as possible.

Push system
The push system (Figure 9.5) works where there is an advantage in buying bulk quantities rather than making several small orders. An example for an importer would be to compare the cost of making several small air-freighted orders compared to one large sea-freight container load.

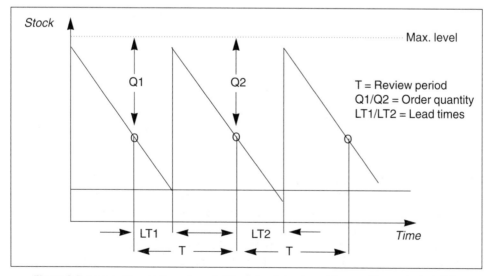
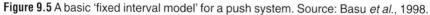

Figure 9.5 A basic 'fixed interval model' for a push system. Source: Basu *et al.*, 1998.

With a total supply, or value, chain management approach as discussed in Chapter 4 (Figure 4.1) the customer, the retailer and the supplier are considered as one system. The aim is to be more responsive to customer needs, to reduce stock holding and to develop a close relationship with suppliers. With a well-managed value chain, the right quantity of product is always delivered on time and is always exactly as specified. In the past little loyalty was shown to suppliers, and the purchasing department, usually a separate function from operations management, would see their role as being to screw the best price possible out of suppliers and to 'shop around' for best deals. Consequently the supplier was never certain as to their future relationship with the buyer, and little loyalty was shown by either party. As explained in Chapter 4, with the value chain approach the supplier becomes part of the team and is judged on their loyalty, ability to perform on time and to specification, with cost being still important but no longer the key issue. Needless to say it follows that purchasing should not be separated from operations but should be considered as an integral part of the operations function.

Balance date/stocktakes, or 'Where did the stock go?'
Organizations with large amounts of stock holdings will always be concerned about how accurate the stock records are. The only true way of knowing what is really on hand is to physically count it. The problem at balance date is that when the auditors count the stock and compare it to stock records generally there will be a discrepancy. Stock discrepancies only occur for a limited number of reasons:

1. The stock was never received (short deliveries or over-invoiced).
2. The stock was sold but the sale was not recorded.
3. Stock has been stolen.
4. Stock has been damaged or disposed of but disposal has not been recorded.
5. Stock has been miscoded on receipt or when sold (e.g. 200 hoses booked in, but actually 200 hose-clips received).
6. The stock was sold before it was booked in.
7. Stock has been 'borrowed' (in the sale representative's van for display/ demonstration purposes).

The rules I recommend (developed from bitter personal experience) to overcome these sorts of problems are:

1. Stock orders to be entered into the system.
2. Stock must be booked into the system when received. The system should be able to verify that goods received match those ordered (see Step 1).
3. Stock not to be sold before it is booked in.
4. Sales must be entered through the system.
5. Payment to be triggered by the system, not by suppliers' invoices. Let the suppliers do the reconciling; you will only be paying for what you ordered and for what you have received.
6. Carry out rolling stock-takes on a portion of the inventory on a weekly, fortnightly or monthly basis. This should overcome the drama of an annual stocktake, and should also reduce your audit account.

The above system relies on a standard computerized system.

With an integrated supply chain approach a heavy reliance is placed on the information technology system. Thus if goods are bar coded as they pass over the sensor at point of sale, the customer's statement is updated, a delivery docket and invoice raised, stock records of the retailer are updated, sales figures and margins calculated and recorded, and a re-order is triggered. If suppliers are tied into the system then the supplier will also be automatically notified of a replacement re-order. Figure 9.6 depicts an integrated inventory system.

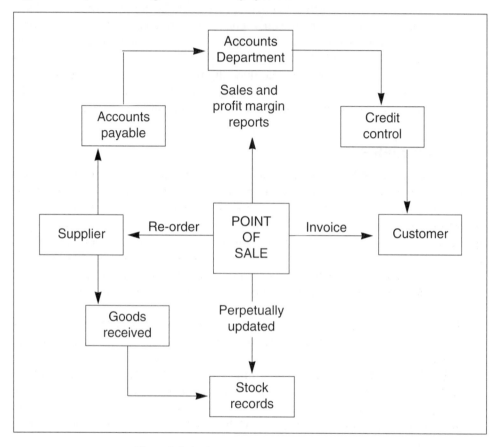

Figure 9.6: An integrated point-of-sale system

 EXAMPLE

Variation on a theme

An advertising agency had great difficulty in reconciling invoices and statements received from radio, TV and print media. Their answer had been to increase the number of accounting clerks, but still they got behind and not only were they losing commission but they were in danger of losing their accreditation.

My solution was to recommend that when the agency raised an 'order' on the media the system would automatically record a payment advice calculated at the media's rate of charge. Subsequently when the due date arrived the computer system would tally the advertisements ordered with the rates and automatically print a cheque that would be attached to a summary of payments. Invoices and statements from the various media companies then became irrelevant. The philosophy was to only pay for what was ordered, and to rely on the media to fulfil orders. Generally it was found that the media ran advertisements on the TV and radio more often than had been ordered and seldom was the agency short-changed.

The result was that within four months of the new system being put into place the accounts staff were reduced by fourteen people, and office space was able to be sub-let. Additionally accounts were being paid on time and the relationships with the media had never been better. The only concern was that of the auditors who had difficulty in ignoring the media's statements, invoices and credit notes. Eventually I was able to convince them that the agency were paying for what was ordered and nothing else was relevant.

Time management

We began this chapter by identifying that the two key issues of scheduling are timing (when) and how much resource is required. For customer satisfaction we identified the key issues as being specification, time and cost. Again, when considering resource utilization, time was also found to be an important element. In this section we are going to consider how you personally can manage *your* time better. As with all operation management problems the first step is to know what the objectives are, and the steps or activities needed to achieve the objectives. It is also important to prioritize objectives and steps. A five-step approach to personal time management is as follows:

1. List the problems/tasks facing you. Sort those that will advance the organization's interests and those that don't really add value to the business. Discard those that don't add value.
2. Prioritize; that is, determine which objectives are the most important and the order in which they should be done. This includes deciding which cannot be delayed, and which are not important. Sometimes it is possible to get rid of several small tasks in a short space of time, but don't get bogged down with a trivial task.
3. Having decided the order of objectives, then in the same manner list the tasks required for each objective and assign priorities to them.
4. Make a schedule of jobs to be done, and in brackets allot time to each.
5. Tick off items as they are completed (this is the best bit!).

This approach can be done at the beginning of each week, and then checked and reset each morning, but don't waste all morning reworking your schedule!

Most managers achieve 80 per cent of their important results in only 20 per cent of their time. In other words 80 per cent of their time is spent on unimportant or time-wasting tasks. It is easy to go home feeling that you have been busy all day, but in reality having achieved very little of value. Some writers suggest setting a regular amount of time aside each day for talking to staff, for checking the voice-mail, making phone calls, checking incoming e-mails and sending e-mails. If you are working across time zones a message sent at 10 a.m. in the UK will arrive at 10 p.m. in New Zealand, thus messages don't have to be answered immediately.

By the same token you should try and make it a rule that all voice-mails, e-mails and faxes are replied to on the day received, if only just to acknowledge receipt. Technology is wonderful but don't be deluded into thinking that just because you have sent a message it has arrived. Somewhere in the IT link a server can be down, and although you have not received a 'message returned' advice this does not mean that your message has gone all the way down the so-called superhighway. If you don't get a reply in a reasonable amount of time don't be shy in sending a message asking for confirmation.

Meetings don't have to be a waste of time

The greatest time-waster of the 1990s has proved to be meetings. A poorly-run meeting can run on for hours, waste everyone's time and achieve nothing. Minutes of meetings should only cover actions to be taken by members. At the next meeting the first task should be to check if actions have been completed, and then to discuss what else has to be done, what should be done, and to agree a fresh list of actions. Unless any action follows from a meeting, why have it? One suggestion for running a meeting is to have no chairs; if everyone has to stand for the duration of the meeting it is surprising how quickly the meeting finishes. If this is too revolutionary, at least try not serving coffee; a meeting is not a social occasion – if it *is* a social occasion it should be billed as such, and we should not expect to achieve any worthwhile business.

CHAPTER SUMMARY

In this chapter we have considered the key task of scheduling work. We showed that scheduling includes arranging resources and setting time frames so as to achieve objectives as efficiently as possible.

- Techniques and methods of scheduling were considered.
- The importance of stock management and basic approaches were explained.
- Finally we discussed the importance of managing our own time.

We conclude this chapter with the thought that time is a precious commodity, and whether you are doing time, marking time, or spending time, believe us time is running out. Your only hope is to do it now, procrastination is the thief of time.

CD ROM CASE STUDY

The CD ROM cases that apply to this chapter and in fact cover several preceding chapters are Wiggo Kongstad (Denmark) and The Open Polytechnic (New Zealand).

Part Five

In Part Three the overall approach to planning, implementation and control was covered. It was seen that for control to be effective, measurement in the form of standards and budgets was necessary. In Part Five the philosophy required to achieve a total quality management operation and the measurements that are needed is detailed.

- **Chapter 10** concentrates on the quality philosophy. It is acknowledged that there are many approaches to the subject of quality. It is argued that quality is not a separate discipline, such as accounting or marketing, but quality is an integral part of all management activities. It is shown that quality issues and the level of quality provided to customers, and the way in which the quality philosophy can be used to increase the efficient use of resources, is a matter of business policy.

- **Chapter 11** continues with the quality theme, the need to add value and to reduce non-value-adding activities. In this chapter it is shown that unless there are standards and measurement of performance, control will be less than perfect, and without measurement it will not be possible to know if performance is improving or not. The taking of measurements will take effort and therefore cost money; the taking of measurements alone does not add value to an organization. The bigger the organization, the more opportunities exist for well-meaning managers to seek returns, statistics and measurements, and not all of this effort will be justified. It is accepted that some non-value-adding measurements, such as required by government departments, have to be maintained. In this chapter, measurements that are important and measurements which should be taken are considered.

Chapter 10

Quality performance

Objectives for this chapter

This chapter considers the subject of quality. In particular the following issues are examined:

- Definitions of quality.
- Who determines levels of quality and service, and why.
- The cost of quality, including conformance and non-conformance costs.
- Levels of quality management.
- ISO 9000.
- Quality initiatives such as *kaizen*.
- Establishing quality controls.

Introduction

In this chapter the subject of quality is considered. There have been volumes of books and learned papers on the subject of quality. Some universities now offer quality as a separate subject or programme, the inference being that quality has become a discipline or subject in its own right which can be studied in isolation from other disciplines. My approach is different; I believe that in the management of operations, quality has always been important, and is inseparable from any management action. Quality cannot be put into a separate compartment, to be picked up and put down when the occasion or management situation demands. The management situation in today's global economy will always require that quality be an integral part of all management actions. This is especially true in service industries where customers rightly expect high-level service. This book has recognized this, and quality issues have been discussed in each chapter. Our underlying theme has been customer satisfaction and efficient use of resources. Both of these objectives require quality considerations. Customer satisfaction cannot be divorced from an understanding of what quality is, and likewise efficient use of resources requires a total quality management approach.

Having said that quality is an integral part of operations management, it is acknowledged that a separate section is required concerning the philosophy of culture, the costs of quality, and some understanding of specific approaches to quality such as ISO 9000, and of terms such as *kaizen* and quality circles.

EXAMPLE

Marty, after having quoted the wrong rate to a branch office after their third and urgent request, was heard to say in the cafeteria: 'Anything that can go wrong, will go wrong'.

Marty's manager loomed up, glared at Marty and said 'Especially if it involves people' and passed him an e-mail. The e-mail was from the branch and included comments made by their customer (now their ex-customer), which said many things and ended with the words 'and at the worst possible time'.

Definitions of quality

Applying inverse logic to the above, quality could be defined (as it often is) as 'The right thing, at the right place, at the right time'. Another popular definition is 'Get it right first time' and yet another is 'Fitness for purpose'. At first glance, it is difficult to fault any of these definitions but the problem remains 'What does "quality" really mean?'

EXAMPLE

In 1998 Nevan and Joy visited England for six months. On arrival they bought an aging car for £450. After travelling 11,000 miles over the length and breadth of the United Kingdom and over large parts of France, they sold the car for £300. Apart from three punctures, the car never once let them down. It always started first time, motored comfortably at some ten miles per hour above the speed limit, and all the bits and pieces such as the windscreen wipers, the indicators and lights worked. Applying the three definitions to this car we would find that 'The right thing, at the right place, at the right time' definition does not apply and likewise the second definition 'Get it right first time' also does not fit, but 'Fitness for purpose' certainly appears to be appropriate. For Nevan and Joy, the requirement, or specification, was a reliable vehicle that would safely get them around Britain and France. For the six months they had it, that car proved as reliable and as efficient as a vehicle that might have cost ten times as much. And yet, despite its proven record, it was still not worth any more than what they sold it for. Fitness for purpose? – *Yes*. Quality? – *No*. Not even the most optimistic second-hand car dealer could describe a rust-ridden, one hubcap-missing, £300 car as a quality vehicle.

Most people like to have a car that they can have some pride in. They are fussy about the model, the colour, the sound system, and they like to keep it clean. They are prepared to pay large amounts of money for the vehicle that best meets their rather ill-defined requirements. Reliability, performance and efficiency are taken for granted. Fitness for purpose is therefore only one aspect of quality. Quality can be divided into two parts – basic requirements and higher-level requirements.

As we saw in Chapter 2, customers have basic requirements of specification, cost and timing.

The example used in Chapter 2 was the commuter bus service. First, unless the bus is travelling more or less to where we want to go (specification) we won't catch it. The second requirement is timing; if we start work at 9 a.m., we will be looking for a bus that gets us to work no later than 9 a.m. and probably not too much earlier. The third consideration is cost. We would classify the route, the time and cost as basic requirements, and probably, depending on circumstances, rank them in that order. The alternatives, if the bus service did not fit our requirements, might be to use our car, share a car with a neighbour, walk some distance and catch a train, buy a bike, or not make the journey at all.

A bus service could meet all the above requirements and still not be a quality service. If the service was unreliable (sometimes late, sometimes early, sometimes did not keep to the route) then we would not consider it to be a reliable quality service. To be a quality service, the bus service needs to meet clients' basic requirements and be reliable (right thing, right place, right time). Supposing the bus did all these things, got you to work on time at a reasonable cost, and was always on time, *but* it was dirty, the driver was surly, the seats were hard and it leaked exhaust fumes. Then, although it met the criteria of right thing, right time, right place, there is no way you would describe that service as a quality service. Thus apart from the basic needs there are certain higher-order needs that must be met. In this case, we would look for polite service, a clean bus, reasonably comfortable seating, and certainly no exhaust fumes. A truly high-quality bus might be spotlessly clean, have carpets on the floor and piped music as well as all the other attributes. But, no matter how comfortable the ride, how polite the service, how cheap the fare, unless the bus is going 'our way' we won't be interested in catching it. In other words the specification must be reasonably satisfied.

The other definition, 'Get it right first time' is more of a slogan aimed at encouraging a sense of responsibility amongst lower-level staff to be accurate in their work (rather than relying on someone else to find an error). For anyone to be expected to do something right first time, they first have to know exactly what they are meant to be doing.

EXAMPLE

When Joy's car had a puncture, Tom, a young friendly and helpful mechanic, fitted a new tyre. A week later, the new tyre was damaged when Nevan hit a concrete block on the motorway. When Nevan jacked the car up and tried to undo the wheel nuts he found that they were so tight that he was unable to move them. The RAC came to the rescue and, by applying leverage, were able to solve the problem. The RAC man advised that over-tight wheel nuts were a common problem.

If young Tom had been instructed that the purpose of wheel nuts was to keep the wheel on and, to be effective they must be done up tight, Tom had got it right first time. Add the fact that he was pleasant and helpful, his manager probably thought that Tom was providing a quality service and indeed, for the space of a week, Joy and Nevan thought so too. It could be argued that Tom didn't get it right first time, because the nuts were too tight. But he didn't know that, nor did his manager and, for a time, nor did the customer.

Thus the slogan 'Get it right first time' means that to get it right, we need to know what is right. In other words, a standard has to be set and the operator has to be informed as to what the standard is. Furthermore, there has to be some way in which the operator can check his or her work to ensure that the standard has been achieved.

Consider the case where Tom has now been informed of the correct tension to which to tighten the wheel nuts. Say the customer is in a hurry, but has been told to come back in an hour, and when the customer comes back, finds the job hasn't been started. Tom is at tea, the foreman calls him, and with bad grace the job is performed. Tom duly carries out the job to specification. But not only was Tom surly, he left grease on the steering wheel and also didn't replace the hubcap properly. Later, the hubcap comes off and is damaged. The customer would not regard this as quality service. In fact, the quality of the job was superior to the first scenario where subsequently it had proved impossible for the customer to remove the nuts.

'Fitness for purpose', 'Getting it right first time', or 'Right thing, right place, right time' may all fit the basic requirements. However, in the customer's eyes, these are the minimum requirements that the customer expects. Without satisfying the basics, you won't be able to give an acceptable level of service. To have your service or product described as a quality product, the customer will expect higher-level benefits, such as courtesy, attention to detail, pleasant surroundings and so on. These higher-level benefits are what gives an organization a competitive edge, and often the difference costs very little to achieve.

However, there is no point in an organization concentrating on friendly, clean service in the hope that this will make the difference if the service or product does not meet the basic specifications, costs too much, or is not available when the customer wants it.

 EXAMPLE

The restaurant is in a good location, the decor is tasteful, the wine list is good and not too expensive, the menu is varied and interesting, the waiting staff are well-groomed and helpful, *but* the food is poorly cooked, almost uneatable. You don't go back and you will tell many people of your experience, and in turn these people will pass the bad news on, often with embellishments.

No one knows how many potential customers are lost as the result of sub-quality products or inferior service. Such a figure cannot be quantified, it is unknown and unknowable.

Who determines quality?

When asked, 'Who determines quality?', most people will say, 'The customer'. But this is not the case.

In most cases, the level of quality that your organization will aim for is determined by what your competition is offering. If you are a reasonable-sized player in your market, then you will be influencing the level of quality, and the competition will be reacting to your initiatives. Even where you are seen to be leading the market in setting quality standards, the very reason that you will be doing so is because of your perceptions of what the competition is likely to do and your desire to stay in front. 'But,' you might ask, 'isn't what the competition does, and consequently what you do, a response to what the customer wants?' Up to a point the answer is yes, but only to a limited extent.

EXAMPLE

When using an airline service most customers (unless they are travelling on the expense account, i.e. someone else is paying) want the cheapest airfare possible and to travel at a convenient time. If the customer was deciding the level of service they would probably like free car parks at the airport, business class seats and service, and fares to be reduced by 50 per cent. This is, of course, not possible. No airline could afford to provide such extras. Each airline will provide prices and services similar to the competition.

Let us therefore accept that the customer's wishes are not always paramount!

Thus the quality offered is determined in light of what the competition is offering and what the service provider can *afford* to give.

Cost to the supplier of a service is, and always will be, a limiting factor in the determination of the level of quality provided. Or, looking at it from another angle, any organization, no matter how inefficient it is, can, for a short period of time, provide a top-quality service or product if it ignores the cost of doing so. However, in the final analysis, unless that organization is making a profit, it will not survive. Thus, we are not likely to see free valet parking at the airport for economy-class passengers, nor will air fares drop to the extent that the airline does not, in the long term, make a profit.

You will note that in our perception of how an airline passenger judges quality, we have not listed all the basic requirements, such as getting you, together with your luggage, to the right destination safely and on time. Such requirements are essential and are taken for granted by the customer. These will not form the basis by which the customer will judge quality. The customer's expectations will be greater than the mere satisfaction of the essentials. Quality will be judged by the price, plus intangibles such as friendly service, but most of all, by the 'extras' provided. And the extent of the extras which any organization can provide will be limited by the cost which the organization is prepared or able to accept.

Social and political requirements

Other influences on the level of quality to be provided are political (for example, minimum levels of safety, hygiene, pollution and consumer protection can, and usually are, legislated for), and social opinion, including health and environmental concerns. Where social issues have not been legislated for, organizations like to be seen to have a social conscience. Frequently, in meeting the social needs, the provider will be just one step ahead of the legislators.

Technology

Another determinant of quality is technology. Technological advances, and how the competition uses the advances, will provide further opportunities or challenges to increase quality. But the greatest determinant on how much quality, or the level of quality an organization will give, is *cost*.

Efficient use of resources

In operations management, the classic conflict is between customer service and efficient utilization of resources. We saw in Chapter 1 that tangible resources and inputs to the service system are materials, machines, equipment, real estate and people, and intangible assets include time and information. As seen in Chapters 8 and 9, at one extreme if the policy is for resources to be fully employed (i.e. there is no spare capacity), customers will be expected to wait or queue. At the other extreme, if the aim is to have no queues of customers, surplus (idle) capacity will be required. Generally it can be assumed, from the customer's perspective, that queuing is not synonymous with quality.

In the context of the level of quality to be provided, the onus is on the organization supplying the service to determine a standard for the level of quality it aims, and can afford, to provide. The standard has to be clear and communicated to staff, ideally with an explanation of why service standards have been set at that level.

Determination of service level

As a provider of services, the question 'What market do we want to be in and why?' has to be periodically asked. The next question is 'What is the competition doing?' Logically the next question is 'What share of the market do we want and how can we hope to achieve this share?' The answers will be limited by what is feasible given the system structure and capacity of the organization. One of the main issues you will now find yourself looking at is quality; that is, quality as currently provided by the competition, and by your organization. Next you might go further and attempt to find out what the customers want. Having done this and discovered what the competitors are doing, and having attempted to gauge what the customers expect, you will be able to determine what level of quality is required and attempt to balance that against the level you can afford to provide.

Remember: 'Many organizations have gone bankrupt despite having loyal and satisfied customers' for 'given infinite resources any system, however badly managed, might provide adequate customer service . . . at least for a time' (Wild, 1995).

Quality decision is not the customers'

The quality decision will be yours, not that of your customers or of anyone else. Your decision will be based on what you can afford and what you are capable of doing. Of course, unless you provide the basic essentials as expected by the customer, you will lose market share. On the other hand, if you want to gain a competitive edge and increase market share, you can readily do so by increasing your level of quality. The secret is finding out what you are capable of achieving. If cost is your greatest constraint (as it most certainly will be), then surely the solution must be in reducing costs. Thus the level of quality is determined by your own actions.

The importance of quality is that, to hold your place in the market, you must at least provide the same level of quality as the competition. To improve your position in the market, you need to demonstrate an increased and sustained level of improved quality above that of the competition. Quality, then, is the competitive edge that we are all looking for. The problem is of course that customers expect and, indeed, take for granted the basic requirements. They take for granted that food will be hygienically prepared, that a bus is roadworthy and that the driver is licensed. Quality in the eyes of the customers is the extras. Some extras cost little (courtesy, cleanliness), other extras cost money and cost will be the inhibiting factor as to how much quality can be afforded. But if the competition increases its extras, then, to hold your place in the market, it is essential that in some manner you step up your service just to keep your position.

Once extras have been provided by one player in the market and copied by the rest of the market, customers will take these extras for granted. What bank could afford not to provide automatic (hole-in-the-wall) banking? Which supermarket cannot afford to provide free car parking if a competitor opens up and provides plenty of free car parking?

Extras are provided to gain a competitive edge, but in service industries are generally easily copied by the competition. Often any extra market share gained by the introduction of an extra is short-lived, but once given it is difficult not to continue providing the increased service. (No marketing manager would be brave enough to try.)

How can organizations afford to provide extra services? The answer is found in increased efficiency and productivity. This has been achieved by a combination of:

- Taking advantage of advances in technology such as information technology, office systems and communications systems.
- The development of 'new' management techniques and philosophies to reduce cost and, at the same time, increase the speed and efficiency of service.
- Identification and elimination of costs or processes that don't add value, or the minimization of such costs where it was found they could not be totally eliminated.
- The adoption of philosophies such as total quality management, continuous improvement (*kaizen*), restructuring, empowerment and delayering of management (business process re-engineering) all of which require a change in organizational culture and a degree of carefully planned change management. Chapter 12 discusses change management in some detail.

The need to continually increase benefits and services to keep up with the market or to gain a competitive edge on the market, but without an increase in price to the customer, has led to the need to eliminate any cost that does not add value. The pressure to provide the customer with more for less will cost the service provider and will also set higher future expectations. *The level of quality provided must be a strategic decision based on what the competition is doing and what can be afforded, with a clear appreciation that once started there is no turning back.*

The cost of quality

Quality does not come cheaply. It is not free. To instill a quality culture into an organization will take time, require total commitment and will cost money. But the alternative is to lose your place in the market, and eventually your organization will be no more. The payback for the investment in quality is in the long term, and benefits of higher quality are the reduction of costs, higher profits, growth and survival.

Non-conformance costs

Non-conformance is when work or service is not performed to the standard set by the organization, and has to be corrected, done again or the customer has to be recompensed. The costs will include waste of wages for re-doing work, wasted time and perhaps waste of materials. Such costs should be captured and recorded. If we know how much extra expense we incur because of mistakes, then errors can be analysed and procedures changed to make sure that such mistakes are not repeated.

Flow-on effects resulting from mistakes include stock-outs in warehouses, and overtime worked as a result of errors. These costs may not be readily apparent but can be calculated after perhaps a lot of soul-searching and recriminations. However, the costs of lost opportunities and loss of enthusiasm by workers cannot be measured. For eventually, if errors and second-rate performance become the norm, morale will be such that there will be a general unwillingness to accept responsibility and an attitude of fatalism will pervade. The worst cost, however, cannot be measured, and that is the unknown cost of lost customers and lost opportunities. A really bad experience by a customer is likely to be repeated to at least ten other people, and the story will often grow in the telling.

So far we have discussed the usual costs of quality. Now let us explore the cost of quality from another perspective. Hopefully we agree that, if jobs are properly specified, if staff members understand what is required and are trained to do the job, and are prepared to accept responsibility, then supervision should not be needed. Checking and correcting of their work will be the staff member's own responsibility. Ideally, jobs will be done right every time, and the customer will receive excellent service.

In operations management, the aim is to efficiently use resources to transform inputs into useful outputs. This is known as the transformation process. Anything that is done that doesn't add to the transformation is regarded as inefficient.

Consider a simple process in an office where an invoice is received in the mail and is eventually paid. The lapsed time, or cycle time, between receipt and the raising of the cheque and mailing out might be three weeks. During that time, the actual amount of time spent on processing the invoice might be 30 minutes. Some of the actions taken might be: validity checked, that is goods and services received; amount and price checked, discounts correct; then the cheque requisition is raised, the cheque is issued, and finally posted out. The balance of the time (three weeks less 30 minutes) the invoice will be waiting for processing. In the case of most invoices, some delay in payment might not matter, but in other cases discount will be lost or charges will be levied for late payment.

YOUR TURN!

Make a list of costs of non-conformance to quality standards for your department.

Supposing you believe your organization is achieving 99.9 per cent quality; that is, 99.9 per cent of the time, you achieve exactly what you have set out to achieve. I would imagine that you would probably think you were doing pretty well. Thought of in this way, 99.9 per cent quality in the United Kingdom would mean:

- One hour of unsafe drinking water per month.
- Two unsafe landings at Heathrow airport per month.
- 12,000 lost items of mail per day.
- 300 incorrect surgical operations per week.
- 15,000 babies dropped by the doctor at birth each year.

For a typical management college, 99.9 per cent would mean 25 mislaid exam or assessment test papers a year. Because 99.9 per cent is simply not acceptable in some areas (such as how a college accounts for exam papers or how drinking water is controlled), the 'statistics' above refer only to what might be if standards were relaxed. This does not mean to say that any organization is 100 per cent efficient in all areas of its operations, but in crucial areas it has to be.

I am sure you can think of examples of waste and expense that has been well publicized, such as the new road and flyover that was built for access to a refuse landfill. The only problem was that planning permission had not been obtained. Two years and £6 million later the road and tip were finally opened. Of course, government bodies can make large mistakes – they won't go out of business as a result. But what happens to a private company in a highly competitive world?

Conformance costs

How are such costs prevented? In some cases, a modicum of common sense might help. Generally, second-rate organizations – that is, those that have not embraced the philosophy of getting things right first time, or of giving all levels of staff responsibility for their actions – will resort to inspections, tests, close supervision and audits. These costs can be grouped under the heading of conformance. They are the costs of inspection and checking.

EXAMPLE

How much is your audit account? If you know in advance what the auditors want it is possible that you could reduce your account by up to 50 per cent. This will require schedules to be properly prepared, support information to be ready, inventory count to be correct, debtors and the bank accounts reconciled; in short, the figures should add up and be in a convenient form for the auditors.

YOUR TURN!

In your organization how many supervisors do you have? What is the cost of supervision? Would you need supervisors at all if every member of the company knew what they were meant to be doing, did it right first time, and were confident enough to take action or to seek advice if they thought things were not going the way they should be? If a staff member is bold enough to raise a concern but their fears are proved groundless, and the supervisor is sarcastic or disparaging, it will make the employee reluctant to speak up or make suggestions next time.

EXAMPLE

We began this chapter with Marty's dilemma. Marty used the wrong manual when quoting an insurance rate; does this mean that Marty needs more supervision? Or, does it mean that if Marty had been properly trained, the job was correctly specified, and if Marty knew the consequences of his actions, then perhaps no supervision at all would be necessary?

Supervision strategy

There are two possible strategies: the first is to increase supervision to prevent mistakes (increased ongoing cost); the second is to reduce the cost of supervision and to spend more time (one-off cost) on training. Which strategy do you think would be the most profitable in the long run?

EXAMPLE

In one advertising agency, now out of business, the handling of invoices was so poor that accounts weren't paid when due, not because of lack of cash flow but because of inefficiency. Eventually the agency's telephones were disconnected. Imagine an advertising agency, a business that depends on communication, without a telephone. What did that do for the customers' perception of the efficiency of the organization?

Levels of quality management

The four levels of quality management are:

1. Inspection.
2. Control.
3. Assurance.
4. Total quality.

Quality inspection and quality control

Quality inspection and control rely on supervision to make sure that no mistakes are made. The most basic approach to quality is inspection and correction of errors; the next stage, quality control, is to inspect, correct, investigate and find the causes of problems and to take actions to prevent errors reoccurring. Both methods rely on supervision and inspection.

Quality assurance

Quality assurance includes the setting of standards with documentation and also includes the documentation of the *method* of checking against the specified standards. Quality assurance generally also includes a third-party approval from a recognized authority, such as ISO. With quality assurance, inspection and control are still the basic approach, but in addition one would also expect a comprehensive quality manual, recording of quality costs, perhaps use of statistical process control and the use of sampling techniques for random checking (see Chapter 11 for statistical control and sampling), and the overall auditing of quality systems.

Quality inspection and control and quality assurance are aimed at achieving an agreed consistent level of quality, first by testing and inspection, then by rigid conformance to standards and procedures, and finally by efforts to eliminate causes of errors so that the defined accepted level will be achieved. *This is a cold and often sterile approach to quality.* It implies that once a sufficient level of quality has been achieved, then, apart from maintaining that level which in itself might be hard work, little more need be done. This does not mean that management is not taking into account what the customer wants or is ignoring what the competition is doing; it just means that the managers believe they know what is best and how this can be achieved. To this end, supervision and inspection become an important method of achieving the aim, with little input expected from staff members.

Total quality management

Total quality management (TQM) is on a different plane. Total quality management does, of course, include all the previous levels of setting standards and the means of measuring conformance to standards. In doing this, statistical process control (SPC) may be used, systems will be documented, and accurate and timely feedback of results will be given. With TQM, ISO accreditation might be sought, but an organization that truly has embraced TQM does not need the ISO stamp of approval.

Any organization aspiring to TQM will have a vision of quality which goes far beyond mere conformance to a standard. TQM requires a culture whereby every member of the organization believes that not a single day should go by without the organization in some way improving the quality of its goods and services. The vision of TQM must begin with the chief executive. If the chief executive has a passion for quality and continuous improvement, and if this passion can be transmitted down through the organization, then paradoxically, the ongoing driving force will be from the bottom up.

Figure 10.1 depicts a TQM culture, wherein management has the vision, which is communicated to and accepted by all levels of the organization. Once the quality culture has been ingrained in the organization the ongoing driving force is 'bottom up'.

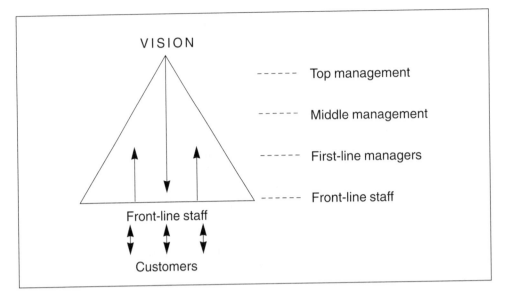

Figure 10.1: Quality and the driving force

Generally it is the lower-paid members of the organization who will be physically interfacing with the customers or providing the service, and it is the sum of the efforts that each individual puts into their part of the finished service which will determine the overall quality as experienced by the customer. Likewise, generally it is the lower-paid staff members, such as shop assistants, telephone operators and van drivers who are the contact point with the customer and the wider public. They too have a huge part to play in how the customer perceives an organization. It is on the lower level then that an organization must rely for the continuing daily level of quality. Quality, once the culture of quality has become ingrained, will be driven from bottom up rather than achieved by direction or control from the top. Management will naturally have to continue to be responsible for planning and for providing the resources to enable the workers to do the job. But unless the shop assistants, the telephone operators, the cleaning staff, the van driver, and the junior account clerk are fully committed to quality, TQM will never happen.

TQM, however, goes beyond the staff of the organization; it goes outside the organization and involves suppliers, customers and the general public.

Japan and TQM

Total quality management has its origins in Japan. (The acronym used in Japan is TQC – total quality control. TQC is synonymous with TQM.) In the 1960s, Japan went through a quality revolution. Prior to this, 'Made in Japan' meant cheap or shoddy consumer goods.

The approach Japan used in the 1950s and 1960s to improve quality standards was to employ consultants from America, notably Dr W. Edwards Deming. Deming's philosophy was to establish the best current practices within an organization, establish the best practice as standard procedure, and train the workers in the best way. In this manner, everyone would be using the same best way.

Deming's approach was to involve everyone in the organization and to win them over. He believed that quality was everyone's business. Deming said that to find the best way meant getting the facts, collecting data, setting standard procedures, measuring results and getting prompt and accurate feedback of results. He saw this as a continuous cycle: the continuous spinning of the quality wheel of plan, control, do, and act. Deming argued that once a consistent standard or stable condition has been determined, control is achieved by reducing variability in the processes and that this can only occur if the results are promptly and accurately fed back so corrective action can be taken to eliminate variations to the standard (Deming, 1986).

Deming emphasized that people can only be won over if there is trust at all levels. This means that management are prepared to allow and encourage employees to take responsibility, and that employees are prepared to accept responsibility. Employee participation, through understanding processes and contributing through improvement suggestions, is a serious part of the Deming philosophy.

American and European approaches

In the United States and in Europe – perhaps because senior management, bankers and investors are concerned with the annual report, the bottom line and the share price, and perhaps because increasingly senior management calls upon consultants for immediate fixes – the tendency is to expect instant results. The time frame is short-term, and if results are not readily apparent, there will be a move to some other solution. The Japanese, however, know that success is rarely an overnight phenomenon. The implementation of TQM, because it requires a total change in management thinking and a major change in culture, will take years to internalize. Thus TQM has lost favour with some organizations, because results are not instant. Where results are apparent in a short space of time, they may not always seem to be major. How, though, can you tell if there have been benefits and whether they are significant or not?

EXAMPLE

If after adopting TQM an organization is still in business and the results are slightly up on the previous year, is this something to be excited by? Maybe the shareholders won't see this as a triumph. But it may well be. If the organization had not begun its quality revolution, perhaps the results would have been much worse.

Sometimes, just a change in attitude and recognition of key problem areas can be sufficient to make a big difference. For example, when Jan Carlzon took over SAS, the airline was about to lose $US20 million. Within twelve months, by establishing where the moments of truth were between customers and front-line staff, he was able to turn a $20 million loss into a $40 million profit. Carlzon and moments of truth are discussed in more detail in Chapter 12. But this example is an exception: most benefits are incremental, and goals are long term. The philosophy of TQM is to look for a continuous improvement, not major breakthroughs; any major breakthrough will be a bonus. No organization can ever say that TQM has been achieved – the quest for improvement is never ending.

ISO 9000

The International Standard Organization 9000 series (ISO 9000) is the most recent international standard and is accepted as the world standard. Its predecessor was the British Standard BS 5750 (introduced in 1979 to set standard specifications for military suppliers). To gain certification, an organization has to meet rigorous standards and satisfy a third party, the accreditation authority.

Total quality management means more than just the basics as outlined in ISO 9000; indeed ISO 9000 could be seen as running contrary to the philosophy of TQM. As Allan J. Sayle (1991) points out:

> It is important to recognize the limitations of the ISO 9000 series. They are not and do not profess to be a panacea for the business's ills. Many companies have misguidedly expected that by adopting an ISO 9000 standard they will achieve success comparable to that of the over-publicized Japanese. One must not forget that the ISO 9000 standards did not exist when the Japanese quality performance improved so spectacularly: many Japanese firms did not need such written standards, and probably still don't.

What does ISO 9000 achieve?

ISO 9000 exists to give the customer confidence that the product or service being provided will meet certain specified standards of performance and that the product or service will always be consistent with those standards. ISO 9000, then, gives the customer confidence, so much so that some customers will insist that suppliers of services are ISO accredited. But what of the organization seeking ISO 9000 certification; are there any internal benefits?

First, by adopting ISO 9000, the methodology of the ISO system will show an organization how to go about establishing and documenting a quality improvement system. To achieve accreditation, an organization has to prove that every step of the process is documented and that the specifications and check procedures shown in the documentation are always complied with. The recording and documenting of each step is a long and tedious job. Perhaps the most difficult stage is agreeing on what exactly the standard procedure is.

If an organization does not have a standard way of doing things, trying to document will prove difficult and many interesting facts will emerge. The act of recording exactly what is happening and then determining what the one set method should be from now on will in itself be a useful exercise. Wasteful activities should be unearthed and, hopefully, overall a more efficient method will emerge and be adopted as standard procedure. Determining a standard does not imply that the most efficient method is being used. The standard adopted only means that there is now a standard method (not necessarily the most efficient), that the method is recorded, and that the recorded method will be used every time. The standard method not only includes the steps taken in the process but will list the checks and tests that will be carried out as part of the process. This will often require the design of new and increased check procedures and a method of recording that each check or test has been done.

From this it can be seen that the adoption of ISO 9000, rather than streamlining an organization can actually serve to increase the need for audits and supervision. ISO 9000, to this extent, can therefore be seen to be contrary to the philosophy of TQM. With TQM, staff members are encouraged to do their own checking and to be responsible for getting it right first time, and the need for supervision becomes almost superfluous. With ISO 9000, the standard method will likely be set by management edict and, once set in place, the bureaucracy of agreeing and recording improvements may stultify creative improvements.

ISO tends to be driven from the top down and relies on documentation, checks, and tests to achieve a standard, somewhat bland level of quality assurance. TQM on the other hand, once established, relies on bottom-up initiatives to keep the impetus of continual improvement. However, as the Deming method of TQM does advocate a stable system from which to advance improvements, the adoption of the ISO 9000 approach will mean that there will be a standard and stable system. To this extent, ISO 9000 will prove a useful base from which to launch TQM.

ISO 9000 – the wedge

As shown in Figure 10.2, ISO 9000 can be depicted as the wedge that prevents quality slipping backwards.

Notwithstanding the benefits of obtaining a standard stable system through ISO procedures, it must be queried why a true quality company should need ISO 9000. If the customer or potential customer is *not* insisting on ISO accreditation, then the time and effort involved (and the effort expended will be a non-recoverable cost) make the value of ISO to an organization highly questionable.

Gaining ISO 9000 accreditation is a long and expensive business. Internally it requires much time and effort, and most organizations underestimate the time and effort involved. Generally, recording the systems alone will require the full-time efforts of at least one person for a period of time likely to be measured not in months but in years.

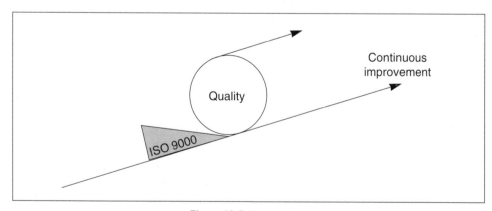

Figure 10.2: The wedge

EXAMPLE

One small print shop employing 20 people, and with one main customer, was sold on the idea of ISO accreditation by a consultant. The management was advised that the process of obtaining accreditation would take nine months. The actual time taken was two years and three months. The main customer had not asked for accreditation, but the difficulties experienced by the print shop in getting accredited led the customer to query the efficiency of the organization and the account was almost lost. What of the expensive consultant? Well, they took their fee and rode off into the sunset.

Internal costs of obtaining accreditation are high – higher than most organizations are prepared to admit. Total internal costs will not be known unless everyone involved in setting up the systems records and costs the time spent, and this is seldom done. The external costs can be equally high. It is not mandatory to hire an external consultant, but there are advantages in doing so. Consultants are not cheap and quotes should be sought from at least three consultants. Briefing the consultants will force an organization to do some preparatory work which if properly approached should help in clarifying the overall purpose and give some indication of the effort that will be involved. Once the consultant is employed, it will be the organization hiring the consultant that will do the work. Consultants point the way. They give guidelines and hold meetings, they will help with the planning; but don't expect them to get their hands dirty. They won't actually do any work – the organization seeking accreditation does the work!

Accreditation can only be obtained through an approved certifying body. The fee charged by the certifying body is relatively small. Fees depend on the size of the organization and the level of accreditation.

The ISO 9000 series has several standards: ISO 9000, 9001, 9002, 9003, 9004, ISO 14000.

ISO 9000 mainly deals with how to choose other ISO series standards for inclusion in a contract between a customer and a supplier.

ISO 9001 should be chosen if there is design work, or changes to designs involved, and/or if after-sales service is required.

ISO 9002 should be chosen if there is no design work involved and/or no after-sales service in the contract. Some people think that ISO 9002 is easier to achieve and that therefore ISO 9002 is a lesser 'qualification' to 9001. This is not so. If there is no design work involved or after-sales service required, then ISO 9002 is appropriate and it is no less onerous than 9001.

ISO 9003 only requires one final check and thus is not a good way of reducing costs of mistakes and of instilling into the organization a quality culture. Of course, ISO 9003 can be amended to include corrective action taken during the process and so on. If such amendments are made, then maybe ISO 9002 may be more appropriate.

ISO 9004 extensively uses the word 'should'. This means that an organization is not required to actually do anything included in the standard. ISO 9004 can only be regarded as an advisory introduction paper to quality management. It is not so much that what ISO 9004 covers is wrong; it is the lack of compulsion that makes ISO 9004 of little value for contract purposes. If a customer were to use ISO 9004 in a contract document, then wherever 'should' appears, 'shall' ought to be substituted.

The latest ISO standard being touted (ISO 14000)concerns environmental (green) issues. Again, if an organization has a social conscience and is environmentally aware, why would it need ISO accreditation!

Throughout the ISO 9000 series, reference is made to documentation. To meet the ISO requirements, it is not necessary to have hard copies of quality plans, quality manuals and procedures. Indeed, when people have a computer terminal at hand, they are more likely to search the computer rather than leaf through large manuals. Also, with a computer system, it is easier to update the records with the latest procedures and to ensure that the user acknowledges receipt of change when using the system. In this way the system can be kept almost instantly updated.

The other important aspect of ISO is audits. Audits can be carried out internally and/or by external auditors. ISO 9001 and 9002 generally only require internal audits. The audit requirements of the ISO 9000 series are more towards compliance checks after an activity has started or been completed. This type of check confirms that procedures are being kept to, or that an outcome complies with the standard. Where mistakes are found, they are retrospective. They will highlight where errors have occurred and thus indicate the need for corrective action for the future, but they don't stop the error happening in the first place. The most effective audit is the audit carried out before an activity occurs, with the aim being to prevent mistakes happening. ISO 9000 does not require this type of audit.

To be effective, the internal quality auditor should be trained in audit procedures and the purpose of auditing. Auditors should be there to help and guide, not to trap and catch. If the audit takes place before the event or process, it is preventative, and so much the better.

To summarize this discussion about ISO 9000, with TQM the aim is continuous improvement, with the continuing impetus for quality improvement being driven from bottom up. ISO 9000 will not achieve this. At best, ISO can be seen as a step on the way to TQM. At worst, it might actually inhibit TQM, as it relies on the setting of top-down standards and controls. A true TQM organization does not need ISO but, if ISO is insisted on by a customer, it can be made to fit into the overall TQM plan.

Quality initiatives

Kaizen

The Japanese have a word for continuous improvement: it is *kaizen*. The word is derived from a philosophy of gradual day-by-day betterment of life and spiritual enlightenment towards a long-term goal. *Kaizen* has been adopted by Japanese business to denote gradual unending improvement, but with a firm goal in mind. The philosophy is the doing of little things better to achieve a long-term objective. *Kaizen* is 'the single most important concept in Japanese management – the key to Japanese competitive success' (Masaaki Imai, 1986).

Kaizen moves the organization's focus away from the bottom line, and the fitful stops and starts that come from major changes, towards a continuous improvement of service. Japanese firms have, for many years, taken quality for granted. *Kaizen* is now so deeply ingrained that people do not even realize that they are thinking *kaizen*. The philosophy is that not one day should go by without some kind of improvement being made somewhere in the company. The far-reaching nature of *kaizen* can now be seen in Japanese government and social programmes.

Zero defects

The core belief of TQM is that it is possible to get things right the first time: zero defects can happen. To make this happen, an organization has to know at every level exactly what the goals are and how to achieve them. There has to be a prompt and accurate method of feedback, there has to be a philosophy of continuous improvement, and everyone at every level should be looking daily for ways to make improvements.

Paradigm change

All this means trust. The managers have to stop being bosses and trust the staff; the staff must believe in the managers. This may require a major paradigm change for some people. The end goal is to gain a competitive edge by reducing costs and by improving the quality of the service. To determine the level of quality to aim for, it is first necessary to find out what the customer wants and to be very mindful of what the competition is doing.

The daily aim should be accepted as being *kaizen*; that is, some improvement somewhere in the business.

Quality circles

In the 1960s, Juran said 'The quality-circle movement is a tremendous one which no other country seems to be able to imitate. Through the development of this movement, Japan will be swept to world leadership in quality' (Juran, 1988).

Certainly, Japan did make a rapid advance in quality standards from the 1960s onwards and quality circles were part of this advance. But quality circles were only one part of the Japanese quality revolution.

Quality circles have been tried in the United States and Europe – often with poor results. From first-hand experience of quality circles in Australasia and in the United Kingdom I believe that quality circles will work if the following rules are applied:

1. The circle should only consist of volunteers.
2. The members of the circle should all be from the one functional area.
3. The problem to be studied should be chosen by the team, and not imposed by management. Problems looked at by the circle may not always be directly related to quality or, initially, be seen as important by management.
4. Management must wholeheartedly support the circle, even where initially decisions and recommendations made by the circle are of an apparently trivial nature or could cost the company money (such as a recommendation for monogrammed overalls).
5. The members of the circle will need to be trained in problem-solving techniques and in how to present reports. The basic method study approach of asking Why, What, Where, When, Who, and How? (see Chapter 6) is a standard quality circle approach to problem solving.

6. The leader of the circle and the internal management of the circle should be decided by its members.

The overall tenor of these rules is trust and empowerment. Management of the organization have to be seen to be willing to trust the members of the circle to act responsibly and then must be active in supporting the circle. Although, initially, the circle may not appear to be addressing hard quality issues, as the confidence of the members increases very real benefits can be expected.

Side benefits of quality circles, but nonetheless important, are the fostering of a supportive environment which encourages workers to become involved in increasing quality and productivity and the development of the problem-solving and reporting skills of lower-level staff.

In Japan, the quality circle traditionally meets in its own time rather than during normal working hours. Not only do circles concern themselves with quality improvement but they also become a social group engaged in sporting activities and outings. It is not expected, in a European country, that a quality circle would meet in the members' own time; few workers are that committed to an organization. However, there is no reason why, once the quality circle is up and running, management could not support and encourage social outings for a circle, perhaps in recognition of an achievement.

Quality project teams

A problem experienced in the United Kingdom with quality circles was the blurring of circles and quality project teams. The project-team approach was top down, that is management selected a hard quality problem and designated staff from various sections to be members of the team. The top-down, conscription approach might appear to be more focused than the quality circle approach, but the fundamental benefits of a voluntary team approach are lost. With the pure, bottom-up quality circle approach, the members are volunteers and the circles consist of people who work well together and who want to contribute to the success of the organization.

Ishikawa (Fishbone technique) or cause and effect

The Ishikawa diagram, named after its inventor Kaoru Ishikawa (1979, 1985) or the cause-and-effect diagram is designed for group work. It is a useful method of identifying causes and provides a good reference point for brainstorming (brainstorming is discussed below).

The usual approach is for the group to agree on a problem or *effect*. Then a diagram is drawn consisting of a 'backbone' and four (sometimes more) fishbones are shown to identify likely *causes*. Common starting points are *people, equipment, method* and *material* (see Figure 10.3a).

The following eight causes cover most situations:

1. Money (funding).
2. Method.
3. Machines (equipment).
4. Material.

5. Marketing.
6. Measurements.
7. Management and mystery (lack of communication, secret agendas etc.).
8. Maxims (rules and regulations).

Example

Let us consider a situation where customers of a large international travel agency sometimes find that when arriving at their destination the hotel has no knowledge of their booking

In this case, to get started, the quality circle might begin with four basic possible causes: people, equipment, method and supplier (Figure 10.3b).

The circle will now have a clear picture of the possible problem areas and the linkages. The diagram will point the way for collection of data. (In this example, training and standard procedures would appear to be worthwhile areas to follow up, a second likely cause might lie with the suppliers (hotel systems), and finally the e-mail system might need checking. In a more detailed problem, sub-causes may need further breakdown until the true cause of the effect is determined. As in the basic method study examine stage (see Chapter 6) the main question is: 'Why?'

Brainstorming

Brainstorming should be considered as a fun way of identifying all the causes of a problem. It consists of a group of people being given a problem to consider with every person encouraged to make at least one suggestion.

Before the actual brainstorm process begins, it is important that the subject be defined and that the rules of the session are agreed. Members of the team will need at least five minutes of thinking time before the brainstorming proper begins.

Some rules for successful brainstorming are:

- One person to be responsible for recording suggestions on a whiteboard or large flipchart.
- Encourage everyone in the team to 'freewheel'. There should be no criticism of seemingly silly suggestions.
- Everyone in the team should come up with at least one suggestion, and other members of the team should not interrupt or make comments.
- Take suggestions by working around the room so that everyone has a turn.
- If someone is unable to contribute first time round, pass on to the next person.
- Typically, there will be a lot of suggestions in the first twenty minutes, then there will be a lull. Don't stop when this lull occurs but keep going, as usually there will then be another burst of ideas. Often the second burst provides the most creative ideas.
- Keep the initial ideas in front of the team until the end of the brainstorming session.

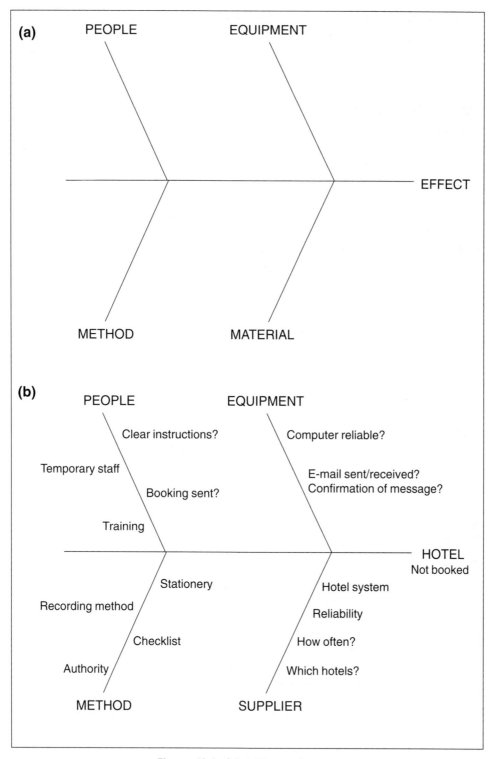

Figures 10.3a & b: Ishikawa diagram

- When suggestions have dried up, the team should review the suggestions made and sort them into logical groups. Some suggestions will be found to be duplications and can be eliminated. One method of sorting the suggestions is to use a form of the cause-and-effect diagram.

Establishing quality controls

The classic approach to management control is for management to measure and correct the performance of subordinates to make sure that progress towards the organizational objectives is being made. Planning, it is said, creates standards of action, and controlling keeps the plans and actions in line. Control is therefore the function whereby every manager, from senior management to the supervisor, makes sure that what is being done is what is intended. However, because this system of control relies on feedback of results, control tends to be in the past tense rather than in the present. That is, the manager checks after the event to see that what *has* been done is what was intended. In this model the manager cannot control without having plans and goals. A manager will use the plan, consisting of goals and targets, to measure whether subordinates are operating in the desired way. The more detailed the plan, the more precise the control will be.

The control process can be at two levels. The traditional method is for the manager to attempt to control, top down. The alternative method, the TQM approach, is to empower the worker, or a team of workers, so that control is exercised on the spot where the activity is being carried out.

For any activity, no matter how the control is exercised, whether it is through a top-down approach (where the aim is to control the activities of subordinates) or whether control is exercised directly by the staff, the same three control elements apply. The elements are: setting standards of performance; measuring performance against the standards; and correction of deviation from the standards.

Measurements and standards are covered in Chapter 11.

 CHAPTER SUMMARY

This chapter has covered the question of quality. Our approach is that quality is not a new or separate discipline, but that quality pervades all management actions. Our philosophy is that quality is too important to be left to the managers: it is everybody's concern, not only of those in the organization, but also of customers and suppliers and any other stake-holder.

Quality has two main aspects: it can be measured from the customer's perspective – customer satisfaction; and it can be viewed from the perspective of efficient use of resources. These two seemingly separate objectives are in fact inseparable when quality is considered. An organization that wishes to compete in the global market must be efficient and provide a high level of customer satisfaction. No organization will be able to afford to provide world-class service unless its use of resources is efficient and non-value-adding activities have been minimized.

The level of quality an organization sets for itself is a policy decision, and to a large extent the decision is driven by what the competition is doing or is likely to do.

In this chapter we also discussed the various approaches to quality, including ISO 9000 and the total quality management approach. Specific techniques such as quality circles and cause-and-effect analysis were also introduced. We concluded by reiterating the need for control and by outlining the basic control process.

CD ROM CASE STUDY

The CD ROM case study which applies to this chapter is New Zealand Post.

Chapter 11

Measurement of performance

Objectives for this chapter

In this chapter it is shown that measurement is needed:

- For control.
- To show that progress is being made.

The following key areas for measurement are considered:

- Profitability.
- Market performance.
- Resource utilization.
- People performance.

Additionally the following methods of measuring are considered:

- Score cards.
- Statistical process control.
- Benchmarking.

Introduction

This chapter is concerned with the need for quantifiable measurements to:

- Determine if progress/improvements are being made;
- Effect control.

The importance of qualitative measurements, especially in relationship to customer service, is considered. Key measurements are identified and methods of interpreting measurements, including basic financial ratios, are discussed.

Some people might believe that measurement is the province of the accountants and not an important area of concern for operations managers. While it is accepted that figures are not everyone's strong point, nonetheless unless standards are set which can be measured and results recorded, it will not be known if progress is being made or not. If all measurements are left to the accountants then control is abdicated to such an extent that they will drive major policy decisions. In Chapter 5 the financial imperative was discussed, along with hard (quantitative) and soft (qualitative) measurements of service. The need for measurement was further discussed in Chapter 10, our 'quality' chapter. Now in Chapter 11, the contention is made that rather than the accountants pressing Operations for returns and figures it should be the operations manager who is pressing the accountants to provide information.

This chapter therefore determines which measurements are operationally important and how the operations manager can use these figures to the overall advantage of the organization.

Measurement for control

The setting of standards is closely connected to planning and the setting of objectives. Standards have to be precise and communicated to and understood by all the members of the organization. Once the standards have been set feedback of actual performance and variations from standards are important. Feedback has to be made to senior management so that they can see if the overall objectives are being met, and to lower-level staff directly responsible for activities so that control can be exercised at the time, or close to the time when activities are taking place. In this sense control refers to determining progress in achieving the plan and taking corrective action as deviations to the plan occur. Figure 11.1 expands on the control cycle shown in Chapter 5 (Figure 5.1) to show that feedback is required at two different levels. Detailed feedback is required at lower levels where the activity is occurring, and overall (global) information is required for senior management. At the operational level the day-to-day measurements which matter are those which set a standard *benchmark*, and those which provide feedback to let the person responsible for a particular task or activity know when something is slipping below (or in some cases too far above) the benchmark.

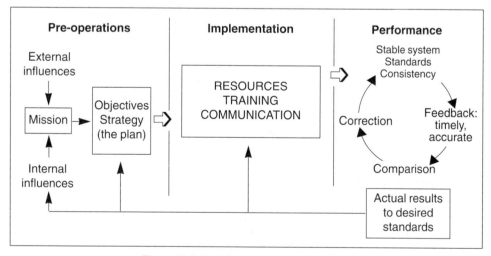

Figure 11.1: Feedback in the control cycle

Measurement should not inhibit creativity

In some organizations, especially those relying on the skill, expertise and creativity of staff, standards are often poorly defined and variation from standards is a matter of perception rather than measurable. Too much measurement and too many standards are likely to stultify creativity; thus it is important to keep measurement restricted to the areas where it will do the most good. Care has to be taken not to impose detailed measurement on people who have been hired for their creative ability.

Key areas for measurement

The key areas for measurement in operations management are:

- Profitability, or (for non-profit organizations) not exceeding budget allocations.
- Market performance.
- Resource utilization.
- People performance.

Stable systems

Before any standards can be set, a stable system must exist; that is, each individual and the team must know what is currently being achieved and what can consistently be achieved. Once the existing standard is known, and the method of achieving this standard has been agreed, the basic standard (to measure against) can be set.

Profitability

We would all recognize that if any undertaking is to stay in business it has to make sufficient profit to:

- service its debts;
- make a return to the owners;
- invest in new resources for future growth.

For non-profit organizations efficiency has to be demonstrated and management have to be accountable for the funds and assets that have been provided.

Most people would see that recording and reporting profitability and/or being accountable for funds used is the responsibility of the accountants; however, every manager, in particular operations managers, must know how the figures are compiled and must be able to read standard accounting reports.

Accounting requirements

Much of the information gathered by accountants is not relevant to adding value to the service or the product. To be fair to the accountants, they must meet demands made from outside the organization, such as the Inland Revenue, the company's office, the stock exchange and other regulatory bodies. Obviously regulatory and statutory requirements have to be met too. Likewise, people such as investors and bankers will also insist on financial reports that have been verified by external auditors. The collection of and the demands for any other information by accountants should be queried strenuously. For example, does internal charging between departments add anything to the value of the service or product? One question which should be asked is how does the time and effort required to collect and record a particular piece of information add to the value of the service being provided to the customer? In short, if this effort was not expended, what difference would it make to the customer?

Generally the customer won't care at all how costs are internally apportioned. The answer might be given that it is important to know what each section of the organization is costing, so we can control those costs. But if the costs are inevitable, then knowing the electricity cost for one department does not really make any difference. If analysed in this fashion, you might well be surprised how much information that is currently painstakingly gathered, reported and then queried with further information required is in fact of little, if any use whatsoever!

EXAMPLE

One education institution records every piece of paper that is photocopied, and charges the cost to the various sections in each faculty. At the end of the day the cost of photocopying does not change, but the wages of one clerk has been paid to track this useless piece of information. Occasionally an edict will come out that the overall cost of photocopying is too high and all staff (irrespective of which section) are urged to make all copying double-sided.

EXAMPLE

An accountant in an insurance office calculated that the cost of each policy issued, after all the transfer costs were calculated and a share of overheads were apportioned, was £88. He was puzzled when it was explained that using this logic to save money, we should halve the number of policies sent out, thus if 1,000 policies cost £88,000 then using his figures 500 policies would only cost £44,000, a saving of £44,000. The truth is, of course, that the direct cost of each policy is the paper and printing, the envelope and the stamp. In short each policy cost £2 to mail out, thus the saving would only be £1,000 if all the other transfer costs and overhead costs (including a share of his wages) were still there!

Most accounting departments could be cut by at least 50 per cent, and probably more, if they were restricted to recording what the operations managers wanted. The point is that while accountants keep themselves busy demanding useless information and challenging every other function for explanations and more detail, the other functions don't have the knowledge or time to challenge them.

YOUR TURN!

How much does the accounting function cost your organization? If you don't know (and most likely you won't) ask the accountants for this information, then ask them how they plan to reduce *their* costs by 10 per cent. Explain to them that internal charges are not to be included in their calculations.

Traditionally accountants have seen themselves as the major channel through which quantitative information flows to management. Accountants work on historical data of what has happened, and their reports cover arbitrarily set periods of time, with little allowance for the fact that business activities do not stop on the 30th of June or the 31st of December (or whatever other date has been designated as the time to take a snapshot of the financial position of the business). From a conventional point of view, and from the point of view of stakeholders such as shareholders and bank managers, there has to be a way of measuring the performance of an organization, and currently there is no better method than accounting reports. It follows therefore, that for accountants to do their job of reporting to meet the conventional and regulatory requirements, information will be required from the operating arm of the business. This cannot be disputed. Therefore if information is being provided, then it is useful to try and use that information to improve the efficiency of the organization.

Some information, such as that required for tax returns and annual returns, although it does not add value, has to be gathered. The question is: how can this expensive information be used to further the aims of the organization?

Basic financial measures
We will not delve into the sophisticated world of financial management involving the methods of financing, tax implications, currency hedging etc. However it is important that key financial concepts are understood, so that they are not used against what you are trying to achieve, i.e. the purchase of an important new piece of equipment.

Some key accounting terms are:

Sales or revenue
The total income of the business in money terms.

Net profit
The money made by the business after charging out all costs. This can be shown as before tax or after tax.

Equity
Equity or shareholders' funds, equals the total of all the assets less all the liabilities. Thus equity is the net worth of an organization. The equation is: assets – liabilities = equity (ALE).

Working capital
Working capital refers to the funds available, and is the difference between current

assets (debtors, inventory, bank balances and cash) less current liabilities (creditors, short-term loans, overdrafts, and the current portion of long-term loans). The equation for working capital is:

$$\text{Current assets} - \text{Current liabilities} = \text{Working capital}$$

It refers to the amount of money that would be still available if all short-term debts were paid and all short-term assets were turned into cash.

Increased working capital can only come from:

- Profits from operations.
- Sale of fixed assets.
- Long-term borrowing.
- Increase of shareholders' funds through the issue of shares.

A decrease in working capital can only be due to:

- Losses from operations.
- Purchase of fixed assets.
- Repayment of long-term loans.
- Distribution of profits (dividends).

The key indices relating to the financial objectives of a business are:

Trading margin	=	Net profit/Sales value × 100
Asset turn	=	Sales value/Capital employed
Return on investment (ROI)	=	Net profit/Capital employed × 100

Cash flow statements

Cash flow statements show where and how the working capital has increased or decreased.

Balance sheet (position statement) ratios

The balance sheet shows the financial position of an organization at a given date. It shows the assets, liabilities and equity (assets – liabilities = equity). The balance sheet is in effect a statement of financial position as at a given date. Many organizations now use the term 'position statement' rather than 'balance sheet'.

 EXAMPLE

Below is a simplified example of balance sheet figures. The numbers shown are to the nearest thousand to reduce the number of zeros for ease of reading and in making calculations.

Position statement as at 31 December 1999:

	£'000			£'000
Capital:				
Ordinary fully called	8,000	Fixed assets		14,000
Unappropriated profits	2,000	Current assets:		
Equity	10,000	Stock	4,000	
Term debentures – 7%	6,000	Debtors	1,000	
Current liabilities	4,000	Cash	1,000	6,000
Total funds employed	20,000	Total assets		20,000

Note: Assets – liabilities = equity.

Assets 20,000 minus debentures and current liabilities = equity 10,000.

1. Solvency ratios – these show the extent to which a company can meet its current commitments (i.e. pay accounts as they fall due and remain solvent).

Current ratio	=	current assets	current liabilities
	=	6,000	4,000
	=	1.5 :	1

This shows for every £1 owed there is £1.5 of current assets.

The working capital is 6,000 – 4,000 = 2,000.

Liquid ratio	=	liquid assets	current liabilities
	=	2,000	4,000
	=	0.50 :	1

For every £1 owed there is only 50p of 'quick' assets available to pay accounts as they fall due. Quick assets are cash and debtors. Stocks (of goods and materials) will take time to turn into cash.

2. Equity ratios – these show the extent to which the company is financed by shareholders:

Equity/total capital (funds) employed = 10,000/20,000 = 0.5
Debt 10,000 Equity 10,000   Debt: Equity = 1:1

This shows that the shareholders' funds are 50 per cent of the total funds invested in the business. The balance of the funds has been provided by creditors and term debentures. If equity is less than 50 per cent the business is said to be highly geared, and in effect the creditors would have a higher percentage of the funding of the organization than would the shareholders. With high gearing the future of the business depends on the continued support of the creditors and financiers.

3. Operating ratios – these show operating performance in terms of sales and capital employed:

The performance statement, or profit and loss statement, shows the operating results/performance for a given period.

Performance statement for twelve months ended 31 December 1999:

	£'000
Sales	12,000
Cost of goods sold	8,000
Gross profit (margin)	4,000
Operating expenses	2,000
Interest	500
Net profit	1,500

Return. (For these examples net profit is before tax. Some organizations use net profit after tax.)

Return on investment	=	net profit/total funds employed
	=	$(1,500/20,000) \times 100$
	=	7.5%

Return on investment (ROI), which is the same as return on assets (ROA), shows the earnings on the total funds employed. Return on investment is an indication of efficiency and can be used for benchmarking against other similar organizations. Return on investment is also used to assess the validity of further capital expenditure, such as an important piece of new equipment.

Return on shareholders' funds	=	net profit/equity
	=	$(1,500/10,000) \times 100$
	=	15%

In this example the business is returning 15 per cent on shareholders' funds. The actual dividend declared might well be less than this.

Return on sales	=	$(1,500/12,000) \times 100$
	=	12.5%

This is another measure of efficiency, and can be used for comparing with other similar organizations.

Gross profit or margin %	=	Gross profit as a percentage of sales
	=	$(4,000/12,000) \times 100$
	=	33.33%

The key measure is return on investment (synonymous with return on assets). If the return is to be improved there are four areas which can be examined:

1. Increase the gross profit margin. This only applies to organizations that sell goods; the margin can be increased by increasing the price without increasing the costs.
2. Reduce operating expenses. The aim is to be more efficient in the use of resources, i.e. less rent, wages, energy costs, delivery costs and so on. Operations managers should always be aware of costs getting too high and should be taking the initiative to control costs, otherwise it is likely (if costs are deemed to be too high) that senior management will make decisions for them. This leads to costs being cut that shouldn't be cut. For example, a 10 per cent across-the-board reduction of staff will lead to loss of morale, and the best (most marketable) staff are likely to be lost. If in our example expenses could be reduced by £120,000, profit would also increase by £120,000. Reduction of expenses of £120,000 has, in this example, the same effect on the profit as would an increase of sales of £360,000 (£360,000 additional sales at a margin of 33.33 per cent = £120,000). The same increase in profit could also be achieved by increasing the margin by 1 per cent from 33.33 per cent to 34.33 per cent. Sales of £12,000,000 at 34.33 per cent = £4,120 (an increase of £120,000).
3. Reduce fixed assets. This can be achieved by selling off assets, outsourcing (for example selling off your delivery fleet and using contractors), relocating to cheaper premises and so on. Selling of assets and then outsourcing may not always be the best business decision in the long term, although in the short term return on assets will improve as will the ratios of working capital and equity.
4. Reduce working capital. A negative working capital has to be avoided, otherwise creditors cannot be paid when they fall due. But if working capital is high then debtors' collection might have to be improved, and the amount of stock held would need to be looked at. In our example debtors at balance date are £1,000,000 and sales for the year are £12,000,000, thus debtors equal one month of sales. If debtors had been £3,000,000 then this would show that debtors are taking three months to pay. Stock is £4,000,000 and the cost of sales (stock) is £8,000,000 which means at balance date we are holding six months of stock. This could well indicate that we are overstocked and stock holdings and inventory systems should be looked at.

Market performance

The first measure is the sales and the growth of sales, compared to market share. These measurements should readily be provided by the accounts department (sales, sales by service category or branch, and sales growth). The accounts department should also be able to furnish information on who are the biggest customers and whether these customers are increasing or decreasing their spending with the organization. One would expect that the marketing department would also be passionately interested in this information, and would have it at their fingertips!

Chapter 4 discussed the requirements of the marketing department and

Chapter 8 explained how important it was for marketing to provide accurate demand forecasts. Much of the information marketing requires will need measurement expressed in terms of delivery times, cycle times, length of queues and so on. These types of measurement should also be a 'must' for the operations manager.

Customer focus

Sorting out what is useful and what isn't can be a problem. Usually what happens is that we rely on the accountants to tell us what they believe the key indicators to be. What an accountant sees as being important rarely has a customer focus. One method of determining which measurements are important in the market is to approach key customers and ask what they value; if speed of service is the criterion then we should set standards for speed of service and measure if we are achieving our objectives.

Resource utilization

Using budgets to allocate resources

The master budget for an organization should be the means of allocating resources to various areas of the organization to best achieve the overall objectives of the organization. In Chapter 3 we discussed how business policy was set. Once the policy has been set then resources have to be allocated to make the policy happen. The budget can be the means of doing this.

The budget can be used to:

- communicate to all departments the overall objectives;
- determine what actions each department will have to take to achieve the objectives;
- enable each department to bid for the resources necessary to make it all happen.

Resources will never be unlimited, thus ideally resources will be allocated to the areas where they are most needed, or will do the most good. In this way any activity that does not directly advance the cause of the organization should receive few – if any – resources.

The budget should never be set on the basis of what was spent last year (plus 10 per cent), nor should bids for resources be made from a desire to increase one's importance by having a large department (office politics are counter-productive).

If the budget is to be a positive activity each department manager has to have a clear understanding of the goals and all should be working towards the best way of achieving those common goals. By working together each manager will gain a good understanding of the needs of other departments. The final budget will be the culmination of discussion and agreement between the whole management group and should be seen as a positive way of giving practical expression to the aims and policy of the business. Once set, it is important that the budget is kept to. For this to happen feedback of actual results has to be prompt and accurate. Ideally only summarized figures should be provided to operations managers as a matter of course; and, to prevent paralysis by analysis, only if there are variations to the budget should the operational manager call for detailed figures. As shown in the example in Chapter 5 panic measures to reduce expenses and time spent on writing reports to justify why expenses are above budget are not productive, do not add value and merely add to the overall costs.

Measure only that which really matters and from which real action can be taken.

Budgetary control: negative aspects

One of the dangers of budgetary control is that the system takes over and the accountants go to ridiculous lengths to budget.

Remember that accountants' time is expensive. Don't forget the hidden costs of time and effort in meeting the accountants' requirements. Any cost that does not add value to the service or the product is a wasted cost.

If the budget is imposed without consultation and the operations manager is measured by his or her ability to keep to the budget, then budgetary control becomes a form of power play. The implication is that if the budget is not achieved, for example if there are not sufficient charge-out hours in a lawyer's office (revenue is not high enough), questions will be asked. Measurement for control purposes alone will not foster a climate of empowerment and is contrary to a culture where quality is the philosophy. Under such a method, many of the measurements will have nothing whatsoever to do with adding value to the product but will be designed to control and to police.

Cost cutting

Cost cutting or cost-reduction exercises, if they are panic driven (or 'chairman's ten per cent reduction across the board') will only give short-term results and will cause imbalances and disruptions in operations. Other concerns will be the negative effect on quality, innovation and customer service. The real business focus should be to survive and to retain the capability of competing in the future. Although strategy and innovation are important, the hard fact is that unless there is a positive operational cash flow the business cannot plan for the future. Therefore it is vital to have cost improvement even in a profitable company, but the approach must be cost effectiveness, not cost cutting.

Cost effectiveness

The key principles of a cost-effectiveness programme are:

- Understanding the strategic drivers of cost, i.e. volume/capacity, variety and variation and their impact in the marketplace and on competition.
- Evaluation of the effect of any saving measures on quality, safety and customer service.
- Identification of the leverage of cost structure and the setting of priorities for effort. As a rough guide the amount of effort allocated to manufacturing cost reduction should be proportional to the rest of the costs of the company.

Cost effectiveness is a continuous process for all organizations, but some businesses may require a quick and significant change in their cost structure. If so it may be expedient to form study or project teams to carry out *ad hoc* exercises, such as large-scale value analysis, restructuring or site rationalization (which might include branch and office closures).

People performance

Hard and soft measures

Measurement criteria can be 'hard' and 'soft'. Hard (quantifiable) criteria are those which can readily be measured. Measurements such as quantity, size, numbers of mistakes, numbers of customer complaints, days taken to collect money from debtors, cycle time of customers in a service system, delivery days, are hard criteria. If a system of recording is in place, hard criteria are easily gathered, easily checked and easily understood.

From the customer's point of view, it is often the soft criteria that will determine whether the customer comes back or refers your service or product to others. Examples of soft criteria include aesthetics. Depending on the product or service, this includes colour, taste, smell, ambiance, feel, as well as levels of finish (no rough edges, evenness of colour, flush fittings and so on). Other soft criteria include empathy, political sensitivity and genuineness of people (is the smile real? Do they mean what they are saying? Once the sale is completed will they still want to know me?) With a true quality culture the staff will all genuinely believe in the value of their product and service. The soft criteria will automatically be covered without the worker consciously thinking about what they are saying or doing.

Training for soft criteria

Obviously, some people will need training in new skills which may include grooming, acceptable language, basic manners and so on. However, a genuine desire to help, and faith in the product or service being offered, will overcome most social shortcomings. In any event, no manner of control from above can substitute for people who want to get things right and who want to improve quality, provided that they are empowered to do so.

Basic standards

First though, basic standards of the hard criteria have to be determined and agreed so that everyone knows the minimum level that is acceptable. The criteria should be to only measure what is important, and only if it has a direct bearing on the quality of the product or service.

 EXAMPLE

Within a building society it is possible to measure what staff are doing. For example, how many customer contacts per clerk, how long on average each contact takes, the number of accounts per head of staff, the number of transactions processed per day, and of course the control of expenses to budget. It is not so simple to measure waste in a building society or in most other service industries.

But how would the customer measure a building society's performance?

One large building society took a minimum of three weeks, but usually longer, to approve an application for a mortgage. No one in the society knew the average turn-round time but they all thought that three weeks would be better than average. All the staff knew this and all the staff agreed that the customers were not happy with this time frame, but the cycle time for the turn-round of a mortgage was not seen by management as a key measurement. There were other in-house measures, all designed to control and police, but none at all designed with the customer in mind. What a difference it would make to that building society if all other measures were scrapped and the only measure taken was the turn-round of a mortgage application, especially if the target was set at 48 hours!

Does it matter if Judy is ten minutes late to work on Monday, or if Doris takes Wednesday afternoon off to see her son's head teacher? Who cares if Charlie is back fifteen minutes late from lunch on Friday? The manager had a system whereby staff checked in and out on a time clock and the results were carefully tabulated and checked each week; an excellent example of non-value-adding work.

Need for score cards

All the big names in quality – Deming, Juran, Crosby, Feigenbaum and Peters – agree that measurement is important in achieving quality. Without a score card, it is not possible to see if improvement is being made. And further, if the organization is a group of 30 decentralized empowered teams, all striving to improve, it is highly unlikely that all will improve at the same rate. Therefore, by keeping a score card, it should be possible to easily see which ones are making outstanding progress, find out what they are doing, and then pass the information on to the others. One of the greatest motivators for a team is to be the best, and to be recognized as the best. This can only happen if there is a means of scoring and if the scoring is meaningful and is result-oriented (customer focus, not cost saving).

Meaningful measurements
Meaningful measurements should be decided from three directions:

1. Top down.
2. Bottom up.
3. Customers: internal and external.

1. Top down
Management's responsibility is to provide leadership and to determine the strategy for the organization. Overall goals and targets are also management's responsibility. The key figure for profit-making organizations will be *sales*. Sales targets should be broken down into product groups and into customer groups using Pareto analysis. Pareto analysis will show the top 20 per cent customers which make up 80 per cent of

the sales value and will also show the top 20 per cent products which make up 80 per cent of the sales value. The next stage of the analysis should then be to determine if the mix of products and clients has changed from the previous twelve months. For example, if twelve months ago a client was in the top 20 per cent of customers but this year is seldom using our services then we would need to know why. The answer is not what our staff might expect the reason to be. Glib explanations cannot be accepted. The only way to find out why is to ask the customer directly 'What has happened? Are you not happy with our service? How can we improve?' Such questions cannot of course be asked in a confrontational way, but they have to be seen to be a genuine desire to help and to improve the service. If your organization does not know who the top customers are, then these can easily be found from accounting records. Just sort through last year's statements.

For non-profit organizations, such as government-funded departments, or organizations such as publicly funded hospitals and schools, the key measurement might be numbers of patients treated, students' pass rates, and for a court the number of cases heard and so on.

Non-conformance measures

Following on from the sales figures, we should also keep statistics of sales non-conformance costs; for example: how many orders are delivered late, or how many deliveries are wrong in quantity, quality, or even totally the wrong product? Likewise we could ask how long we took to get the invoice to the customer, and was the invoice correct? We should also monitor the number of days that the client takes to pay the invoice. You might say that these are not sales statistics – these figures would come from several different departments. So what? These are the measurements by which your customer will judge you. The customer doesn't care which of your internal departments has got it wrong, for, as far as the customer is concerned, the XYZ company has fumbled again. And remember, it doesn't matter that 99 per cent of the time you get things right. It is when things go wrong that the customer judges you. When it suits them, customers have a long memory.

Non-conformance measures should be made to identify areas where extra effort is required so that problems do not recur, but never with the prime aim to catch out and punish.

YOUR TURN!

Were you aware that according to research carried out by the Co-operative Bank (reported by the *Daily Mail*, 23 November 1998), office workers spend 45 hours every year stuck on hold, waiting for their phone call to be dealt with? Steve Jennings of the Bank's Business Direct team was quoted as saying that 'customers often get their first impressions of a business by the way telephone calls are handled'.

What is the policy in your organization over telephone answering?

As a customer, what are your views on voice-mail systems? (Consider positives and negatives and what else could be done.)

2. Bottom up

If an organization is serious about quality, it won't take long for the organization collectively to sit down and to agree what measurements are important. Once the overall targets and strategy for the organization have been communicated from top down, measurements that matter can be decided by individual departments/teams. The setting of standards and the way in which conformance to the standards is measured will, therefore, be agreed from the bottom. These measurements will be smaller and will in some cases be self-directed and meaningful to the individual but bordering on the trivial to the organization as a whole.

Key measurements are those that are important in setting meaningful standards with the end view of satisfying the customer. It follows that measurements that matter are those where the impact of the outcome will be felt by the customer. These are the measurements which must be identified and which should be widely circulated. Score cards should be kept and trend graphs should be highly visible in each department.

Other necessary measurements

There are of course other measurements which must be kept, mainly of a regulatory nature such as some accounting information and health and safety records. Such records should be kept to a bare minimum. Ways of using such information to improve the overall process should be investigated. If possible, those records, originally kept for another purpose, will now become part of the key measurement data.

3. Internal customers

The test for measurement is to ask if what is being measured adds to the quality of the product or service as seen from the customer's perspective. This is where the concept of internal customers becomes important. At the individual level an internal customer is the next person in the process, or the person who gives you work to do.

 EXAMPLE

An author passes a manuscript to a word processor. At this stage the author should consider the word processor as the 'customer'. The author should supply the word-processor with the correct material and the material should be as user-friendly as possible. The word processor will judge the author by how legible the manuscript is and by how many times the manuscript has to be retyped. If there is to be a measure in this area, then it will be for the word processor, as the customer, to advise what measurements and what quality level is expected. The measurement could well be how many times it is reasonable for the word processor to have to type the same manuscript. The measurement will then be agreed between the supplier and the 'customer' and a benchmark agreed. A simple example certainly and, in most organizations, setting measurements by word processors will not be seen as a key measurement for the organization as a whole. But in an organization employing a team of twenty word processors, to be efficient, they do need the best possible quality of raw material to work from. *Note:* When the manuscript returns to the author then the author in turn becomes the 'customer'.

Quality has to be practised and measured at every level within the organization. The point is that key measurements and benchmarks should be determined from the customer's perspective. Internally, the customer is the next person in the process and, for many people in an organization, the customer will be internal rather than external. Measurements that do not help the organization to turn out a better end product are not key measurements and should be minimized. Key measurements should be highly visible for all to see.

Pareto analysis

Using Pareto analysis (see Chapter 4), the aim is to identify areas upon which to focus effort so as to gain the maximum results.

Some areas of measurement that could point the way for Pareto analysis are:

- Frequency of effort.
- Amount of errors.
- Overtime generated by the need to correct errors.
- Number of customer complaints.

Statistical process control (SPC)

Statistical process control uses statistical sampling to determine if the outputs of a stage, or stages, of a process are conforming to a standard. With this technique, an upper and a lower limit are set. The sampling is to determine if the process is operating within these defined limits.

Sampling can also be used at the end of a process. This is known as acceptance sampling. In this method, a sample is drawn at random and tested for conformance or accuracy. Examples of acceptance sampling are: the checking of entries on a computer printout, the checking of final documents for accuracy, or an auditor's check such as testing a batch of invoices.

Two methods of statistical control can be used together: random checks during the process and random checks at the end of the process.

The procedure for statistical process control within a TQM environment is:

- Define the requirements, including upper and lower levels of acceptance.
- Set up a process which will achieve the requirements.
- Provide the staff member with a means of measurement for the process.
- Train the staff member to recognize deviations.
- Enable the member to take corrective action.

With TQM, once the person carrying out the task accepts the responsibility for the quality of the product, supervision and inspection can be phased out.

The basic statistical technique used is the calculation of the mean and the standard deviation. The upper control level is the mean plus three standard deviations, and the lower level is the mean less three standard deviations. Statistically, with a normal probability distribution plus or minus three standard deviations will include 99.7 per cent of all of the cases. In effect virtually all cases will fall within plus or minus three standard deviations of the mean, likewise 95 per cent of all cases will be between plus or minus two standard deviations, and 68 per cent of the cases will be within plus or minus one standard deviation of the mean. In practice it is not necessary to calculate standard deviations, and a range of upper and lower limits is used as a measure of variability in place of the standard deviation. Figure 11.2 shows how results of a sample can be plotted on a control chart to show variations from set limits.

EXAMPLE

The policy in a service system is not to have more than two staff idle at any one time (the lower limit), and not to have queues of more than five customers (the upper limit), the ideal situation being no queues and no idle staff. The result of the random samples as plotted on the control chart shown in Figure 11.2 reveals that at least two of the four staff were always fully employed and only on two occasions was there some idle capacity, and that the idle capacity fell within the acceptable limit of up to two people idle. On the other hand the target set for customer satisfaction has not been met. On four occasions more than four customers were queuing for service.

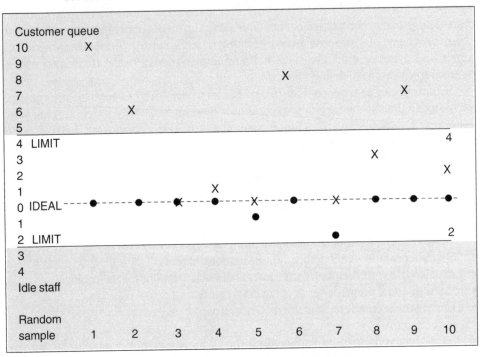

Figure 11.2: A service system control chart

The application of statistical process control requires two things: first, the process must be in a stable situation to be controlled; second, some knowledge of statistical techniques is necessary. It is strongly recommended that specialist advice be sought when setting up a statistical control system. Once the control charts have been established, then the maintenance of them becomes a fairly straightforward matter.

Those who wish to explore the subject of statistical quality control in depth are referred to *Production and Operations Management* (Wild, 1995, Chapter 20).

Benchmarking

Benchmarking can be done in several ways. The purpose of benchmarking is to measure your organization against another organization. The other company may not necessarily be in your field.

The accountant's method of benchmarking is to compare published annual financial reports. It is fairly simple to obtain your competitors' audited accounts and compare them with yours by means of ratios and by looking at various key figures, such as stock turn, return on investment, cost of sales and so on. It doesn't matter if company 'x' has £50 million sales and company 'y' and 'z' have £200 and £80 million sales respectively. If all three are in the same industry it could be expected that the percentage of costs to sales should be roughly the same.

Another example of benchmarking is given by British Airways who use the technique to spur action. They found that a Japanese airline could turn round a Boeing 747 in 40 minutes, but it took British engineers three hours to do the same task.

Unilever in England have entered into benchmarking agreements with other world-class manufacturers whereby the participants have agreed to exchange information about critical success factors. Some of the participants are American companies and some are European. The names of the organizations are not publicized and the participants enter into confidentiality agreements. In this type of benchmarking, the measure is not against competitors as such but against other manufacturers. The information given is used internally to highlight areas for improvement. Using this type of benchmarking, Xerox found, in their distribution system, that they had an additional layer of stockholding that could be eliminated.

Internally benchmarking can be achieved by comparing key measures of like departments, or even over the organization as a whole. Absenteeism could be a benchmark (if it was considered that this was a problem area).

Benchmarking is a form of measurement and is useful in highlighting areas that can be improved. However, there is little benefit in knowing that another organization is more efficient than your own unless the method of improvement used by the other organization can be determined.

True quality companies are generally happy to share their experiences. Their philosophy is that the more efficient the competition, the more efficient they will be themselves.

In other cases it is found that the competition is not always happy to share information, and even when they do the circumstances in each organization will not be the same. Recognizing this, Basu and Wright in *Total Manufacturing Solutions* (1998) developed a new approach to benchmarking against world-class standards.

Although aimed at manufacturers their methodology is easily adapted for service industries.

CHAPTER SUMMARY

In this chapter we have urged that operations managers have to take responsibility for deciding what should be measured and why. If there is no advantage to be gained from keeping a particular record then the gathering of that information should cease. No record gathering in itself adds value; all record gathering is an additional cost. It is accepted that accountants are required to gather and record some regulatory information for government agencies and for other stakeholders such as financiers, the stock exchange and so on. Where information has to be gathered then the operations manger should examine whether such information can be turned to an operational advantage. While there is some truth in the adage that 'if it can't be measured it can't be managed', on the other hand too much measurement will stultify, and lead to extra expense and perhaps even inhibit creativity. Measurement should be used positively to advance the policy of the organization and not as a means of power play to rule and subjugate.

CD ROM CASE STUDY

The CD ROM case relevant to this chapter is Tex Rob (Israel).

Part Six

This part consists of **Chapter 12**, which considers change and change management.

As stated in the Preface, the central theme of this book is that people make the difference in providing an efficient and 'quality' service. However, not all people in an organization have a passion for the mission of the organization, even when they know what it is and understand it. Some people come to work only for the money and do just sufficient to keep their jobs. They do not want to be empowered, they shun responsibility and consider management as being on a different plane. This attitude does not only apply to lower-level staff; there are plenty of examples of middle managers who are content to shuffle paper and wait for pay-day or retirement. In the twenty-first century, organizations with staff of this type will not survive for long.

This Part shows how to re-engineer an organization, first by getting the structure right, and second by achieving a cultural fit with the people of the organization so that everyone buys into the one vision and mission for the organization.

Chapter 12

Change and change management

Objective for this chapter

The objective of this chapter is to excite and to stimulate. The subject for debate is that change is inevitable. Means of change, especially of corporate culture, are explored. As this is the final chapter, much of what has been discussed in preceding chapters is referred to.

Issues looked at are:

- Structure of organizations and re-engineering of structures.
- TQM, vision and cultural fit.
- Using the mission statement for change.
- Model for change.
- Project management for change.
- Training and communication.

Introduction

We live in a period of accelerating change. Great political events change our perception of the world. Fundamental changes in society restructure our lives. New technology means that the impossible becomes commonplace. Change is all around us and the capacity to manage change effectively is the crucial attribute of a successful manager in today's organizations. (Carnall, 1993)

There is no doubt that people today are more travelled, better educated and consequently more discerning than ever before in history. Quality service, value for money and accountability are now taken for granted. Likewise, although innovation and technological advances are soon copied and any competitive advantage gained is only short-lived, failure to keep pace with changing technology could well prove to be a false economy.

Competitors are global, standards are world class, and organizations that are not striving to meet world-class standards will soon be found out. The breaking down of national barriers (with the elimination of protective tariffs) and the opening up of worldwide competition is seen by some as a threat, and by others as a great opportunity.

What was adequate in the past when information and communication were slower is no longer adequate for today. To reap the benefits of the new technology and the opportunities of the global market organizations must have the appropriate structures and systems in place. Knowing what the appropriate structure should be requires a re-evaluation of: what the organization is trying to achieve (its core mission), what the customers want and what the regulators expect, and what the suppliers can provide.

The organization has to be structured around the whole extended process from supplier through to customer – ever mindful of technological changes and the competition – with the focus on adding value and the elimination of non-value-adding activities. In short the organization has to be re-engineered.

In this chapter it is shown that re-engineering is not just redundancies and cost cutting. It is also shown that re-engineering requires major transformational change.

Needless to say the operations manager is at the cutting edge of competitive and technological change, and will be vitally concerned with both the process and the outcome of re-engineering.

For operations managers in service industries there are two basic types of change. One is the continuous and controlled change associated with the incremental philosophy of total quality management, and the other is major transformational change as brought about by the need to re-engineer to meet strong external forces.

Unless carefully managed, any change will lead to confusion. Elements of continuous improvement (incremental change) and the total quality management philosophy have been covered in Chapters 7 and 10. This chapter deals with the management of major transformational change and the overall change management process.

Communication revolution

Shareholders and other stakeholders can be excused for expecting that the rapid technological communication revolution of the last ten years would have by now resulted in increased performance, reduced costs and greater profits or surpluses. After all, communication of information is now meant to be instant, accurate and freely available. At the same time, with the well-publicized advances and promised benefits of technology, customers have come to expect, even to demand, improved service at less cost.

Management has been caught two ways: first by the need to justify by results through heavy investment in technology; and second by the expectations of the market for better service (including speed of delivery and up-to-date information).

Why then is it that so few organizations are seemingly no more profitable, and service is generally no better, than it was ten years ago? Figure 12.1 summarizes the operations manager's dilemma and indicates that the problem lies in organizational structures and communication blocks.

Unstructured reactions to change

Some organizations (perhaps many organizations) have taken an *ad hoc* approach to change with a series of knee-jerk reactions to major external threats and/or opportunities. With others there has been a reluctance to change and, as a compromise, matrix-type solutions have been superimposed on existing bureaucratic structures. In other cases rushed major changes, in the guise of

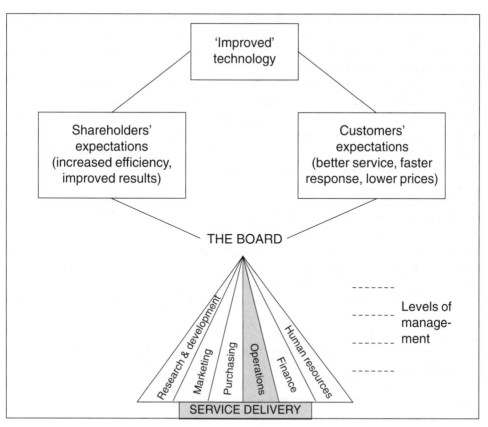

Figure 12.1: Service delivery

re-engineering, have been forced through without adequate planning and with very little appreciation of what the long-term effects might be. In most cases, whatever the approach to the changing environment has been, there has been a general lack of understanding of the magnitude of the changes that have occurred in the last ten years, and little appreciation of what is entailed in the *management* of change.

Change cannot be departmentalized

It has first to be appreciated that any change of a major nature cannot be limited to one department; for example it is not possible to increase service by concentrating on efficiency in one backroom department in isolation from the rest of the organization. Effective change has to be organization-wide at all levels, and the structure has to be such that it supports the intended changes.

Structure of organizations

Large organizations are still generally structured in the traditional hierarchical manner with defined functions, such as human resources, accounting, marketing, sales and operations, with each clearly separated into vertical departments. Typically each functional department is budget driven, and each divisional manager guards their department from other departments and tries to get as large a share as possible of the budget irrespective of the legitimacy of other departments' requirements. This departmentalization can be compared to bunkers or silos where each department considers itself distinct and closed off from the other departments. In some cases departments become suspicious of the motives of other departments, power is jealously guarded and, in short, a bunker mentality emerges. Departments tend to become inward looking with their main concern being to meet the budget. Apart from the duplication of effort and wasted time in fighting other departments and in guarding borders and responsibilities, it is equally likely that customers seeking information will be passed from department to department with no one wanting to accept responsibility.

The main problem, where the hierarchical structure of functional silos or bunkers is retained, is that improved communications technology has only served to speed up data collected within the silos, but communication blocks between departments have not broken down. In short the silos or bunkers now have more data, but information dissemination is no better than previously, and the power of each department has been most assiduously retained.

While organizations retain functional departments the benefits of improved communication and the real progress offered by becoming more open and more team-orientated will be squandered.

Another organizational approach that attempts to break down communication blocks between departments is the matrix structure. With this approach people who work in one department are assigned responsibilities which are cross-functional. This approach attempts to superimpose a cross-functional team onto a rigid budget-driven departmental structure. The problems of the matrix approach are the divided loyalty of members of teams, arguments over priorities, and of course the wrangling that arises from transfer of costs between departments and teams.

The budget-driven bureaucratic model is shown in Figure 12.2 and the matrix structure is shown in Figure 12.3.

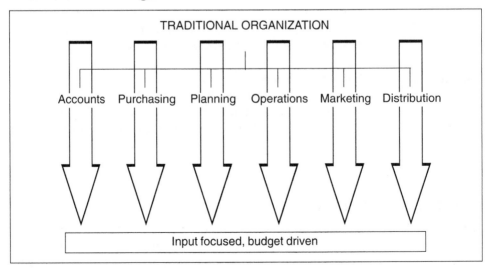

Figure 12.2: The budget-driven bureaucratic model

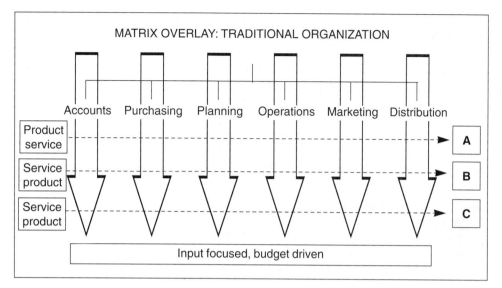

Figure 12.3: The matrix structure

Small organizations

The smaller the organization, the less opportunity there is to develop an organization consisting of separate functions. Very small organizations will of necessity be borderless with every member market focused (rather than budget driven), and each member will have a duty to satisfy a customer's query.

EXAMPLE

A small business employing fewer than twenty people will not need a human resources department, a planning department, or a marketing department. Certainly each person might have specialized tasks – one person might keep the accounts and pay the wages, another might be responsible for purchasing, and so on – but *all* will be customer focused. There will be little time for formal meetings with keeping of minutes, little time to write protective memos to justify actions taken, and no time to maintain records and statistics which are never read or used. Each person will be too busy satisfying the customers' needs.

Re-engineering structures

'Re-engineering' means breaking down the silos and re-organizing around the process to gain real advantages from the investment in technology. This might sound dramatic, and it is. Indeed, Hammer and Champy (1993) describe their book *Re-engineering the Corporation* as a manifesto for business revolution.

The term 're-engineering' emerged during the 1990s but many people are now confused as to what the term means. Many companies, especially in the United States, claim to be re-engineering but are, in reality, using the term to describe cost reduction and major restructuring. Major restructuring, involving the elimination of several layers of management and the creation of massive redundancies, is not re-engineering *if* the basic functional silos are still retained.

Re-engineering, properly applied, means that any activity that doesn't add value to the product, or any organizational or communication block that gets in the way of satisfying the customer, or anything that costs money without truly adding value is eliminated. This means the whole organization has to be questioned and re-aligned. It means getting a blank piece of paper and starting from the beginning as if nothing existed.

It is not an exercise in trying to make fit what we already have. It is an exercise aimed at scrapping what exists and starting again. Re-engineering is not about incremental changes: re-engineering aims at quantum tenfold leaps in performance.

EXAMPLES

IBM, without huge reductions in the workforce, claim to have saved £4.5 million a year by re-engineering, and Gateway Foodmarkets in the USA claim to have increased sales by 50 per cent and the margin on sales by 30 per cent.

Once re-engineering has taken place, then pressure has to be maintained to keep the new structure in place. Once stability has been achieved then a culture of continual (incremental) improvements has to be fostered.

People can change

The revolution should not start by scrapping all the middle managers (and then subsequently hiring young graduates straight out of university). Many organizations are today regretting this approach. Loyalty and knowledge are hard to recreate. Some firms believe the only way to get a new culture is by getting rid of the existing staff (it is thought that they will be set in their ways) and hiring new people with open minds, the belief being that it is human nature to resist change or that it is simply not possible for people to change. The people who hold these sentiments naturally don't believe that it applies to them; they, of course, are the enlightened ones – they can change, it is everyone else who can't.

YOUR TURN!

Are you personally capable of changing and of accepting new responsibilities?

Of course it is possible for people to change. People can adapt *if they know the reason for change and they can see a place for themselves in the new order of things.* There is considerable evidence to show that a mature, experienced manager is more likely to cope with major change than younger managers who have not previously experienced change.

The only thing that happens if managers are fired without anything else changing (assuming that the managers who are dispensed with were actually doing something) is that, given time, the layers of management will return. Changing titles and changing people doesn't change anything; it is like re-arranging the deck chairs on the *Titanic* – an exercise in futility.

EXAMPLE

In 1995 a service industry went through the agony of restructuring. Once there were fourteen managers reporting to the Chief Executive, after restructuring took place the fourteen were reduced to three, with some redundancies, some early retirements and some reductions in the ranks. The whole exercise caused uncertainty, a drop in morale and in overall effectiveness. Some good people, who had not been targeted for redundancy, resigned because they were suspicious of general management and felt it was better to jump before they were pushed. A massive investment was made in information technology. Now there are 33 managers. True, only six report to the Chief Executive, but these six have all in turn appointed managers to report to them, thus creating a new layer of management that hadn't existed prior to the restructuring! Although this organization believes it has re-engineered, and despite the heavy investment in technology and restructuring, income is only marginally up on the 1995 figures, costs have escalated and morale is still way down. And, worse, market share is steadily declining.

Re-engineering: more than redundancies and restructuring

Re-engineering is more than restructuring and redundancies and it is more than the adoption of a horizontal, flatter structure with fewer levels of managers (this being, however, one likely and desirable outcome of re-structuring). With re-engineering, the structure is designed to support the process. For instance, it might take on a circular form with several teams, each supporting a process, loosely connected, and communicating electronically (see Figure 12.4). Obeng and Crainer (1994) suggest re-engineering produces a fist-full of dynamic processes more akin to a fist-full of writhing snakes as shown in Figure 12.5.

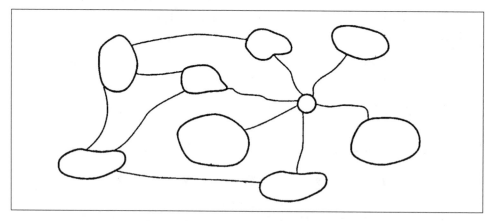

Figure 12.4 : Loosely connected structure

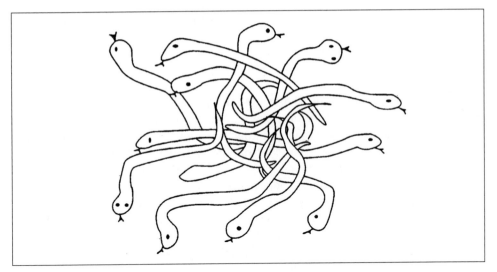

Figure 12.5: Dynamic process structure

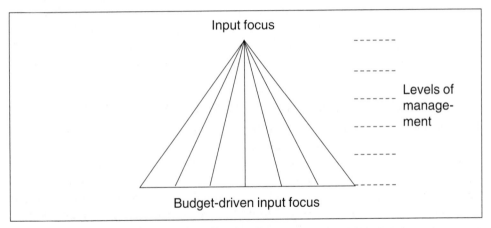

Figure 12.6: Bureaucratic budget-driven structure

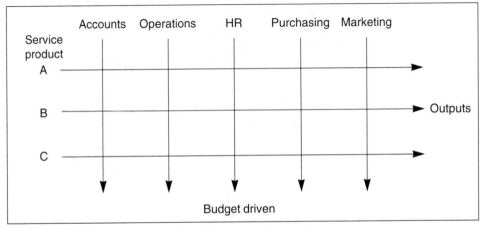

Figure 12.7: Matrix approach

Focus of re-engineering

The essence of re-engineering is an appreciation that the focus is the satisfaction of the customer through increased quality and by the reduction of costs that don't add value. Work is organized around processes and outcomes and not around tasks.

Re-engineering and structure

The old organizations were organized around functions and the flow of information. It was important for people at the top to have information about what was happening down the line. The bigger the organization, the further the information had to flow. Information was pushed up the line until it reached a person in the organization who had the authority to make a decision (see Figure 12.6).

Today with cell phones, faxes, electronic mail and its derivatives (Internet, Lotus Notes, AB Inform, and so on) information is just a fingertip away. Information is instant, accurate, global and cheap. This gets rid of one structural shibboleth. As Obeng and Crainer (ibid.) say 'The structure of the organization no longer needs to be the same as the information or reporting structure.'

Likewise, in most organizations, control is *managed* by setting departmental budgets and targets and by the allocation of resources to departments. Departments therefore are organized to fulfil a function and are usually groupings of specialists, such as accountants plus various levels of bookkeepers in one group, marketing people in another group, and so on. The result is that each individual is set targets and then measured against these targets by their managers. Thus the aim is to keep to budget with the first priority being the function and not the overall process. (The process is only completed and the service supplied to the customer after several functions have had a direct or indirect input.) Likewise the matrix structure, although designed to provide an output focus, is still very budget-driven (see Figure 12.7).

With re-engineering, one of the approaches is first to determine the key processes, secondly to recognize what has to be done and what resources and inputs are needed, and then to make those processes happen as efficiently as possible, always with the customer in mind. Attention will be paid to what really happens, and how the information networks exchange information and become meshed to make the process happen. In doing this, suppliers are regarded as part of the process. The functional structure is ignored in this analysis.

Adding value – quality of service and efficiency of operations – is seen as everybody's responsibility. Churchill once said that war is too important to be left to the generals. So too with adding value: everyone in the organization has to be involved and everyone, in the words of Tom Peters, must have a passion for excellence (Peters and Austin, 1986). But efficiency is more than an in-house concern; it is the concern of all involved in the extended supply chain. The supply chain begins with the suppliers of material and flows through the process to the customer (see Figure 12.8). Anything in the process where value is added to the product or service makes up the supply or value chain. Anything that doesn't directly add value to the product or service is outside the supply chain.

In the supply chain approach, not only are all members of the organization involved in quality and have the aim of making a daily improvement to the level of quality, but the suppliers are also expected to be imbued with the same enthusiasm.

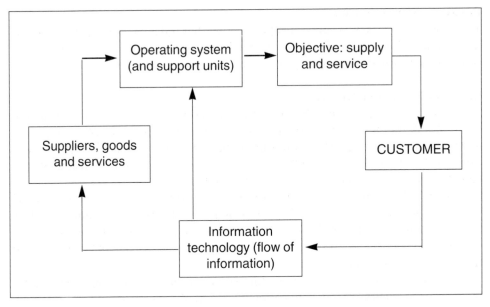

Figure 12.8: The supply chain approach

Likewise, if customers can be involved in advising and specifying what changes or improvements they would like, they too are a part of the supply chain and consequently are expected to be an integral part of the quality culture.

In this sense, the suppliers and the customers will, along with the in-house people involved in adding value to the product, be expected to incrementally force quality improvement on a daily ongoing basis. This is the basis of TQM: quality is everybody's business – not just the managers'.

Nothing is sacred
With re-engineering, nothing is sacred. *This is the main drawback.* Organizations that have been successful tend to look backwards for what is tried and true. The only problem is that conditions that apply today are not the same as those of even five years ago, let alone ten years ago.

Change is inevitable
We live in times of unprecedented change: organizations can no longer afford not to change. Those who ten years ago adopted TQM (see Chapter 10) have gone a long way towards re-engineering without the agony. For a start, they will have a culture that accepts change and is used to the self-empowered team approach. They will be in a good position to carefully assess how best to take advantage of technology with the aim of improving their product and reducing non-value-adding costs.

No organization can afford to be complacent. Change is here to stay.

The new structure

EXAMPLE

A chain of 40 retail stores, each employing up to twenty people, does not have a centralized purchasing department; each branch is authorized to phone, fax or e-mail their needs on a daily basis to designated suppliers. Goods are delivered directly to the branch and booked into the computer system by use of bar code wands. As each branch is electronically linked, stock transfer between branches is facilitated by the ease of access to information by any member of the group. Head Office can monitor stock holdings at any time, but their prime responsibility is not to police stock holdings and stock turns, but to evaluate suppliers, look for new products and to negotiate global (discounted) prices. Each branch and department of this organization works as a self-directed team, there is no large Head Office Human Resources Department (see Figure 12.9). The Human Resources Department consists of one manager and one clerk. They co-ordinate broad policies and issue one small, easy-to-read human resources manual. They also administer the payroll. Each branch manager, known as team leader, acts as personnel manager, and is responsible for recruitment, training of team members, and for dismissals. Team leaders do not see themselves as supervisors but believe that their role is to chase Head Office to ensure that the branches have every thing that they need to perform efficiently. Team leaders and team members are encouraged to

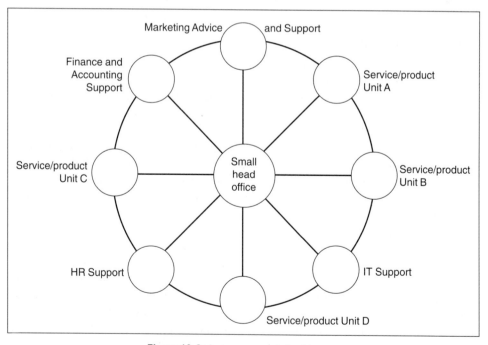

Figure 12.9: Autonomous linked teams

speak out if they think Head Office is not performing. The overall thrust is that front-line staff will suffer as little interference as possible; rules that exist are minimal. An organization such as this requires a culture where lower-level staff take control and accept responsibility for their activities. It doesn't mean fewer people working twice as hard, but it does mean the elimination of several levels of management and it does get rid of the matrix of responsibility for human resources and other 'service' or staff departments as shown on the old-fashioned organization charts. With fewer levels of management, communication has become less confused and responsibilities (and areas of mistakes) have become much more obvious. (Mistakes are publicized for all to learn from, and likewise improvements are not guarded but shared.)

TQM culture

To achieve a TQM culture will require a vision of total quality from top management. Top management has to sell the vision and the rank and file has to buy into its vision. Once the rank and file is won over it will be the force driving the quality bandwagon. Once the culture of quality has been firmly entrenched within the organization it will permeate outwards to embrace suppliers and customers. Once this happens management will no longer be attempting to dictate the level of quality and directing how the level might be achieved. Customers, suppliers and in-house, lower-level staff will be making daily incremental improvements and giving suggestions to management for larger, far-reaching improvements. As stated in Chapter 10 the drive will now be from the bottom up rather than enforced from above, and with everyone sharing the same vision.

Vision and cultural fit

The word 'vision' suggests almost a mystical occurrence (Joan of Arc), or an ideal (such as expressed by Martin Luther King: 'I have a dream'). The same connotation is found when looking at vision in the organizational context. A leader with a vision is a leader with a passion for an ideal. But unless the vision can happen, it will be nothing more than a dream; see Wright (1996).

To make a vision happen within an organization, there has to be a cultural fit. Corporate culture is the amalgam of existing beliefs, norms and values of the individuals who make up the organization ('the way we do things around here'). The leader may be the one who articulates the vision and makes it legitimate but, unless it mirrors the goals and aspirations of the members of the organization at all levels, the vision won't happen.

Culture and values are deep seated and may not always be obvious to members. As well as the seemingly normal aversion to change by individuals, often there is a vested interest for members of an organization to resist change. Often middle management is more likely to resist change than are other members. Machiavelli (1513) wrote 'It must be considered that there is nothing more difficult to carry out, nor more doubtful to success, nor more dangerous to handle, than to initiate a new order of things.' Human nature hasn't really changed much since the sixteenth century!

Organizations are made up of many individuals, each with their own set of values. The culture of an organization is how people react or do things when confronted with the need to make a decision. As shown in Chapter 7, if the organization has a strong culture, each individual will instinctively know how things are done and what is expected. Conversely, if the corporate culture is weak, the individual may not react in the manner that management would hope.

Engineering a culture

To engineer or change a culture there has to be leadership from the top. Leading by example might seem to be a cliché but, unless the chief executive can clearly communicate and demonstrate by example a clear policy, how will the rest of the people know what is expected?

Mission statement and change

In Chapter 7 we noted that often a new chief executive will issue a new mission statement ostensibly to signal a change in direction (although the real reason might only be to let everyone know that they have a new boss). Signalling a change in direction is a valid reason for the issue of a new mission statement, and any effort to change an organization's culture is likely to require the articulation of a new mission. To be effective, as discussed in Chapter 7, it is important that the new mission is in tune with what the people of the organization believe. To achieve a mission that fits the culture it would seem to be sensible to get the involvement and interest of all the staff in the writing of the new mission. Thus a change in culture could well begin with the determination and the 'buying in' of staff into a new mission.

Effecting a change in culture

To effect a change, there has to be leadership and a clear statement by the chief executive of exactly what is expected. Leadership does not have to be charismatic, but it has to be honest. Leadership does not rely on power and control. In Chapter 7 we stated that real leaders communicate face to face, not by memos.

Learning for change

If employees, organization-wide, are going to accept change, and themselves individually change, they will need to learn certain skills, such as:

- understanding work processes;
- solving problems;
- making decisions;
- working with others in a positive way.

All these types of skills can be taught. The main message that has to be taught is the need for cultural change, and for people to trust each other; in particular management have to win the trust of lower-level staff and have to learn how to change from autocratic management to becoming coach and mentor. Lower-level staff, in turn, have to learn to trust management.

Hammer and Champy (1993) have defined five roles which they consider essential to make business process engineering happen. These are:

1. *The leader* – a senior executive who authorizes and motivates the overall effort.
2. *The process owner* – a manager with the responsibility for a specific process for re-engineering.
3. *The re-engineering team* – a group of individuals dedicated to the re-engineering of a particular process who diagnose the existing process and who oversee the re-design and the subsequent implementation.
4. *The re-engineering committee* – a policy body of senior managers who develop the organization's overall re-engineering strategy and who monitor its process.
5. *The re-engineering czar* – an individual responsible for developing re-engineering tools and techniques within the company and for achieving synergy across separate projects.

All of Hammer and Champy's roles are required to support the three constituents of the change process:

1. *Why* (the vision and reason for the change).
2. *What* (the aspects that have to be changed).
3. *How* (the method of change including communication, training and the step-by-step implementation of the overall change programme).

Change is painful
Change will be painful and it will not happen overnight. Most writers and management consultants will agree that to change a corporate culture will take at least three years. Change requires careful planning, harmonious collaboration and a willingness to listen and to accept criticism and suggestions. The first step for a chief executive will be to win the Board over, then senior managers have to be convinced. Until there is wholehearted agreement and a determination at senior management level it won't be possible to sell the changes to the lower levels. At this stage, it is likely that some senior managers will opt for early retirement or will move on. Change and the 'giving up' of power will be too difficult for them to handle. As the change cascades down through the organization, it is likely that some middle managers and quite a few supervisors will also opt to leave. The problem is that for too long organizations have been built around those who give orders and those who take orders and it is hard for people to give up power and to trust the lower echelons to get things right. Some, too, will find it difficult to give up the trappings of power. The company car, the car park, the private office are all treasured and outward evidence of power and success, not only within the organization but to friends and family.

As the re-engineering process takes hold (together with the philosophy of total quality and value adding), *and* is accepted at all levels, executive privileges will become less important.

A leader leads by example; a leader does not need a separate office; a true leader will want interaction and to be where the action is.

The action is on the front line

The action is not to pore over figures and budgets and draw up new mission statements; the action is on the front line. With a quality culture, there is no room for people or for expenses that do not add value to the process. It is best to let people go who don't want or who can't change. This will be one of the hard decisions that will have to be taken.

'Structural teams provide the best means of distributing authority and accountability; thus they facilitate leadership that operates bottom up as well as top down' (Bill Creech, 1994). Creech believes that a decentralized team approach permits empowerment at all levels, especially on the front line, 'so that enthusiastic involvement and common purpose are realities, not slogans'. He adds that it doesn't matter how often the word 'empowerment' is used in the annual report, as long as centralized control is retained, leadership will not be able to operate from the bottom to the top.

Agreeing the need to change

The method for obtaining commitment and acceptance of change is, first, for senior management to agree on the need for change. Once the need is agreed, understood and accepted, the changes can be rolled down through the organization. This will involve strong leadership, discussion and agreement at all levels.

Schein (1988) points out that any change process involves not only learning and believing in something new, but unlearning something that is already present. Thus, no change will take place unless there is a motivation to change and the need for change is fully understood. All changes have to be negotiated, that is agreed to, before a stable change can take place.

Loose cannons are dangerous

Empowerment is one thing but loose cannons are dangerous. As shown in Chapter 10 it is not for a staff member to decide a change in policy or to commit the organization to a course of action when they don't have the authority. The staff member must know what the policy is and what their individual level of authority is. Empowered staff are those who are encouraged to show initiative and to make suggestions for changes to policy; they don't unilaterally make spur-of-the-moment changes to policies.

 EXAMPLE

A car salesperson will have authority to 'do deals' when selling cars, *up to a certain level*. The car salesperson does not have unlimited authority to make huge discounts or to give over-generous allowances on trade-ins. Part of the job satisfaction for top car salespeople is in negotiating and 'doing a good deal', thus a good experienced salesperson will be given more latitude to deal than will a less experienced person.

A car saleperson's actions might well be isolated from the rest of the organization. In other cases, where a staff member is part of a larger process, then the dangers of unilateral decision-making will be obvious. Thus people cannot take it upon themselves to make a change that will impact on another staff member or on another department; such changes have to be approved at a higher level where the impact of changes throughout the system can be evaluated.

In a stable system – where standards are known and consistency of performance is being achieved – staff should be empowered to make corrections at the lowest possible level. For this to happen people have to know what is expected, feedback of results has to be accurate and timely, and staff have to know what corrective actions they can take.

EXAMPLE

Scandinavian Airlines (SAS) was a very efficient organization. They knew their business – transporting goods and people by air – and they did this with clinical efficiency. But when Jan Carlzon took over as President of SAS he found that the company was about to lose $US20 million. Within one year, he had turned the loss of $20 million into a profit of $54 million.

Carlzon determined that the airline had sufficient resources and well-trained staff and that ten million passengers were carried each year. He then established that for each passenger there were five occasions when the passenger came into contact with front-line employees and that this contact lasted on average fifteen seconds. He called these contact times 'moments of truth'. 'Last year ten million customers came into contact with approximately five SAS employees, and this contact lasted an average of fifteen seconds each time. Thus, "SAS" is "created" in the minds of the customers 50 million times a year, fifteen seconds at a time. These 50 million "moments of truth" are the moments that ultimately determine whether SAS will succeed or fail as a company. They are moments when we must prove to our customers that SAS is their best alternative' (Carlzon, 1989).

YOUR TURN!

When do 'moments of truth' occur in your organization? When does your customer come into direct contact with your organization?

For some organizations, the moment of truth might only be three times: once when the order is placed with the salesperson, once when delivery is taken, and once when the invoice is received. In many service organizations there might only be one moment of truth: that is, the service will be provided and paid for at the same time. No matter how many moments of truth your customers have, there won't be many and they don't last long – as Carlzon discovered. And once the 'golden' moment has passed it cannot be recaptured.

A moment of truth is a moment when your staff have an opportunity to prove to the client that your organization is the best. Usually the person the customer will come into contact with will be one of the lower-paid members of an organization. It could be the telephone operator, it could be the cashier, or the check-out person in the supermarket. Or it could be the driver of the van, which has your name emblazoned on it, who dangerously overtakes a potential customer. It is a good idea to have your name in large letters on the van, but not if the driver is an aggressive youth with seemingly suicidal/homicidal tendencies.

Establishing which staff are the contact points should not be hard to do. Training them in simple courtesy, good grooming, and perhaps providing them with a smart uniform would be a good start. It would also be a sound investment to train these people in basic product knowledge, where to go for help, and how to handle difficult customers. Such investment will be well rewarded. It should be stressed that the customer is not always right, and that the staff member must therefore know what can be given or offered.

Continuous improvement should be to encourage – but as a team approach, not by one person 'doing their own thing'.

Specification

In considering Carlzon's moments of truth, it must be remembered that SAS was efficient in moving people and goods. Perhaps they weren't so good at distinguishing people from goods, but the basics were all there. Goods and people got to their destinations safely and on time. The corollary to this is that it is no good having polite and efficient front-line staff, if the product or service is not up to the customer's specifications.

 EXAMPLE

Consider the restaurant where the owners have got the right location, spent a fortune on the decor, had the furniture ergonomically designed and a lighting expert determine the right level to eat by. The string quartet is obvious but not obtrusive and the serving staff are well groomed, courteous and helpful. Despite all of this, if the food is cold or overcooked the moment of truth will be very negative. The basics have to be right and the product or service provided must be what the customer wants.

 EXAMPLE

Recently a dentist took over an existing practice. She asked advice on how to improve her service. Her own opinion was that the waiting room was shabby and needed upgrading. New carpet, a coat of paint, comfortable chairs, pot plants, current magazines, and perhaps piped music; these were all improvements that she was considering. Without seeing the waiting room, my comment was 'but people don't want to be sitting in the waiting room at all. You should concentrate on keeping to your appointment timetable – this surely is more important that the comfort of the waiting room'.

In a dentist's surgery it is desirable to keep the moments of truth as short as possible!

Once basics are being regularly and consistently achieved, moments of truth will help in selling the image that you want to your customers, but the basics must first be satisfied.

Adding value

Does the customer care if the boss's office is well furnished? What benefit is it to the customer that the accounting section has pot plants and that the accountant has a new desk? The only concern to the customer is that the product or service is fit for their purpose, that is, it does what they want, is provided at the right time, the price is right and the staff they deal with are knowledgeable, helpful and pleasant. For the customer anything else is not important: they simply don't want to know. Within an organization, any money that is spent that does not add value to the service or product or which will not eventually add value (such as research and development) is a cost that should be queried and then queried again. Certainly you might be able to show that contented staff will give better service to the customer and therefore an up-market cafeteria is justified, but first it is essential to define the key points: *where is value added?* and *where do moments of truth occur?*

EXAMPLE

Nevan plays golf (but not very well . . . Joy). Sometimes he loses a golf ball (often . . . Joy). This means that, in a moment of stress (having just lost a ball, and taken the required penalty stroke), he extracts from his bag a small box containing a new ball wrapped in tissue paper. Why do new golf balls come wrapped in a piece of tissue paper inside a small square box? From a customer's point of view, the paper and the box do not add value. A golf ball is not a delicate object, it is designed to be hit hard with a piece of steel. It does not need the protection of being wrapped in tissue, nor does it have to be cradled in a box. There is no useful purpose for either the tissue paper or for the box, and they are both pieces of rubbish that Nevan is stuck with, just when he doesn't need any further stress. They certainly do not add value, but they most certainly have added to the supplier's cost. Only the customer can judge if a moment of truth is positive, only the customer knows what they want.

Learning for change

Having agreed that change has to be organization-wide, requires the development of a strong corporate culture, and that people can change, what is required of managers? Managers will have to learn how to make the transition from being autocratic to becoming a mentor and coach. What of staff? Staff have to be given the opportunity to learn new skills and new technology. They also have to develop the skills of working with people and working as a team. These issues were discussed in Chapter 7.

Model for change

Many organizations start a change programme without going through the earlier stages of identifying the real requirements. Change programmes that are not carefully planned and managed are doomed to failure, because not only is it likely that the improvement strategy will be wrong but also the necessary commitment and culture will not have been developed.

Making changes and improvements should be a continuous process, but to sustain continuous change is as difficult as initiating and implementing change. To keep the momentum going, it is necessary to evaluate if the change process has produced results and to keep developing ongoing improvement activities.

The success of any project is underpinned by management commitment, organization and resources. Building a commitment for all the stakeholders, inside and outside the company, involves the understanding of why improvement is needed and the nature of improvement. It is a common phenomenon for various factions to appreciate why a change is required but at the same time to believe that the need to change does not necessarily apply to them. As we have said in earlier chapters, the culture of the organization has to be such that everyon, from the cleaner to the chief executive, believes that they have a personal part to play in making changes. The prerequisite for change is the vision and the will to change based on a culture that will accept change.

It is vital that detailed discussion and agreement occurs throughout the company as to what, how, when and where change should take place and whom should be involved.

The model for change given below is based on that developed by Basu and Wright (1998) and consists of four phases:

1. Start-up.
2. Self-analysis.
3. Making changes.
4. Feedback.

1. Start-up

The key task for senior management is to decide what improvement opportunity areas have the greatest impact for the business. However, a significant number of companies that initiate a change programme do so because they feel their survival is threatened. Our recommendation is that before any improvement is attempted, self-analysis takes place to identify the weaknesses and the gaps in performance. A self-analysis process does not start on its own. Any benchmarking programme requires full commitment, preparation and planning. The start-up phase contains three major steps:

- Recognition of need for change.
- Organization.
- Launch.

Recognition of need for change
It is vital that top management and the Board wholeheartedly recognize the need for a change programme. This recognition may be prompted by a reaction to current company performance, a threat from a new competitor or a strategic change (e.g. a merger or an internal report from any of the key stakeholders). The Board and management must believe that serious action has to be taken. Major, panic-driven changes can destroy a company. Poorly planned change is worse than no change. Change has to be planned, methodical and relentless.

At this stage it may be helpful to conduct a limited number of consultation workshops with key stakeholders to acquire agreement and understanding about the need to change. The outcome of this will be the full commitment of top management and the support of the stakeholders. The programme begins with the formation of a project team.

Project management for change
The organization phase involves a clear project brief, appointment of a project team and a project plan. The project brief must clearly state the purpose of the project and the deliverables expected from the project. There is no rigid model for the structure of the project team. Basic elements of Basu and Wright's (1998) recommended project structure are shown in Figure 12.10.

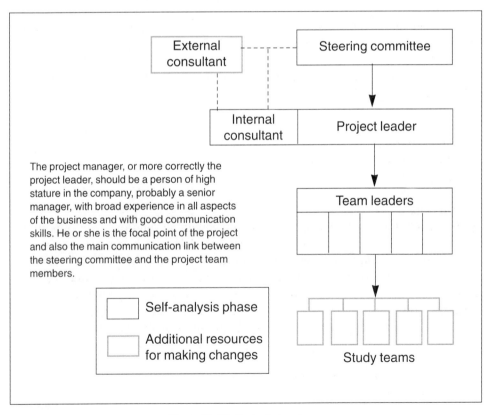

Figure 12.10: Project structure

Steering committee

To ensure a high level of commitment and ownership to the project the steering committee should be drawn from members of the Board and include senior management. Their role is to provide support and resources, define the scope of the project consistent with corporate goals, set priorities and consider and approve the project team's recommendations.

Project leader

The project leader should be a senior manager, with broad experience in all aspects of the business and with good communication skills. He or she is the focal point of the project and also the main communication link between the steering committee and the project team members.

The role of the project leader can be likened to that of a consultant. However, if a line manager is given the task of project leadership as an additional responsibility to his or her normal job, then an experienced staff manager can be co-opted to support the leader. The project leader's role (similar to Hammer and Champy's czar – see above) is to:

* provide necessary awareness and training for the project team, especially regarding multi-functional issues;
* facilitate the work of various project groups and help them develop design changes;
* interface with other departments.

In addition to the careful selection of the project leader, two other factors are important in forming the team. First, the membership size should be kept within manageable limits. Second, the members should bring with them not only analytical skills but also in-depth knowledge of the total business covering marketing, finance, information technology and human resources. The minimum number of team members should be three, and the maximum number should be six. Any more than six can lead to difficulties in arranging meetings, communicating and in keeping to deadlines. The dynamics within a group of more than six people allows sub-groups to develop. The team should function as an action group, rather than as a committee that deliberates and makes decisions. Their role is:

* to provide objective input in the areas of their expertise during the self-analysis phase;
* to lead activities during the making-changes phase.

For the project leader the responsibilities of the project include:

* education of all the members of the company;
* establishing study teams to recommend changes;
* regular reporting to the steering committee;
* regular reporting of progress company-wide to all the members of the company.

Obviously the project leaders cannot do all this work themselves; but they have to be the type of people who know how to make things happen and who can motivate people to help make things happen. To assist in various phases, study teams should be formed to work with the project leader.

We strongly recommend Eddie Obeng's book *All Change! The Project Leader's Secret Handbook* (1994) as essential reading for project leaders.

Study teams
In general, study teams should be formed after the self-analysis phase, but in selected areas. However, some members of study teams can assist in the original data-collection phase and also in the analysis phase. The members of the study team represent all levels of employees in the organization and are the key agents for making changes. Their role is to develop design changes and submit recommendations to the project leader.

External consultants
The use of an external consultant at various stages of the project might be useful to supplement your own resources. However, a consultant cannot know your company as well as your own staff do. It could be argued that a consultant not only brings his or her expertise and experience but will also act as a catalyst during the total implementation process. Likewise, in the initial stages, consultants can be effectively used in training the staff of organizations in both analytical tools and in assisting with culture change. In my opinion the best time to employ a consultant is probably after self-analysis has been completed and after the selection of a change strategy has been made.

Launch
It is critical that all stakeholders (managers, employees, unions, suppliers and key customers) who may be immediately impacted by the programme are clearly identified. Internal stakeholders must be consulted and kept fully informed at every stage of the programme. After the organization phase the next milestone is the formal launching of the programme. The nature of launching can be either low key or a big bang. It is recommended that before self-analysis a low-key, but not a secretive, approach is more appropriate. Too much excitement and too high an expectation could be counter-productive if it leads to uncertainty. It will be only after self-analysis that an improvement strategy can be finalized. A high-profile launch would therefore be more appropriate once the change strategy has been approved by the steering committee.

The nature of the launch sets the tone for how future communication will take place. It is absolutely essential that senior management give strong and visible support.

2. Self-analysis
After the launch the project team will be involved with the self-analysis of the organization. This is basically do-it-yourself benchmarking. The steps are to establish key measures as discussed in Chapter 11 and analyse how well the organization is performing against these measures. Additionally, obtain reports on the best

organizations known to you in your field and try to judge your performance against theirs. Identify the vision, mission and key values of your organization. How does actual performance compare to the stated vision and mission? Are resources, system structure and your people capable or sufficient to meet your service objectives? How is quality determined and measured? And so on. Once a questioning attitude such as this has been introduced it will be surprising how many weaknesses will be discovered. However, it is not only weaknesses that must be recognized, it is equally important to know your strengths. Remember, this is not a witch-hunt but an honest attempt to recognize the need for change and what has to be changed.

3. Making changes

In this phase the change process moves on to the action programme to make the changes happen. Having chosen the improvement strategy, the detailed work of implementing the changes will be influenced by the strategy. We have found it to be effective to name the total initiative (e.g. Project 2002) so that everyone in the organization can identify it as a 'single issue improvement culture' that transcends divisional boundaries.

4. Feedback

It is possible that after spending several weeks with the self-analysis phase employees outside the core project group may demonstrate scepticism. If this shows signs of occurring it may be necessary for top management to re-launch the initiative, for example '2001 Stage Two'.

If this is done the project team will need reconfirmation. There is an obvious advantage in continuing with some of the same people involved in '2002 Stage One'. Their experience, new-found company-wide knowledge, and their belief in the recommendations should not be undervalued.

The project leader will be responsible for writing implementation plans indicating key tasks, responsibilities, deliverables, resource requirements and target dates. It is recommended that the project plan will include a critical path, and that periodic reviews and reports by the project leader be made to the steering committee.

Process design

Process design relates to the actual transformation of an operation, procedure, organization or facilities from the current state to a desirable future state.

The steering committee should be kept informed of all changes and their progress. There is no advantage to be gained by being secretive. A world-class organization does not have secrets or hidden agendas.

Training and communication

Training and communication of people throughout the organization is essential. Key points are:

1. The objective is to share information and change processes among the stakeholders at all levels of the organization, e.g.:

- Top management, and the Board, must understand enough about the improvement programmes to know how the changes will affect the business. They must know what is happening and show leadership so things will happen.
- Project team education. The study team needs to have a detailed understanding of what is planned for their area and a good overall understanding of the big picture. They are the ones who will be responsible for working with and training people in process design changes in sections and units of the company.
- Middle management and staff education. While everyone cannot be on project teams, everyone has a role to play in the improvement programme. Therefore everyone on the staff must be informed of how their work will be affected.
- Employee training. No change process will work if the employees in the front office oppose it either directly or indirectly. Employee involvement and training are vital to the success of an implementation plan.
- Communication to trade unions. It is critical that the representatives of unions and other staff representative bodies are kept informed at critical stages of the implementation of how the change process will affect their members.

2. The communication among the stakeholders should be full and open. A change programme cannot be built upon any false pretence. Success depends on trust. Secret agendas don't remain secret for long. Leaked information is always more damaging than official information. Damage limitation can be costly and time-consuming.

3. Learning programmes should be properly structured.
   - There should be a learning manager with a focused role.
   - On-the-job learning should be accomplished through team leaders.
   - An external human resources consultant may be valuable in guiding the learning and to effect a culture change.

Installation

The installation phase involves the planning and physical actions necessary for putting the changes into place. Separate capital proposals may be required, and these should be channelled through the steering committee. Other likely expenditure will include modification of premises and office layouts. It is important that proper authorization be obtained for any expenditure before it is incurred. The project has to lead by example and cannot be seen to be taking short cuts.

The installation stage consists of a large number of concurrent and parallel activities including selection of equipment, revising layout, improvement of process capability, commissioning, training and so on. It is useful to prepare a project schedule showing the critical path and all the necessary resources.

Some people understand a system conceptually but cannot accept it unless they can see it in action. Pilot projects can demonstrate results and validate the purpose of the change. It can be a great advantage to move along the learning curve by a trial at a group of branches rather than going organization-wide in one hit.

Feedback

The phase of feedback involves the continuous need to sustain what has been achieved and to identify further opportunities for improvement.

It is at least as difficult to sustain changes as it is to design and install them. Keeping the change process going by regular feedback is a different process from that of making changes. It usually calls for different approaches and sometimes the responsibility of this phase may shift to a different team.

The feedback phase contains two inter-related milestones – evaluation and continuous development.

The progress of the changes should be monitored at regular intervals, usually by comparing the actual results with target performance levels.

All the staff of the organization have to understand the purpose of the project, believe in it and wholeheartedly support it. It goes without saying that the lead must come from the top of the organization. To get the full commitment of the whole organization might mean a major change in culture. Changing the culture is likely to be part of the improvement strategy.

CHAPTER SUMMARY

This chapter has covered the need for change, the process for re-engineering, the need for an organizational structure which will support re-engineering and the constituents of a successful change programme. Again we have found that in service industries the most important element for success in an organization is the people. People include management and staff at all levels. As has been stressed elsewhere in this book, if the overall culture is right then there is very little that an organization cannot achieve.

CD ROM CASE STUDY

The case study which is relevant to this and earlier chapters is Trinidad Highways.

References

Basu, R. and Wright, J. Nevan (1998) *Total Manufacturing Solutions*, Oxford, Butterworth-Heinemann.

Bateman, T. S. and Zeithaml, C. P. (1993) *Management Function and Strategy*, Illinois, Irwin.

Berry, L. L., Parasuraman, A. and Zeithaml, V. A. (1988) The Service Quality Puzzle, *Business Horizons*, July–August, pp. 35–43.

Bogan, C. E. and English, M. J. (1994) *Benchmarking for Best Practices*, New York, McGraw Hill.

Carlzon, J. (1989) *Moments of Truth*, New York, Harper Row.

Carnall, C. (1993) *Managing Change*, London, Routledge.

Christopher, M. (1992) *Logistics and Supply Chain Management*, Pitman Publishing.

Creech, B. (1994) *The Five Pillars of TQM*, New York, Truman Talley Books/Dutton.

Deming, W. E. (1986) *Out of the Crisis*, Cambridge: Mass., MIT Centre for Advanced Engineering.

Dulewicz, V., MacMillan, K. and Herbert, P. (1995) Appraising and Developing the Effectiveness of Boards and their Directors, *Journal of General Management*, Vol. 20, No. 3, Spring, pp. 1–19.

Hammer, M. and Champy, J. (1993) *Re-engineering The Corporation*, London, Nicholas Brealey Publishing.

Herzberg, F. (1966) *Work and the Nature of Man*, Cleveland, World Publishing.

Herzberg, F. (1968) One More Time: How Do You Motivate Employees?, *Harvard Business Review*, January–February, pp. 53–62.

Ishikawa, K. (1979) *Guide to Quality Control*, Tokyo, Asian Productivity Organization.

Ishikawa. K. (1985) *What is Total Quality Control? The Japanese Way*, trans. D. J. Lu, Englewood Cliffs, Prentice Hall.

Juran, J. M. (1988) *Juran on Planning for Quality*, New York, Free Press.

Kotler, P. (1997) *Marketing Management*, New Jersey, Prentice Hall.

Lewis, B. R. (1994) in B. G. Dale (ed.), *Managing Quality*, London, Prentice Hall.

Machiavelli, N. (1513) *The Prince*, trans. Luigi Ricci, revised by E. R. P. Vincent, New York, New American Library of World Literature (1952).

Masaaki, Imai (1986) *Kaizen: The Key to Japan's Competitive Success*, New Jersey, Random House.

Maslow, A. H. (1943) A Theory of Human Motivation, *Psychological Review*, Vol. 50, pp. 370–96.

Obeng, E. (1994) *All Change! The Project Leader's Secret Handbook*, London, Pitman.

Obeng, E. and Crainer, S. (1994) *Making Re-engineering Happen*, London, Pitman.

Parasuraman, A., Zeithaml,V. A. and Berry, L. L. (1985) 'A Conceptual Model of Service Quality and its Implications for Future Research', *Journal of Marketing*, 49, Fall, pp. 41–50.

Parasuraman, A., Zeithaml, V. A. and Berry, L. L. (1991) 'Understanding Customer Expectations of Service', *Sloan Management Review*, 32(3), pp. 39–48.

Peters, T. and Waterman, J. R. Jnr (1982) *In Search of Excellence*, New York, Harper Row.

Peters, T. and Austin, N. (1986) *A Passion for Excellence*, London, Fortune.

Porter, M. E. (1990) *The Competitive Advantage of Nations*, London, MacMillan.

Sayle, A. J. (1991) *Meeting ISO 9000 in a TQM World*, AJSL.

Schein, E. H. (1988) *Organizational Psychology*, Englewood Cliffs, Prentice Hall.

Schein, E. H. (1991) *Organizational Culture: A Dynamic View*, San Francisco, Josey Bass.

Schonberger, R. (1986) *World Class Manufacturing*, New York, Free Press.

Skinner, B. F. (1971) *Contingencies of Re-inforcement*, Norwalk CT, Appleton-Century-Crofts.

Smith, A. (1776) *An Enquiry into The Nature and Causes of the Wealth of Nations*, Book One, London, Methuen, 6th edition, 1950.

Taylor, F. W. (1987) in Boone, L. E. and Bowen, D. D., *The Great Writings in Management and Organizational Behaviour*, New York, McGraw Hill.

Tompkins, J. A. (1989) *Winning Manufacturing*, New York, Free Press.

US Bureau of the Census (1990).

Vroom, V. H. and Yetton, P. W. (1973) *Leadership and Decision Making*, Pittsburg, University of Pittsburg.

Vroom, V. H. and Jago, A. G. (1988) *The New Leadership: Managing Participation in Organizations*, New Jersey, Prentice Hall.

Wild, R. (1995) *Production and Operations Management* (5th edition), London, Cassell.

Wright, J. Nevan (1996) 'Creating a Quality Culture', *Journal of General Management*, Vol. 21, No. 3, Spring.

Wright, R. (1995) *Managing Labour Relations in a New Economy*. Canada, The Conference Branch of Canada.

Zeithaml, V. A., Parasuraman, A. and Berry, L. L. (1990) *Delivering Quality Service: Balancing Customer Perceptions and Expectations*, New York, The Free Press.

Index

The Management of Service Operations

The installation process installs Acrobat Reader and some other required files on your hard disk. Once you access the material you will be given instructions on how to proceed and an explanation of the symbols used for navigation.

Installation Instructions

Close any applications that are running. Place the CD in your CD disk drive. If your CD drive is not D, substitute the appropriate letter in the following instructions.

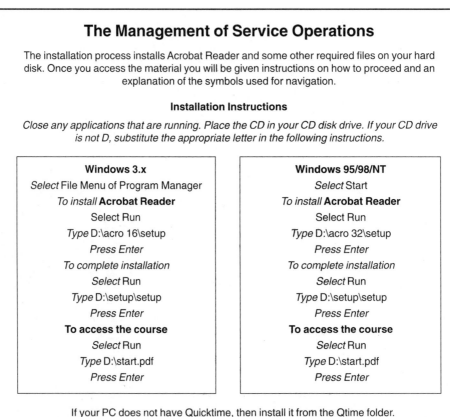

Windows 3.x	Windows 95/98/NT
Select File Menu of Program Manager	*Select* Start
To install **Acrobat Reader**	*To install* **Acrobat Reader**
Select Run	Select Run
Type D:\acro 16\setup	*Type* D:\acro 32\setup
Press Enter	*Press Enter*
To complete installation	*To complete installation*
Select Run	*Select* Run
Type D:\setup\setup	*Type* D:\setup\setup
Press Enter	*Press Enter*
To access the course	**To access the course**
Select Run	*Select* Run
Type D:\start.pdf	*Type* D:\start.pdf
Press Enter	*Press Enter*

If your PC does not have Quicktime, then install it from the Qtime folder.
Recommended requirements: 486 8mb multimedia PC, Windows 3.x or 95/98/NT
2x CD ROM drive, 800 x 600 display, 16-bit colour